A SCOT GOES SOUTH

By the same author

Scot Free
A journey from the Arctic to New Mexico

A SCOT
GOES SOUTH

A journey from Mexico to Ayers Rock

Alastair Scott

JOHN MURRAY

To Jane

© Alastair Scott, 1988

First published 1988
by John Murray (Publishers) Ltd
50 Albemarle Street, London W1X 4BD

Typeset by Inforum Ltd, Portsmouth
Printed and bound in Great Britain
at The Bath Press, Avon

British Library Cataloguing in Publication Data

Scott, Alastair, *1954–*
A Scot goes south : a journey from
Mexico to Ayers Rock.
1. Latin America——Description and travel
——1981–
I. Title
918'.0438   F1409.3

ISBN 0–7195–4392–4

Contents

Illustrations

Maps

Photographs in colour

Who was I? An Englishman? Ah, an Irishman, then?

'No,' I said, 'a Scotsman.'

A Scotsman? Ah, he had never seen a Scotsman before. And he looked me all over, his good honest, brawny countenance shining with interest, as a boy might look upon a lion or an alligator.

ROBERT LOUIS STEVENSON, *Travels with a Donkey in the Cevennes*

O wad some Pow'r the giftie gie us
To see oursels as others see us!
It wad frae monie a blunder free us
    An foolish notion;

ROBERT BURNS, *To a Louse*

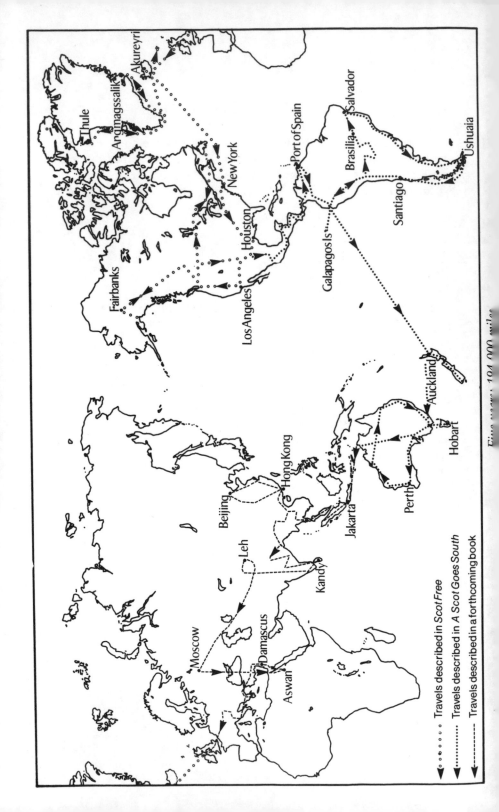

Fine maps: 104,000 miles

Travels described in *Scot Free*

Travels described in *A Scot Goes South*

Travels described in a forthcoming book

Prologue

According to the legends of the Aboriginal Dreamtime, Australia was the first continent to exist. Through a lonely bulging rock in the centre of this land, Bulari, the Earth-Mother, gave birth to the rest of our world. Amongst her issue were the Pacific Ocean and the Latin American subcontinent, including the ingredients for Machu Picchu. The ruins of this Inca city balance on a mountain saddle 8,000 miles to the east of Ayers Rock but, in the eyes of a Dreamer, they are related through an almost inconceivable feat of maternity.

In my school library was a picture book containing photographs of both places. As I leafed my way through the many parts of the world illustrated, feeling like a penniless windowshopper before an expensive store, these two places repeatedly arrested my attention and held it, taunting my mind with their physical beauty and their puzzling unworldliness. The 'Lost City' was evocative enough by name, but when depicted beside a jagged peak above a near-bottomless valley and (in the close-ups) as a cubist's jigsaw of huge stones neatly shaped and fitted together with such perfection, the text said, that it was impossible to slip a sheet of paper into the joints, Machu Picchu fired my imagination with an irresistible fascination. How had the Incas built it, I wondered, and what were the descendants of one of the world's greatest civilisations like today? Then I would flick over a few pages, 8,000 miles, and gaze at Ayers Rock, red potter's clay beaten into a ball between cupped hands and thrown forcefully onto a vast, flat and empty land. It was smooth and swollen, ominously brooding and pregnant, and in every picture it had mysteriously changed colour. The text said it was constantly flaking in an erosion process akin to rusting, and then it moved on to pictures of Aboriginals. Two stood on a rock gazing into the distance; they carried a spear and an elongated boomerang quite unlike the type that had once appeared in my Christmas stocking and nearly fractured my wrist on the only occasion of its voluntary return. I tried to visualise the lifestyle of these people and dreamed of the rock where the world had been born.

Now, almost a decade later, travelling had become a reality and I stood in El Paso poised to enter Mexico. I have described in my previous book how two years earlier I had left my home in Scotland intent on wandering the world as freely as possible, without worries about time and without a rigidly planned route. All travellers need a reason to sustain a long journey no matter whether their identity corresponds to that of impecunious tramp or pampered tourist (in third world countries the distinction is unimportant; anyone who can afford to use a passport is privileged). My journey was inspired by an eagerness to see a large part of the world and to sample the lives of a cross-section of its peoples. I chose the level of a shoestring traveller, preferring to spin out my limited but usually adequate means with frugal living, and relinquishing a certain degree of comfort in exchange for insights by moving amongst those outside the luxury of privacy. These motives were reinforced by my ambitions as a photographer. I had studied photography and worked in a commercial studio before packing a camera case with twenty-eight pounds of equipment (in addition to a thirty-pound pack containing a tent, sleeping blanket, cooker, clothes and a universal bathplug), and setting off to replace the captions and images of a picture book with my own impressions of the world. This sense of purpose proved sufficient to sustain my journey for five years and 194,000 miles.

Carrying a universal bathplug had been a complete waste of energy over the last 50,000 miles but I continued to take it with me in the hope that it might prove useful during one of the remaining miles. But no. Developed countries provided plugs, underdeveloped countries seldom had drains, let alone baths or plugholes (this was fine because they simply had a different method of washing; dipping a jug into a vat of water and pouring a more economical shower – many minor aggravations encountered in a strange culture could be allayed by adopting the attitudes and practices that had evolved to suit its particular environment). A much more useful item amongst my possessions was a kilt. I had worn it for a large part of my travels through the Arctic and North America where it had shown immeasurable worth by identifying me as foreign and a curiosity in some of the world's most hospitable lands, and despite occasional unpleasant moments it had brought me my richest experiences. It seemed only natural to take it from Texas into Latin America, even though I had doubts about its practicality in a hot climate and its reception among a race reputed to have hot blood.

My earnings from jobs along the way had provided me with sufficient funds for at least one year of travel in a relatively cheap subcontinent. This money, held as traveller's cheques in my sporran or in a pocket sewn inside a trouser leg at ankle height, enabled me to arrive at the Mexican border secure in the knowledge that when the string holding my boots together finally broke, I could afford to replace them. (Cobbler's repairs never seemed to last and string was very effective.)

Only a fool enters Latin America without apprehension. The day before entering Mexico, my diary ended with the words: 'In Latin America I will face my biggest challenge for it is host to everything that is hostile to a traveller; revolutions, political oppression, false imprisonment, extortion, corrupt police, excessive bureaucracy, violence, theft, drugs, poverty, unhealthy water, killer and recurring diseases, venomous snakes, biting insects and hordes of parasites. There is a great risk of my films being damaged by heat or lost by unreliable postal services, and I also foresee major problems in carrying so much camera equipment through sensitive military areas.' It was a gloomy view, but it has been said that the difference between the optimist and the pessimist is that the pessimist is usually better informed. I was a postponed optimist, travelling on a dream and a smile.

The proportion of risk that each traveller encounters is governed partly by good sense and partly by the amount sought, but largely by luck. There is only so much one can do in preparation for the unknown and a limit to the degree of caution that one can maintain. If one wishes to be receptive to a new culture then inevitably defences must drop to permit interaction, but this also renders the traveller more vulnerable to predators. I began this stage of the journey believing a sympathetic attitude would attract a sympathetic response in my quest to discover Latin America.

And besides, I had a lucky talisman. I had my kilt.

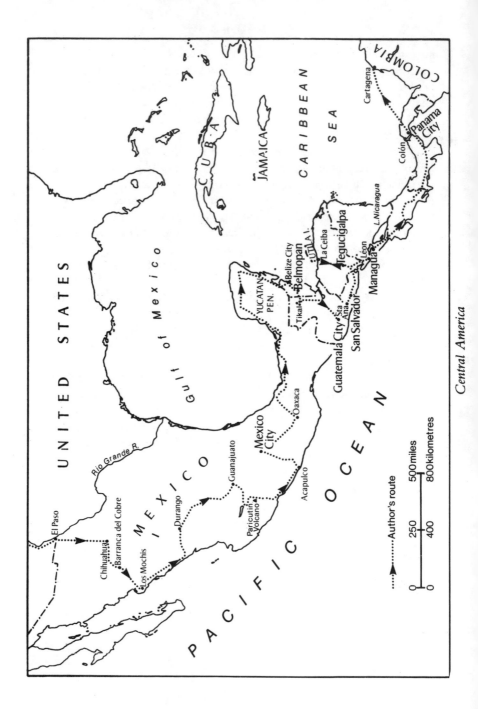

Central America

1 · The Price of Machismo in Mexico

Mexicans do not like kilts.

My kilt was ignored during the bullfight in Mexico City. The fighters were the young up-and-coming toreros (Bizet incorrectly called them 'toreadors') who had yet to prove themselves, and so the seating area was simply full instead of the more usual crush which forced feverish fans to perch on the perimeter wall and to cling to the drainpipes of the stand. A bull had just been messily dispatched with two swords and the torero's incompetence had left the crowd shrieking abuse for ten minutes. They had only been silenced when an announcement came that the torero would fight another bull and pay for it out of his own pocket. The crowd sat down, some people cheered. Only six bulls should have been killed that afternoon, but the pursuit of entertainment is not concerned with justice, and bullfighting arenas are places of execution where the condemned are merely offered the chance to die honourably.

The seventh had been baited and rankled until he kicked and butted, and then he pranced into the ring, snorting, strings of white saliva clinging to his mouth. He was big, lean and muscular, not like the overweight studs that lie around the pleasant English scene, and he stood in the middle staring at the crowd, bewildered, angry and afraid. A rosette was pinned on his back to mark the muscle which the picadors had to pierce. They rode in like frilly conquistadors and lanced the bull. The horses showed no fear, but then they had little means of doing so for they were blindfold and their vocal cords had been cut. The rosette turned crimson and the bull was left shaking his head in rage while blood trickled down his neck, over his chest and dropped to the sand. The crowd applauded. Some spectators close to me felt hungry and bought fried bananas from a passing vendor. The bull's blood was darkening, becoming viscous and matting the tufts on his black coat, the sand at his feet was now stained with dark spots, and I heard the sound of laughter. The air smelt of dust, sweetened by the lingering aroma of fried bananas.

The disgraced torero walked in with two darts, each eighteen inches long and trailing colourful ribbons. The crowd fell silent, voracious for a mistake. The torero faced the bull and stood with his feet together, chest thrown out, body held rigidly erect, arms angled up straight in front of him and holding the two darts, angled down. He made several pompous stiff-legged struts to catch the bull's attention. The bull charged. The torero's movements became gawkish hops, discipline paralysing his limbs as he took to the air, taunting and feinting. He sidestepped the horns, lent over and stabbed the darts into place. They fell out. The crowd booed and yelled insults. 'QUE MIERDA! HIJO DE PUTA!' He tried again. One dart stuck in the flank and the other dropped to the ground. The crowd was on its feet, gesticulating wildly, and the jeers were deafening.

The fighter was upset and struggling to save his name. He grabbed the last two darts from an assistant, ran to the edge of the arena and broke them over the hoarding. It was a rash act of defiance incited by his despair. Shortening the darts made the task of placing them very much harder and more dangerous, and this was now the level of skill demanded to avoid utter humiliation. But he made a poor job of this too and looked alarmed to see that instead of halving them, he had left himself two five-inch darts – almost suicidal. In desperation he waited till the last moment, allowing a horn to crease his tunic. He lent so close over the charging bull that its blood was smeared onto his hips, and placed the darts perfectly. The crowd roared approval, people leapt to their feet and some flowers were thrown into the arena. It had been a particularly brave act. The air was suddenly full of hats being tossed into the ring. The torero was ecstatic. Within seconds he had risen from shame to heroism. He gathered a few flowers and took another bow as he faced his jubilant admirers. The tumultuous roar reached a new peak and some screams penetrated the furor, but by then it was too late. The torero turned as the bull's horns caught him in the small of the back. He was instantly pounded to the ground and butted several times before being thrown in a somersault over the bull's shoulders. Flowers were still clenched in one hand as he lay there twitching, and dying – it was later reported – of internal injuries and a punctured lung. The crowd, still standing, fell silent and 50,000 crosses were carved in the dusty air. There were no feelings of remorse or guilt that these people were in part responsible for his death, and they left the bullring with a feeling of money well spent.

Latin America measured by the hour is confusing. One hour it is passively waiting for mañana and the next it is an explosion of activity. When measured by the minute it is the spectacle of the bullring; life, death, honour, disgrace, anger, amusement and prayer. For men in particular, the minute of honour is the most important; *machismo*. The torero with the punctured lung was all right. He died *macho*. He could have achieved this in other ways, by smoking, drinking excessively, beating his wife, womanising or earning without working; all *macho*.

But a kilt is not *macho*.

'God created a paradise,' I was told, 'and called it Mexico. Then He put Mexicans in it because He knew they would be too lazy to ruin it.' Hernando Cortés did not find it such a paradise when he marched into the unknown territory called New Spain in 1519 with only 600 men. Asked later what the country looked like, he made his famous gesture of crushing a piece of parchment in his hand and holding it out. 'That,' he stated, 'is the map of Mexico.' Neither did he find the inhabitants lazy when his small force was outnumbered by hostile natives at the ratio of 25,000 to one – but Cortés was one of the world's greatest military leaders and a master tactician. He shrewdly manipulated tribal disagreements within the Aztec kingdom to win allies, and his cannons and modest cavalry proved lethal amongst the astonished Indians.

Cortés was also fortunate in the timing of his arrival in Mexico. The Aztec fifty-two-year cycle had just ended and they were waiting to see if the world would be destroyed or if a new cycle would begin. The Aztecs, who had inherited magnificent temple pyramids from earlier civilisations and had developed an advanced social and economic structure, practised ritual cardiectomy, using knives of flint and obsidian to cut open the sacrificial victim's chest before ripping out the still palpitating heart. A warrior's prowess depended on the number of captives he provided for sacrifice, and when the gods had been propitiated with the blood, he received the truncated limbs to eat. (Cortés found 136,000 skulls on a rack beside a temple in what is now Mexico City.) But the powerful Aztec dominion was causing discontent among the populace, and in particular, a growing resentment against the constant demand for sacrificial victims.

In this period of uncertainty the priests turned to Montezuma, their absolute ruler and the representative of the gods. He ordered 12,000 human sacrifices to be offered in one session and although the priests considered this insufficient to ensure a new life cycle, the world did not end. The fear of imminent destruction was still hanging over the empire when reports of white invaders arrived. Montezuma believed it was the fulfilment of a prediction that the god Quetzalcoatl would return from the East, with white skin and a beard. He allowed the Spaniards to advance but by the time he realised the true character of these men, driven by courage, determination and greed, he too had been caught by the horns and overthrown. In 1521 Cortés took control of the country with the help of 150,000 Indian allies. Aztec gold treasures were melted down and sent across the Atlantic; Catholicism, Spanish and bullfighting had reached Central America.

Pre-conquest Mexico had scarcely been a paradise for at least 130,000 poor souls, but centuries of Spanish administration and subsequent independence have done little to redress the inadequacies of the great Aztec civilisation. Today, half of Mexico's sixty-five-million population are peasants who earn less than twenty per cent of the average national income – a hangover from the system which Cortés introduced and to which he too fell victim, dying a pathetic old man begging compensation for his suffering. No monuments stand to his name and all reminders of his trail of conquest have been eradicated in keeping with the ideology of uncompromising national-ism that pervades the country.

But Cortés was all right, because he was *macho*. In a kilt he would not have been tolerated.

Three weeks before the bullfight in Mexico City I spent one night at El Paso's Grand Hotel on the American border, one thousand miles to the north. This hospice did not live up to its name but it helped to prepare me for some of the rough sleeping quarters that were to come later, and I had scarcely expected any more from the brief description in a guidebook. 'Grand Hotel; Billy the Kid shot a man in Rm 24, otherwise friendly and helpful.'

The next morning I approached the Mexican border with my kilt folded up inside a dark green kitbag, which had been converted into a backpack by adding straps, but my crude stitching made them uncomfortable and they rubbed my shoulders with each bounce of my stride. I felt cowardly for wearing jeans but then this was my début as a gringo and discretion persuaded me to allow a period of acclimatisation before appearing as a Scottish gringo. (The word supposedly came from the wars with the United States, in which Mexico eventually lost over half of her territory, around the time of

Davy Crockett and the siege of El Alamo (1836). I was told that Mexicans spying on American soldiers heard them singing a song 'Green grows the grass . . .' as they marched past – but I was told many things.)

The sound of traffic faded as I crossed a bridge over the Rio Grande, an anaemic trickle in a concrete trench, to be replaced by the plodding footsteps of other itinerants and the shuffling of dragged luggage. This noise of friction became more resonant in an enclosed passage of fabricated marble-style slabs where faces behind the windows of bureaucracy scrutinised the no-man's land of migration with relentless suspicion or authoritative boredom. Before confronting my first window I took out my phrasebook. My Spanish was grammatically unsound but competent on an elementary level, and the phrasebook was to help me until my confidence increased. My finger passed over such indispensable phrases as 'Do you have anything in camel hair?' (*Tiene usted algo en pelo de camillo?*) and eventually found the section on border crossings.

'Good morning,' I said cheerfully and, remembering the advice in the introduction, waited for a reply. ('Courteous gestures are a way of life and an exchange of pleasantries should not be rushed.')

'Good morning,' I repeated when the official stopped talking to his colleague several minutes later. He ignored me and resumed his conversation. I waited patiently and then thought of trying, '*Tiene usted algo en pelo de camillo?*', but decided against it. Five minutes later my passport was brusquely stamped and I passed on to the next window without an exchange of pleasantries. Perhaps this reaction had something to do with those behind me for they were mostly Mexican 'wetbacks', illegal emigrants who had sneaked into the United States to find work and were now being forcibly recycled back to redundancy in their homeland. My excitement found no reflection.

'Good morning,' I said to the customs official, but he was only interested in his blackmarket sideline of buying dollars, and his rate of exchange was absurdly low. When I declined to change any money he attacked my luggage with a vengeance and beamed with delight on discovering I had thirty-six rolls of film when only twelve were allowed in duty-free, and indicated that his exchange rate was a better bargain than having to pay the duty. I paid, reluctantly. His country had of course lost an awful lot of gold and silver to the Spaniards, and this form of recuperation was an accepted part of international trade. His colleague was faring even better, shaking his head as two farmers slowly raised their bribe to be allowed in with part of a tractor engine.

No country should be judged by its border towns, for these are entities on their own whose character falls half-way between national and foreign. The less wealthy border town cannot hide its deficiencies but it tries to disguise them in a shop-window where the more ostentatious elements of its neighbour country's trends are displayed in concentration. Border towns are basically shopping centres catering in all things that foreign day-trippers consider cheap, unusual or illegal.

My first sight of Mexico was of narrow streets, shabby buildings, ragged pavements, stalls of bric-à-brac, heavy metal shutters half rolled up to expose shallow shops with wares bulging out into the streets, people bustling about their errands and cars honking at loiterers or gossipers, a loudspeaker furiously churning out oscillating guitar chords from a scratched record, laughter, shouting, a shoeshine pointing at my boots, cigar smoke, monstrous billboards in Spanish and Coca-Cola signs in small but conceited red and white.

I came to a modernised sector where walls were blocks of composite chips, polished and colourful, and the pavement edges were neatly bevelled to impress the visitor and as proof that the masonic skill of the Mayas had not been lost. Here were shops selling gold, silver, onyx Aztecs and sex. There was a nightclub with neon lights still stabbing at the sunlight, and doorways that advertised their services with partially blacked-out photographs or suggestive shades of electric bulb. Further away from the centre the town became more rundown, shops became hole-in-the-wall caches. A woman sat wedged in a stall among a thousand hats and next door a dwarf sold off-the-shelf coffins. He had some in sombre colours with gilt or silver handles, and for those who had a penchant for something more jaunty, there were others painted in pink, purple, yellow and green, and lined with a choice of lace ruffles or imitation velvet or fur. Housewives formed a queue outside a nearby family tortilla factory. The one being served caught the hot pancakes as they fell off a squeaky conveyor belt and stacked them on a square of cloth which she knotted like a bundle of laundry when the stack was tall enough and then wore it as a hat. The aroma of hot dough made my mouth water but the long queue dissuaded me from waiting.

I had convinced myself that Mexico was uniformly hot and all jungle, but crossing the Rio Grande had not produced tropical weather and a cold November wind moaned through the streets of

Ciudad Juárez, sucking at empty alleys where dust spun in eddies and litter rattled against the drab walls. But the cold did not reach me. My thoughts were riding high on the fascination of a new culture. By not peering into it too deeply, by ensuring that I continued to exist outside its grasp, I was able to revel in the privileged observation that poverty was charming, thought-provoking and touching in its simplicity, and high adventure.

A donkey began braying in the distance, its costive, wheezing call jarring the air – and then something slimy grazed my cheek. My head recoiled as a beggar's hand suddenly appeared from behind me. The hand possessed a thumb and a little finger but the other fingers had gone, just bulging knuckles, and a long cut crossed its width. A black scab had formed but it had not closed over the gore of inflamed red, dirt and puce flesh. This weeping wound had left a smear across my cheek.

'Please, señor, one peso.' The man looked wizened, emaciated and old, but beggars always look old, even the children. My hand immediately went to my cheek and then I examined it to see what trace had been left behind, afraid that already some rash or swelling was breaking out. 'Please, señor . . .' I fumbled in my pockets and gave him the coins that were there, not out of compassion but in utter horror, to get rid of this loathsome creature who had touched my clean white skin with his mutilated body. I turned to watch him limp off, my hand involuntarily went back to my cheek and froze there, my throat felt choked and I couldn't swallow – the figure stumbled, stopped to pick up and open out a banana skin, threw it away and hobbled off. Then a torso with no legs appeared from a doorway, balancing on a sort of skateboard and punting along with wooden batons, tipped with rubber pads, which were strapped to handless wrists. The sight was unbearable and I hurried away in shame.

The single peso for which the beggar had asked was just under two pence and would have bought him four tortillas, one large banana or the fingernail of an onyx Aztec. Within my first hour in Mexico I had experienced the forces of corruption and poverty in a land of stark beauty and wealth.

Enough day-trippers, who had probably never ventured beyond a Mexican border town, had persuaded me that this country was full of bandits and swindlers and that it was best to live in distrust and forget hitch-hiking. It went against my nature but it seemed sound advice until I could form an opinion of my own. My plan was to travel by bus and train to the capital in a roundabout way. All south-bound traffic headed for Chihuahua, a large mining city four hours away and the first major crossroads on the map. The bus that took me there was comfortable and as fast as implied by its emblem, an emaciated and extraordinarily elastic greyhound. The other passengers were pre-dominantly men in cowboy hats endlessly meeting each other and shaking hands, a gesture prolonged into an exchange of warmth. It seemed to be a national pastime.

We passed through an expanse of flat desert, tedious sand and scrub with patches of snow as a further reminder that the Tropic of Cancer lay to the south. It was only later when I realised that Chihuahua was situated at an altitude slightly higher than Ben Nevis (4,418 feet) that I placed less faith in imaginary lines based on the angle of the sun as indicators of temperature.

Chihuahua was particularly unattractive when seen under a burst cloud. I spent the night there at a small hotel dangerously cluttered with buckets catching drips from the ceiling. The owner had one of the famous dogs which are believed to have originated from here. It kept me awake most of the night with its yapping, which made me doubt that Chihuahuas were the 'little barkless dogs, castrated and fattened' that Cortés had found for sale in the meat markets. I wished the Indians had preferred eating the barking variety. (In fact there is no proof that dogs existed in Mexico before the conquest. The Spaniards were hopeless naturalists and their reports are unreliable. All animals vaguely similar to dogs, such as gophers, tree-climbing coati-mundis, raccoons and opossums, were just called dogs.)

The next morning found me on the train from Chihuahua to Los Mochis on the Pacific coast, descending through deep gorges and dense forests of fir. I found the homely fragrance of pine needles comforting as it infused through the open windows, breaking the diesel fumes' sultry hold over the air, but the sight of deep pockets of snow and of branches bent under the white crust of winter continued to upset my meteorological expectations.

I had been trying to avoid the only other gringo on the train but he came and sat on the seat opposite mine. This irritated me. He removed the self-indulgent feelings of being unique and a pioneer in a strange land that I had enjoyed for twenty-four hours. He made me feel old hat and too late.

'Here, have a joint, man.'

I shook my head affably and tried to wonder how a pine tree could grow on a vertical wall of rock, but he continued to talk and ignore my distant gaze. He said he came from Alabama but was living in a village near Oaxaca in southern Mexico. He occasionally exported cheap clothes to sell expensively in the United States and was currently returning from a sales trip to marry a village girl, grinning wryly that dual citizenship would be his wedding present. He had come this long way round to look for magic mushrooms which grew in the mountains. All his clothes were black. Black boots, trousers and pullover, and he wore a long black Zapata moustache which drooped down from his chin. If his stetson hat had been removed, he would not have looked out of place lying on an Arctic iceberg.

The train stopped on the edge of the Barranca del Cobre – Mexico's Grand Canyon which is actually one third deeper and four times wider than its more famous counterpart.

'Too bad. It's all misty,' the walrus said. The mist parted as he spoke and began to disperse. The earth appeared to have ended abruptly and we were looking down a sheer drop over one mile in depth. ('Wowee.') The walls were glazed with the sheen of tarnished copper, the metal that gave the canyon its name. Hills covered the bottom of the canyon like bumps in a rug, a rug of matted green trees frequently cut by gorges which revealed a taper of brown river. The train whistle blew and called us back. We climbed aboard.

The fir trees became sparse and were replaced by palms – where they overlapped, the mixture seemed incongruous – and the vegetation grew luxuriously as we entered the verdant farmland of the coastal plains. Winter had suddenly given way to a climate which I could only describe, with a smile, as tropical. Mexico's variety is staggering. In so many ways it is a paradise. Gold, silver and oil are abundant amongst its legion of mineral resources, it has farmland where any crops can grow, it has jungle, deserts and mountains, ports on both Atlantic and Pacific, resplendent beaches for the holiday-maker, and of course, it has its past.

The land is rich but the people are not. Independence merely replaced the Spaniards with native élite and left the colonial structure unchanged. Ninety-seven per cent of the rural population owned no land whatsoever at the outbreak of the 1910 revolution, and the economy had become totally dependent on the United States. ('Poor Mexico. So far from God, and so near to the United States,' Porfirio

Diaz once observed, even though his dictatorship (1876–1910) had helped to foster this situation.)

The walrus had brought up the subject and he finished it. 'Y'know the trouble with this country? They had their goddamned revolution too soon. Sure they got a democracy out of it but it ain't done 'em much good. Country folk still ain't got no land. The whole system could use a shake-up right now, but I guess the last one kinda stole their energy.' He expressed, and felt, a sadness beyond the comfort of magic mushrooms and a successful business.

I began hitch-hiking the next day and found it worked well over the 1300 procrastinating miles to Mexico City. A soft drinks truck took me back up into the central mountain range in the direction of Durango. We crawled up multiple bends for hours and when the engine overheated and there was no water near the road, the driver opened four large Fantas and four large Cokes and poured them into the radiator, alternating the bottles as if the mixture were important. Durango was in an area of spectacular rugged desert which was used as a standard set for many American cowboy films. The classic cartoon cactus stuck up in the barren ruby-tinted landscape like prickly candelabra, tall and green. Huts stood surrounded by another species of cactus which had been cultivated into an impenetrable stockade towering above the tin roofs. At the entrance women paused in their chores and remained motionless, hands on hips, to watch our truck as it passed. Outside one hut a man wearing a poncho stood in the expectant desert, gazing at the ground with one foot cast forwards as if caught in mid-stride, and children ran around him flapping their arms and chasing hens for fun. I hoped we had enough Cokes and Fantas to take us away from this listless place.

The truck-driver let me sleep on the back of his truck that night and then let me out in Guanajuato to see a vault containing fifty mummies which had been found naturally preserved in the cemetery. They stood shoulder to shoulder, naked except a man who wore an open coat and a woman in nothing but thigh-length boots. Their bodies were whole in unashamed detail but the yellow-brown flesh of some heads had flaked away to reveal half a skull emerging from half a face. Their features were twisted and jaws had relaxed to produce leering skulls and faces of soundless screams. I stumbled out into the bright sunlight holding my stomach. A vendor was waiting with a tray of 'sugar mummies', perfect cadaverous replicas in yellow-brown candy for those with a sweet tooth and a perverse imagination. I grimaced and stumbled off, leaving the vendor laughing as if he knew he had been over-optimistic, and made my way along a road that had reputedly been paved with a trail of silver ingots 250 yards long from the world's richest mine to La Valencia church on the wedding day of the mine owner's daughter.

My route continued to follow Cortés's map of crumpled parchment, up and down, passing Paricutin Volcano which grew out of a corn field in 1943 and destroyed two villages as it rose to the height of 4,000 feet. Here a sideroad led me to the weird sight of a church spire sticking out of a mantle of black lava. San Juan church had been engulfed and yet left as the only building to survive the eruption, half consumed and crumbling but standing proud. Finally the road ran downhill all the way to the coast near Acapulco. Empty beaches alternated with sluggish rivers where cast-net fishermen waded up to their waists and flung spiders' webs of nylon into the air, expanding circles which flashed white in the sun and then disappeared into the brackish water. My last lift took me past a bizarre cemetery painted blue and green. The driver explained that the community had felt it was an eyesore and had decided to make it more cheerful as part of their programme to develop the village for tourism.

I reached Acapulco late at night, feeling exhausted. A young man called me over and said it was dangerous to walk in the suburbs after dark – many thieves. I was to sleep in his house. I felt pathetically grateful and too tired to question his friendship or let caution affect my judgment. He made up a bed and I fell asleep with discourteous haste. The next morning I found that he and his wife were in the only bed beside me. They shared the facilities of the house with another family but lived in this one room, and they had been married for one month.

I have received much kindness on my travels but this one act of hospitality, to be offered a corner in the bedroom of a young bridal couple – and in a neglected sector of a tourist's paradise – is a token of Mexico and the Mexicans that I shall never forget.

Otherwise Acapulco did little to impress me. It was a typical resort, full of homogeneous hotels and full of gringos and gringas who hung and waved from flying contraptions pulled by speedboats, and whose prostrate oily bodies weighed gaudy towels to the sand as they slowly turned closer to the colour of those who lived out of sight in the fringe shanty towns. One of its spectacles, however, was unique. On a cliff within the city called La Quebrada, a diver stood poised one hundred and thirty feet above the sea. Hundreds of little flags were fixed to the rocks and he had just placed another beside a small shrine to the Virgin where a candle was burning. A crowd gathered around me and we all gave a donation to the diver's assistant who came along with a money pouch. He gave a signal. The diver stiffened, the flags quivered in a puff of breeze and his hair was stirred. He waited for a wave to approach the shallows below him, contemplating its speed, the timing of his plunge and the vital twist underwater which would deflect his course to the rocky seabed. Then he launched himself out over the void, plummeting with his arms spread out in a graceful swallow-dive, dropping for prolonged seconds before flicking his body to enter the water vertically. Spray leapt up around the hole punched in the surface by his impact and there was an anxious pause before he reappeared and swam ashore. This diver was young and would retire early – not because he could afford to do so but through fear of long-term brain damage which was becoming increasingly evident in those who had been regular performers.

A succession of private cars carried me for seven uphill hours to Mexico City, where I planned to go to a bullfight and try on my kilt.

The capital city, once a collection of islands in a lake and later rebuilt on the drained bed by the Spanish with Order and Extravagance in mind, still displays a flair for artistic architecture, though scant evidence of age, inside a swampy fringe of shacks and the rubbish of fourteen million people. By the year 2000, it is predicted, this area will be the planet's most populous settlement with 32 million inhabitants. Mexico city fills a high-altitude basin (7,350 feet) and creeps up into the surrounding hills which are dominated by the snow-capped volcanoes of Popocatepetl, the warrior, and his less pronounceable lover, Ixtaccihuatl. It is a vibrant noisy city with a pleasant climate and plenty of reasons to give the tourist sore feet. One of its principal streets is fifteen miles long and murderous in design with twin lanes of traffic running in each direction and a single opposing bus lane on either side. To cross this street a pedestrian must look right, left, left, right, right and left before reaching the safety of the far pavement, probably to be knocked down by a cyclist or a horse and cart coming from a completely unpredictable direction. Mexico City has smog, horrendous traffic jams and the world's largest bullring.

It felt strange to be wearing my kilt again. In the privacy of my hostel bedroom it seemed to have travelled well and was not too creased, but in the foyer it obviously didn't look so good. The receptionist openly laughed. My Spanish was already improving.

'Not so many of these are there in Mexico, no?' I said. She managed to reduce her laugh to giggles. 'How is called a *kilt* in Spanish?'

'We call it,' she spluttered, 'a Scottish skirt.' She began quivering behind the handkerchief clamped to her mouth.

I blushed. 'A Scottish skirt? . . . but . . .' I couldn't argue. It had been hard enough explaining the difference between a kilt and a skirt to English-speaking Indians in Canada's Yukon Territory, but it was far beyond my limited vocabulary to do it in Spanish. So I meekly turned and set off walking through the streets that led to the bullring, wearing a Scottish skirt.

The hostel was not far from the ring and the first corrida had already started, so the streets were quiet. The ticket-seller never saw my kilt through the small window which blinkered his vision and I took a place at the back of the crowd. Two hours later the *macho* torero was carried away on a stretcher and another fighter killed the briefly triumphant bull. The stadium was almost deserted of spectators when the dead bull was dragged away by three white horses, and I set off back to the hostel.

I turned a corner into a busy side-street and two men approaching immediately stopped as suddenly as if they had walked into a glass door. Their jaws slackened, their mouths fell open. Expressions of surprise turned to disbelief, to shock and, as I stepped quickly around them, to amusement. Nothing cuts deeper than the sound of mocking laughter, and how they laughed. The pavement was obstructed by a crowded stall. I turned momentarily to see the two men leaning against each other, shoulder to shoulder. One was pointing at me, and they were laughing a forced laugh, the loudest and sharpest laugh of derision. The crowd turned to me, and the driver of a parked car lowered his window to stare. Sensing the gravity of the situation and the volatile nature of those around me, I made my way around the stall with mounting panic. The way was obstructed by several large women peering about to see the cause of the commotion. I barged roughly between them as the laughter caught on and the same jeers, whistles and insults that had tiraded the disgraced torero filled the air. A piece of rotten fruit splattered across the ground in front of my feet. I walked at a trot, afraid, angry and smarting at my bruised pride, and yet aware of faces appearing at shop windows and figures coming out onto overhanging balconies. While they picked up the taunting shouts and carried them further along the street, some children tagged on behind me, chanting scorn that was mercifully incomprehensible. The streets, the stares, the accusing fingers, the laughs and shouts seemed interminable until at last I reached the peaceful refuge of my room.

I had to sit on the bed for a while to calm my nerves, feeling thoroughly shaken by the experience. Later I changed into jeans and went out to a bar where I drank enough tequila to consider the situation objectively, and then more until I didn't care. It was obvious that here a man who wore what always has been and always will be a woman's skirt was such a despicable and worthless specimen of manhood that he deserved all the ill-treatment he could be given. A different set of values was in force among these people and fuelled a fiery temperament. Latin America was going to be hard enough to travel without the kilt making it harder. Reluctantly, I came to a decision. Then I drank more tequila and thought: to hell with them, and to hell with the kilt.

On 12th December each year pilgrims from all over Mexico flock to the capital for the festival of Guadeloupe which takes place around the vast and modern basilica of the same name. The Virgin appeared on this spot three times in 1531 and the anniversary is now the occasion for all-night prayer, colourful Aztec dancing and – for the poor peasants to come and marvel at the wealth of the Church and offer it their miserable savings as penance for whispered sins. The Virgin left her image on a cloak which is now set in gold and kept in a chapel nearby, secure behind a silver portcullis weighing twenty-seven tons. Two snack-bars set in the foundations of the chapel do a brisk trade, and a pool of the sacred spring is lined with submerged plates, presumably by whoever has the task of recovering its good wishes offerings.

Two days after the hostile reaction to my kilt, wearing jeans, I entered the basilica along with 12,000 others by standing on a moving carpet conveyor belt which slowed down the pace of life and took us past a picture of the Virgin at reverential speed. An old woman beside me held out gnarled hands in supplication, muttered and threw a coin while tears seeped from her eyes and slithered down her shrivelled cheeks. At another entrance figures completed the last hundred yards on their knees, holding their bodies erect, chin on chest, as they mounted the steps and entered the great hemisphere with a capacity for 20,000 of their kind. They left on their feet, walking backwards, bowing as they went. Pews had been removed to accommodate the pilgrims, and confession booths were abundant although easily outnumbered by collection boxes.

A small choir was practising to the accompaniment of a sound that I had not heard so intensely since Las Vegas. *Chink, chink, chink* from the money boxes constantly peppered the gentle harmonies. The faith of these people was deep and unquestioning, and it was disturbing to think that their alms paid for extravagant décor, a trendy conveyor belt and twenty-seven tons of silver.

I left the festival early, inhaling the smells of corn on the cob roasting over the charcoal stoves of pavement vendors fringing the basilica and pausing to watch a group of dancers magnificently dressed as raffia birds of paradise. They shook tambourines and leapt around in shoes with iron soles – *clink, clink, clink*. It was whimsical but irresistible to think that fun and absolution were so sonorously related. Lovers of the former could enjoy themselves with a clear conscience because they had paid for the latter. But perhaps that is what Guadeloupe and its conveyor belt was all about. For the price of whatever one could afford as a declaration of good intent, Guadeloupe offered a short ride to a feeling of well-being. It was a rare sensation. I headed for the station to find a train east to the Yucatan.

The station was mobbed with returning pilgrims. The queue for tickets snaked around the platform and I waited at the end, advancing a few feet every minute. The train was packed and although first and second class tickets were sold, there was only one class in reality, crushed class, and the most expensive tickets only let you board the train first so that you could choose where you wanted to be crushed.

For the first four hours after the train's departure there was room to stand but not enough to turn about for a different view of someone else's face, neck or ear. A group of nine gringos somehow became compressed around me, mainly Europeans but no other British amongst the eight nationalities represented. The air was suffocating and the sweat of united nations moved freely through our clothes from one body to the next. We had no option but to wait until the pressure eased. After eight hours we stood with some breathing space. A cock crowed from the luggage rack and then I found myself holding a sleeping Indian baby with a bare bottom. The grateful mother began bottle-feeding the twin. The train rocked steadily, more from an irregular track than speed, and lights flickered outside in the night. After fourteen hours some seats became free. The atmosphere was so humid that sweat flowed over my skin and dripped incessantly to the floor. Dawn came, revealing white egrets dotting the fields and banana trees growing out of lush vegetation entwined with creepers. Jungle! Secretive and intensely wild, it sent a tingling through me for my destination was the Mayan ruins of Tikal deep in the jungle of Guatemala. There were only two approaches and my choice was the one curling round from the east, from Mexico's Yucatan toe, cutting through the newly independent territory of Belize and crossing its far border for the short distance to Tikal.

Most of the other gringos in the coach had travelled extensively in South America and, to my disappointment, they recalled the high-lights with vague and moderate adjectives, and seemed least reticent when pressed to reveal ghastly tales of hardship. Even then they shrugged off calamity with the boredom of a stale nursery rhyme. Emotionally their journeys had been abrasive and travelling rough had blinkered their vision to survival. They mixed a strange blend of fortitude and indifference, could swear in local dialects, knew the price of a large bunch of bananas in ten different currencies and existed forever on their last handful of dollars. They were fascinating but unapproachable and while I had no ambition to be like them, I envied them their knowledge in a land which still held many uncertainties for me. They appeared as awesome leviathans of experience and yet at times dulled and as complacent as pachyderms.

The exception was a German called Hans who had notched up an impressive list of survivals on previous visits to Latin America but had remained a sensitive observer. He travelled for six months and then returned to Stuttgart to finance another journey by driving an ambulance or working as a postman. The previous year he had been to Trinidad for its famous carnival, and I asked him what it had been like. His English was fluent.

'In Austria they say the two highest sensations are firstly making love, and then skiing on powder snow. Carnival in Trinidad would come in the middle.'

I noted that this year's carnival was six weeks away and decided to make my way to Trinidad in time for it. I didn't know it then but Hans was to be a recurring figure during my journey through Central and South America where the trails are sufficiently well-beaten to provide many key junctions and resting places.

Some young Mexicans played a cassette-recorder with fading batteries and Jimmy Hendrix sang bass like an obstructed Louis Armstrong until someone told them to turn it off. Then vendors appeared. They were one of the delights of travelling by train, and the chief delight of this particular journey. They constantly came along shouldering garden buckets packed with ice and soft drinks, great trays of peanuts wrapped in newspaper cones, thermos flasks of ice-cream and baskets of sugared coconut dainties folded up in banana leaves pegged with a splinter. When Hans and I shared our food with the other passengers, some of them brought out bottles secreted under their ponchos and one handed around mescal, the potent spirit made from the tops of the peyote cactus. It pricked my throat but later proved to be a pleasant form of anaesthetic.

A man with an eye-patch began squeezing a tune out of an accordion with more colours than notes. He played with such disinterest that it appeared as instrumental ventriloquism but he inspired someone else to join him and a guitar with three strings was produced. Tequila, pulque and mescal (mostly bottled cactus) had made the travellers appreciative and one banged a tin of tuna against a window, managing to time it to fill the gaps between the honks and twangs. He sang and periodically let out nerve-shattering 'Yeeeeeeee-yooooooochs' through decayed teeth which the lurching train frequently brought dangerously close to the unfortunate accordion-ist's ear.

It was only my tiredness that enabled me to forget that eight hundred miles of bumpy track lay between Mexico City and the Yucatan and that even an express train needed forty-two hours for the journey. And I was at this stage blissfully unaware that the lavatories at either end of the coach had become blocked and the evil-smelling contents were lapping over and steadily advancing down the aisle. I fell asleep thinking about my kilt, wondering where it was at that moment and recalling the day after the bullfight . . .

I had taken it to a post office wrapped in brown paper and bearing a label to a land where it was admired, and even considered *macho*. I hoped to have it sent back to me sometime in South America but for the time being it was merely excess luggage. I had handed it over the counter to be weighed.

'What's inside?' asked the clerkess.

'It's a . . .' No. I wasn't going to say it in Spanish. 'It's a kilt.'

'*Keelt*? What is a *keelt*?'

'It's . . . something Scottish.'

She generously wrote '*una cosa escosesa*' on the customs form, and gave me a smile. I tried to return it but failed, feeling sad that Mexico had made me forfeit something Scottish as payment for *machismo*.

Then I was looking forward to seeing jungle.

2 · Bus Race to El Salvador

Belize adds a slight swelling to the base of the Yucatan Peninsula, the largest carbuncle on the Central American isthmus, and is a sparsely populated country. It is somewhat squashed in shape and has a straight-line border on its western side as if hastily plumbed to give adjacent Guatemala a more angular appearance. Guatemala resents this infringement and has never accepted the division, patiently waiting for the chance to rub out the boundary and absorb Belize. Belize is English-speaking and inhabited by some Indians, some whites, an increasing influx of refugees from war-stricken neighbours, many Creoles, the in-betweens of mestizos and mulattos, and the others whose degree of blackness has been categorised in offensive detail, the quadroons and octoroons.

The predominant Creoles' rockdown and reggae music provides the main pulse of activity in a country of scant employment. The presence of the British army is popular and vital to the country's defence, enabling the stable government to turn to other problems such as discouraging farmers from growing the new and illegal cash crop of marijuana. This has become popular following depressed market prices for the traditional produce of bananas, sugar and citrus fruits, and following the havoc wreaked among many plantations by Hurricane Fifi in 1974. (Hurricanes are always given affectionate names – an attempt by weather-worshipping scientists to flatter and mollify the forces beyond their control.) But it was earlier in 1961, when Hurricane Hattie breezed along in the wake of two disastrous friends, that the government became acutely aware of its wind-prone position and decided it ought to leave Belize City. It moved inland to build its headquarters in the shape of a pyramid, and surrounded it with the new capital, a town called Belmopan. Here the government struggles to reduce the disparities of the country in a conscientious manner but with no money, few resources, a preponderance of bureaucracy and the loneliness of independence – an unfortunate but inevitable legacy of a departed fostermother. You can hear birdsong in Belmopan during rushhour but just reggae and the squabbles of seagulls in Belize City where there is no rushhour.

The boundary with Mexico is marked by a sluggish chocolate river forcing a gap between feathery palm fronds, frayed banana leaves and their dense entourage of less lofty foliage. The border guard inhabited a glorified pillbox beside the river where a converted tourboat had been painted naval grey and was moored to attention. I had to get him to repeat his questions as I was not tuned to Creole. It is a capricious form of English seemingly without grammar, spoken with an accent remarkably similar to Welsh, and bounces around with three times the normal range of intonation. When I had answered the customary questions – Where from? Where to? Why? How long? How much money ('Show me')? – he let me enter the country. I changed some money to Belize dollars at a small bank which had a large safe congested with combination locks, keyholes, a wheel controlling triple-bar snibs and a small notice held on with sellotape: 'Please keep door CLOSED.' A map on the wall showed towns called Tea Kettle, Roaring Creek, Sea Breeze and Spanish Lookout. I took a bus to Orange Walk and then on directly to the principal city.

The road ran beside jungle and swamps, houses perched eight feet off the ground on stilts, skinny children sitting trustingly on the ground below clusters of ripening coconuts, and then a refreshing tang of salt air entered the bus as we passed an empty beach overlooked by curved palm trees. An hour later we were engulfed by the dereliction that is Belize City. A teenage guide offered to take me to a hotel and he led me over a canal which seemed to serve as the town sewer. The air stank and seagulls screamed. 'Keep Belize blood pure – vote P.U.P.', said a wall with red paint. The street became clay and sand, the houses were wooden boxes with rusting tin roofs, precariously standing on stilts or arrested in the act of descending from them. The end house in each row was the vital support preventing the chain-reaction collapse of the entire street. Everything was consumed with the maximum amount of decay compatible with its still managing to hold together – the city was a gift for Hurricane Lolita or whoever was next.

Lanky blacks loitered in the shade and their avid stares instantly saw through my aluminium camera case heavily disguised as a weathered canvas shoulder-bag. They mentally stripped me of all my possessions, their minds swiftly registering and calculating the value of what they saw as mobile loot. Soon we were being followed. We quickened our pace but figures caught up with us. One tried to pick a fight with my guide and he fled. At that moment I spotted the doorway of 'Mrs Haywright's Boarding House', and managed to shake off the hands that were prodding my pack and blunder inside. Mrs Haywright was surprised to find a guest who couldn't produce his money fast enough and would have paid anything, but she was benevolent and welcomed me without doubling the tariff.

'Come right on in,' she said, and then, 'My my! Bless ma socks! Them youths gets purdy boy-ster-oss,' on hearing the reason for my hasty entry. She repeated *boy-ster-oss* as if pleased by the way the syllables bounced, and made me a cup of tea. She was a friendly woman, in her late fifties, slim but top-heavy and giving the impression that tripping would be serious; she had light brown skin and weak mestizo features. She explained that her father had been an English entrepreneur who came to British Honduras, as it was then, in the 1920s to work in the mahogany industry. She had never known him and had been raised by her mother. Her husband had been a fisherman but he had died and now she ran a guest-house to keep busy, although the tourist trade was always sparse.

'Do you like Belize city?' I asked.

'Course! Wouldn't live no place else.'

'But what about the hurricanes, and the boisterous youths?'

'Pwwwehhh.' She blew out air and made her lips vibrate. 'They ain't ever bottered me.' Then she excused herself and sat down to watch television. Belize had only recently begun receiving American broadcasts. I sat in the background reading a tourist brochure on the country which talked about the beauty of the nearby cays and coral gardens, and mentioned that the tapir was the national animal. There followed a dictionary description of the creature: 'a large odd-toed ungulate with short flexible proboscis'. After a while I became bored and tried to practise *pwwwehhh* silently, without matching Mrs Haywright's expertise, and eventually turned to watch television. It was a homely atmosphere, but this land of odd-toed ungulates seemed far removed from Dallas on the screen.

The next morning I continued my journey towards Tikal by bus. The buses seemed to run in one direction every other day and return in between. That particular morning was fortunately an outward journey towards my destination but the driver had doubts as to whether we would get through because of severe flooding. It was mid-December and the rainy season should have ended in October but recent rains had swollen the rivers. We set off and after a short time the road disappeared into a lake in the middle of which a truck stood stranded. The road was on a causeway which was now one foot under water, but our driver carried on without hesitation. He peered at the surface immediately ahead and judged by colours. Dark was deep, light was shallow. I watched in horror as we wobbled over the planks of a narrow submerged bridge which seemed no wider than the width of our bus. We then hit a succession of potholes which made us lean over onto one side so that we were looking straight down into the dark depths.

It had been obvious to everyone except our driver that the truck was not parked in the middle of the lake by choice but was stuck, and therefore blocking the road. He didn't appear to realise this until he pulled up behind it, then his forehead wrinkled and he thought for a moment. Slowly his gaze turned on the horizon of water and then fell to his wing mirror which showed another unbroken expanse of water, and that we now also stood stuck in the middle of the lake. The probability that he would have to reverse his bus back along the causeway and over the narrow submerged bridge, as good as blindfold, registered as a slow, sorrowful nod. He stoically rolled his trousers up to the knees and jumped down from the bus, his legs disappearing up to the thighs in an unusually bad pothole. It was while walking around the side of the truck that he lost his footing and tumbled off the causeway into a dark patch of water. There was a fearful moment of thrashing and yelling before we realised that he couldn't swim. Before any of us could react, the truck–driver had appeared and dragged the poor man out.

I was in a good position to see this because I was squashed next to the driver's seat against the windscreen, beneath a notice stating '55 passengers maximum'. While the bus-driver was spluttering and recovering, having firmly clamped himself to the rear wheel of the truck, I amused myself by counting heads. I had reached 80 for the second time when a little boy squeezed out of the throng of bodies and sat down on the driver's seat. He moaned, whined and burped, producing a very fair imitation of our engine when it had been in action, and was pumping on the accelerator pedal which was shaped in the outline of a foot with independent toes, when the steering wheel lifted up and came away in his hands. This silenced him for a moment and then he giggled fatuously at his mother who calmly told him to stop fooling around and to put it back. I closed my eyes . . .

Within half an hour the damp driver came back smiling. A tractor had appeared from the other side and began slowly towing the truck away in front of us. The driver was unperturbed at finding his steering wheel lying on his seat. He slotted it back onto the column and drove on. A few minutes later he started humming. Latin American bus-drivers have a wonderful ability to forget about disasters of their own ingenious contrivance.

We reached the Guatemalan border shortly before it closed for lunch. The official was uncommunicative, so I had to judge his attitude by the posters in Spanish on his wall. The largest was ominous. 'BELIZE IS OURS', was splashed across a map which showed no boundary, and Belize was a corner shaded in the same colour as the rest of the country. He scowled at me on noticing the coat of arms of the United Kingdom on my passport and then levied an entry fine of five US dollars on me because the United Kingdom had taken his top right-hand corner and wouldn't give it back.

The rest of the journey to Tikal was a joy. The road was scarcely passable, a slabby quagmire of ochre twisting through deep cuttings in jungle-clad hills, but a rough-country timber truck gave me a lift on its trailer. I lay in the sun watching the impenetrable wall of vegetation slip by as we bumped and squelched along, relishing the sensation of space. A toucan flew past, followed by a flurry of green parrots with scarlet heads. For one ludicrous moment I was surprised and thought they must have escaped from a cage.

The Mayas were a race of great builders and intensive farmers, being amongst the earliest Indians to cultivate maize. They were skilled mathematicians and used a calendar more accurate than ours today, but strangely, they built their monumental temples and palaces without the use of the wheel. The Central American Indians certainly knew of its existence but the wheel has only been found on the toys they made for their children. Tikal was one of their largest and oldest cities, inhabited for six centuries until around AD 1000. Then the Mayas are thought to have experienced a decline, and mysteriously deserted Tikal.

Tikal's setting is magnificent. Its temples are grouped around small clearings in the jungle and they tower up out of the dense vegetation as great wedges of stone. Lemurs wander through the ruins, butterflies of vibrant yellow, blue and orange silently hiccup through the air and spider monkeys screech in the trees. They are all-prehensile and use hands, feet and tail to cartwheel through the branches of their illimitable playpen.

Approaching the first temple I noticed a thin brown trail emerging from a hole in the ground and running across the neatly mown lawn towards the ancient hand-hewn stones. My eyes followed endless confused columns of black termites going about their daily chores. The outgoing ones followed the trail to the wall and walked up the vertical face of the obstacle. The back was unadorned and so they had a straightforward climb of 229 feet to the top. (I then went round to the front and used the steps to meet them.) Had they paused on the crest of the structure they would have looked out over a sea of green formed by the canopy ceiling of the jungle running into the distance in every direction, fluorescing in the glow of the evening sun. The canopy was broken only by the dark triangles of nearby pyramids whose tops had been left flat and finally capped with chambers in the shape of tall diadems. The termites didn't stop to admire this view but proceeded down the front of the temple before me, down-along, down-along eighty-eight steps which were so steep that a length of chain had been draped over them as a handhold for humans, until they reached the bottom.

They followed their little path worn directly across the plaza, up and over the carved and once painted standing stone in the middle – one of many stellae which were erected every 52 years and used as a calendar, for every Mayan carving had a precise mathematical significance – and were undaunted by the second pyramid which now stood in their way. Ignoring the central staircase this time, they walked up the tiers which lay on either side, went in and out of the jaws and skirted around the eyes of sculptured jaguar heads – the most revered and occasionally sacrificed animal – up 200 feet, down the back, into the jungle and then up the tallest tree. Here they removed a portion of leaf three times their own size and returned home the same way, trampling over some of the finest examples of Mayan architecture from the Classic Period.

A short shower of rain sent me scurrying for cover under the leaves of a gigantic plant. Jungle in the rain is the next wettest place to a loch. Water pours down branches and tree trunks, forms miniature water-falls from every obstruction and if you can avoid the incessant drips, the splashes reach you and puddles grow out of the ground below your feet. To touch a single plant stem is to release a deluge poised above your head – you just have to accept that in a tropical shower of rain, you get soaked. I felt irresistibly drawn to the jungle's sinister atmosphere, its mood of insidious menace. It waits while you watch but as soon as your back is turned it quickly weaves its inextricable bonds around all that lies in its grasp. A jungle is constantly plotting and never idle. It is a seething mass of rampant fertility and racing decay.

There is little moderation in the lowland tropics. It is either scorching hot or a downpour, completely still or a hurricane, daytime or dark night. Events are switched on and off without prelude and are sometimes regular enough for you to judge the correct time by their arrival and departure – the first drops of rain falling each day with the clockwork precision of nature. The rain suddenly stops: six p.m. The sun sets, twilight comes and instantly vanishes: night.

The air was still warm and sultry when I returned to my tent in the park campsite. The dank vegetation steamed with its exothermic activities, creeping, decomposing, carrying the musty smell of compost and a sweet undercurrent of nectar. Fireflies lit up in the dark, momentarily tracing crazy paths of flight before extinguishing their burning glow, and the insect orchestras struck up their shrill, single-tune recitals. *Neeeeeaaaaay* came in pulses of pure notes and then evolved through *weeeaaay* and *woo-hey* to the relentless inter-rogation of *who-why?*. Others trommelled, buzzed, whirred, clicked, scritched and scraped. The air reverberated as if countless thousands of minuscule Hare Krishna processions were going along every branch and every blade of grass, their strident rattles, jangles and chants ceaselessly drilling the night. But the most eerie part was the way these sounds were coordinated and aware of their combined effect. They too were switched on and off, changed pitch in synchro-nised chorus and rose in conducted crescendos as if this was a deliberate war of attrition, and I, for some reason, had been selected as their victim.

But then their spell was broken by the gentle sound of a flute and guitar duet floating across from some campfire, and I fell asleep under my mosquito net feeling content, and safe from the whining hordes which clamoured for my blood.

After toying with the idea of going to El Salvador and then deciding against it because of reports of renewed violence, I changed my mind again after speaking to the guitar-player, a Dutchman, who had

passed through the previous week without any unpleasantness. The
road from Tikal to Guatemala City was impassable and the only
alternative was to take a domestic flight. Shortly after my arrival in the
capital, which was rent by the fissures of past earthquakes (the one in
1976 lasted forty seconds and killed 23,000 people), I found several
buses about to make the 130-mile trip to El Salvador.

The drivers' assistants were young teenage boys who were
chivvying passers-by and trying to fill their bus quickly by hauling
them aboard. I had been seized by one whose bus was going west to
Panajachel, yelling 'Panapanapanapanaaaaaaaa, but extracted myself
and was bundled into the one heading south-east via Jalapa ('Jalajalajalajalapaaaaaaa'). It was the usual affair, a rehabilitated metal carcass
held together by bright paint and necessity. A crucifix hung from a
rubber suction pad on the windscreen and a plaque above testified to
an additional measure of insurance. 'Lord, into Thy hands I com-
mend my passengers. I sat on a seat for two, jammed between a
portly woman with her money and a packet of cigarettes wedged
inside her extensive cleavage which could have held a lot more, and an
elderly man with a hen on his lap. A pathetic mite of a girl appeared to
tout packets of chiclets and then another vendor came with cakes of
penicillin soap. He harangued his captive audience for a while before
passing around a book of colour photographs showing the most
gruesome rashes and skin disorders in graphic detail, and his soap sold
well.

Departure times were dependent more on the number of passengers than the clock, but the driver took his seat before we were full.
There were still three handholds left to allow more citizens to bulge
out of the open door when we set off, but this premature departure
proved to be because it was a race. The bus of a rival company, Rutas
Lima, running the same route was already moving towards the exit.
Our driver was a small man, scarcely able to see over the dashboard,
but his size concealed great bravado and an eagerness to make time
with true *macho* desperation. His hand swept the bulbous head of the
gear-lever in wide movements covering one yard with each change
and this helped to keep the pressurised crowd of passengers at a
distance. Horn and accelerator seemed controlled by the same pedal.

The assistant began to collect fares as we accelerated, our horn
blasting a passage through the twisty streets and each violent turn
throwing us from buttock to buttock. The assistant was close to what
I had seen in the trees at Tikal, half-human, three-quarters monkey

and definitely not normal. He held dozens of currency notes, each folded in half along its length and tucked according to denomination between the appropriate fingers of one hand. The same hand held an inexhaustible supply of coins and the correct change slipped magically from it. He needed no more than a toehold for balance and frequently conducted his transactions suspended by his free hand from the luggage rack as he squirmed his way through the crowd.

The rival RL bus was ahead of us on the main road when we suddenly veered off down a side alley, sending pedestrians and children fleeing. After five minutes of wheel-shrieking insanity we emerged at a toll booth on the principal highway just ahead of RL. The monkey was out in a flash, running to deliver a bit of paper, and then he leapt back aboard as the bus, which had never stopped, was powering off with the driver's foot flat down on the horn. We kept ahead until a roadside woman flagged us down. She tried to enter with forty pounds of bananas on her head at the same time as another woman tried to leave. They became wedged in the doorway and the driver cursed until the banana woman backed down, and we drove off without her.

The terrain had become more mountainous when we next caught up with RL. We were marginally faster on the gradients and so the driver pulled out to overtake as a motorcyclist appeared over the approaching blind summit. Blind summits were an inconvenience, motorcyclists didn't count. The crucifix rattled against the window and caused the driver to glance up. 'Lord, into Thy hands . . .' The driver was all right. He was insured. The alarmed motorcyclist slowed down as much as time allowed and avoided a collision by taking to the rubble verge, still travelling far too fast. I turned to watch as his front wheel shuddered wildly, his rear wheel slithered and some potholes bucked him into the air. With grim determination he stayed upright and returned to the road, his helmet lying somewhat crookedly across his head. Our driver was oblivious of what had happened, scenting his moment of triumph. Spurred on by the monkey who had found a toehold and was now leaning out horizontally through the driver's side window yelling insults at another monkey, he had brought our bus alongside RL, and, wing mirror to wing mirror (both broken), we crested the blind summit together and hammered on towards a hairpin.

The highway was quiet that morning and it was only one mile later that we encountered any opposition, and then RL magnanimously backed down when it seemed inevitable that it would be nudged off into a yellow canyon by our head-on collision with the oncoming vehicle. RL caught up with us after a flat stretch and again we were neck and neck, monkey to monkey, for the fifth blind summit. The contest was then spoilt by a family on our bus who had reached their destination and wanted out. They were quickly ejected but the monkey had to shin up onto the roof to throw down their luggage. We were off before the last bundle had hit the ground and twenty minutes later we were recovering our lost advantage at 50 mph, when the back door flew open and a pair of feet dangled down. The monkey wriggled in, his shirt billowing in the slipstream and his cheeks slightly blue from the cool air at our altitude of 7,500 feet.

Several miles further on, a loud knocking sound suddenly came from the rear wheels and it felt as if we were passing over a long cattle grid. The driver called for the monkey, handed him a machete and stopped to let him out. We heard the blows of furious hacking, and then he returned. All seemed well when we set off. The knocking sound returned after five minutes and then came the more perilous crunch of metal fatigue. This time we coasted to a halt and the driver changed into a greasy boiler suit. It was apparently going to be a lengthy delay and people got out to stretch their legs. The driver disappeared under the rear axle and I watched as bits of metal were periodically thrown out, and the monkey continued to remove lengths of shredded rubber from the outer layer of one tyre with blows from his large knife. When the collection of metal had mounted and included most of the components of the brake system, the fault was evidently cured with loud raps of a hammer and the pile of metal gradually disappeared. Within half an hour we were once more racing through the mountains at break-neck and break-everything-else speed. My neighbours dozed, the one with her cigarettes still safely crushed, the other with his hen almost equally crushed – it was drowsy and rested its head on his wrist, its eyelids closing from the bottom upwards, until the next jolt startled it to attention.

'Jalajalajalajalapaaaaaaa,' shouted the monkey, and we had arrived. It had been a terrific performance and I couldn't resist going over to shake hands with the driver and the monkey. Then I noted the name on the side of our bus and transferred to another company for the remaining journey to El Salvador.

*   *   *

El Salvador is the smallest, most densely populated, violent, divided and, in my opinion, most beautiful of the isthmus republics. While her two closest neighbours, Guatemala and Honduras, may better epitomise the fundamental tragedy of all Latin America – the need for land reform in countries where most of the cultivable land is held outside the reach of the undernourished peasant communities and lies fallow, inefficiently exploited or used to raise export crops instead of staple foods – El Salvador best shows how an economy can grow and result in no social progress for the masses, how wealth buys power and plutocracy protects itself with armed force and the suppression of rights, health and education. Of the one hundred or so super-rich landowners, fourteen principal families form the hub of power and protect their interests with the support of the army and foreign assistance. Growing resentment of their régime and the injustices which it perpetuates has erupted into a guerilla campaign of resistance, strongest in the north, and a civil war in which over 50,000 Salvadorians have died – a war as volatile as the country's many splendid volcanoes must have once been and in bitter contrast to the tranquillity of her numerous lakes. My passport was hesitantly handed over and pounded with 'Entrada' at a town on the western border.

'No, it's not so bad,' said a smiling girl as our bus toiled up Izalco volcano, taking one and a half hours to cover seven miles. 'Worse in the north, but here it's quiet now.' She worked at the luxury Hotel Montana built by the government at the top of an adjacent mountain so that guests could watch Izalco's display of simmering lava; but the lava had stopped flowing soon after it was completed. The hotel had been empty for years. She insisted on buying me papusas, savoury filled tortillas, at every stop until the vendors seemed to disappear with the cool air. Once the bus's loudspeaker crackled with Al Stewart singing 'Love was a smile away', but the song was in English and only meaningful to me. We looked down on Lake Coatepeque, a placid body of water whose shades of ultramarine were in a constant and subtle state of flux, lying cupped as an almost circular blot among dark green hills. Then Izalco stood before us, a conical pile of smouldering rubble, naked and devastatingly black.

There was no sign of political strife when I later gazed up at the tall spire of Santa Ana's neo-Gothic cathedral, which provided hundreds of neo-Gothic perches for flocks of doves. Neither did my second night cause me any concern when I camped on the edge of the extinct

San Salvador volcano. The mountain was a Russian doll of cones; inside its crater was a smaller cone containing a yet smaller crater and cone. The panorama at dawn showed a graceful array of similar symmetrical mountains, the suburbs of the capital city and the distant breakers of the Pacific. The ocean's white ripples clung to the coast as they endlessly repeated their soothing motion. A lizard was grubbing amongst leaves near the bubbling pan on my stove; the air smelt of early morning succulence and, increasingly, of porridge. Only two soldiers guarding a radio mast on the other side of the summit looked capable of mischief. I descended and swam with carefree Salvadorians in a series of pools built in a natural gorge in the jungle. Families laughed and splashed and dived from large concrete toadstools which sprouted from the riverbed and formed stepping stones across the surface. And I was still unaware of danger as I sat in a hotel that evening, eating fried eggs, beans and tortillas spiced with 'Ana Belly's Hot Sauce' (Made in Guatemala), but it was only when I tried to leave the hotel that the manager came out of the caged reception desk and stopped me as an army truck of soldiers went past.

'Curfew,' he said. 'Everywhere. 8.00 pm to 6.00 am.' He returned to his cage. I went to the door and peeped out. The streets were empty and strangely quiet, as if even the dogs and cocks were observing silence. The tranquillity made the graffiti on the wall opposite appear to shout. 'DEATH TO FIFTY YEARS OF MILITARY DICTA-TORSHIP.'

I went back to my room, wrote up my diary and planned an early night, but after ten o'clock the noise of footsteps in the passage became intolerable. I went down to reception to see what was happening. A queue of late-teenage boys and young men were gathered by the cage and one or two were emerging from rooms, followed by a girl who came to lead away the next in line. It seemed there were plenty of restless men prepared to risk a quick dash across the forbidden streets.

I went over to the manager to complain about the noise. He gave me a lewd wink from behind his bars: 'Very cheap. Five colons (£1), twenty minutes.' I viewed the squalid crowd before me with the distaste of being offered a used handkerchief. The manager mistook my concern. 'No waiting. You go next.'

'That's very kind but I just want to sleep. I would like to have a quieter room at the back.'

'No more rooms – all rooms are occupied.' He grinned with genuine pleasure. A curfew was just the thing for business.

The next day I was apprehensive when I entered the capital, San Salvador (Saint Saviour), whose appearance added to my confusion over whether its saint was active, dormant or extinct. It was a modern city hemmed in by hills and a set of crags called the 'Devil's Doors'. Parts were like any other spacious city, others had the worst hovels I had seen – rows of huts made from cardboard boxes and sheets of plastic – and the main plaza was liberally painted with graffiti. A single sharp report of gunfire made me cringe in my steps and when I looked towards the source, I saw a peasant standing holding his head on the far side of the street. His oxen had stopped and were chewing the cud, the cart behind them was stacked high with logs and had keeled over to one side. The peasant was staring aghast at the cart's old car tyre which had suddenly blown and was on the point of toppling his load.

Students had taken over a modern, budget-conscious church which was daubed with slogans of 'Libertad' and 'Revolución' in red paint, and rock music blared from its windows. A crowd was gathered around more students who performed energetic charades which made them laugh and cheer. Some performers were stripped to the waist, smeared with dirt, and going through the motions of cutting crops while other figures prodded them with imaginary rifles. There wasn't a sign of real soldiers anywhere.

It was only two days later, about to leave the country, that I remembered Christmas. It had been the day I came down from the volcano, swam in the river pools and discovered how many people didn't observe the curfew. Christmas had passed unnoticed. It was easy to lose track of days and dates with a nomadic lifestyle but how I had missed Christmas of all days was a mystery. I was not alone. The last writing on the wall that I saw in beautiful and seductive El Salvador gave the explanation. 'THERE IS NO CHRISTMAS WITH POLITICAL OPPRESSION.'

A few days later the death toll had increased.

Daily encounters with strangers often help to remove a lone traveller's feeling of isolation, but a second encounter with even the briefest of these casual acquaintances assumes the rarity value of a precious friendship. With time on my hands before the carnival in Trinidad, I made my way to the Bay Islands, situated close to the east coast of Honduras. It was there, a week later and quite by chance, that such an encounter took place with an old friend of several weary hours' standing.

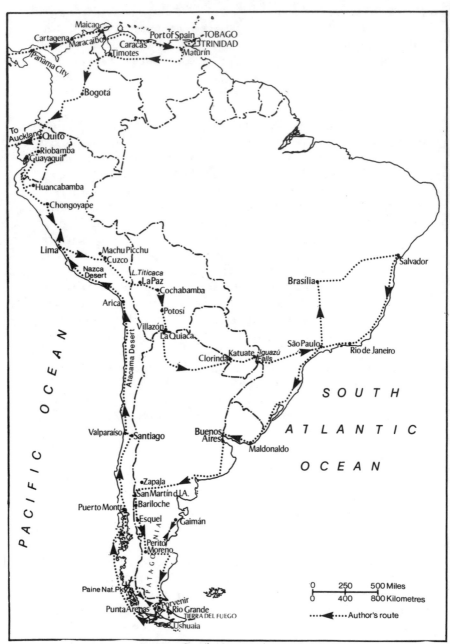

South America

3 · Paradise, and a Pig in Venezuela

Paradise! Once a British possession and a popular haunt of pirates, the Bay Islands have belonged to Honduras for over a century and yet the inhabitants still speak English and consider themselves ethnically closer to Europe than to the mainland twenty miles away. Utila is the most accessible island, lazing in the translucent aquamarine waters of the warm Caribbean Sea and surrounded by coral reefs which are home to a myriad of swimming rainbow colours. One morning in Utila post office a familiar figure was standing in front of me.

Hans was bent over the post office counter trying to stick thirty-two large stamps onto the present he was sending home, a wallet thinly wrapped in paper. It is one of the world's idiosyncrasies that the smallest countries produce the largest stamps. These are usually low denominational values so that the stamps for any international communication heavier than a letter are dispensed by the square foot. (The same practice extends to official rubber stamps. Canada requires a modest corner of a passport for its entry stamp which is the size of two thumbprints, whereas Trinidad and Tobago was to run amok over a full page.) Hans was applying layer upon layer of stamps in overlapping rows in the manner of slating a roof and when he reached the last row, he carefully tore a corner off each stamp. He looked up to see me staring in puzzlement, and after a hearty handshake he explained his odd behaviour.

'I make that to stop someone stealing the stamps. Torn stamps have no value to collectors. In this way it should reach Germany.' He turned to the clerk and insisted that the stamps be postmarked in front of him ('to stop this man from taking off my stamps later and reselling them'). Had it not been for our earlier encounter in Mexico I should have avoided him because he looked like a travelling pachyderm. He was in his mid-twenties, of medium height, fair-haired, stocky, reliable and Teutonically efficient. His face was keen to exaggerate the delivery of a surprising degree of humour, although it frequently went blank in prolonged periods of intense reflection. His most irritating feature was that, with regard to practical matters, he was invariably right. His most likeable qualities were his extensive knowledge and the fact that he never carried a camera.

I was carrying two camera bodies, three lenses, two flashguns, spare light-meter, tripod and handfuls of accessories, and always felt unhappy if I had less than thirty rolls of unexposed film in reserve. This was all housed in my disguised camera case which hung as a lop-sided load from my right shoulder and could do so comfortably for up to eight hours (my left shoulder ached after ten minutes, so I would change and resign myself to walking with a list to the right). Photography was the overriding motive which sustained my interest in travel and my eagerness to see more, but Hans was to make me see the danger that it might suppress my other senses. When my camera was back in its case I immediately felt ready to move on and leave the view in front of me. My objective had been fulfilled. Whereas Hans would witness a scene with no more intention than simply to be there and to savour the experience. He moved freely, unencumbered by excess baggage, absorbing the sights, sounds, smells and atmosphere. An awareness of these components of mood is essential for perceiving an effective photograph, but the traveller obsessed with his camera is liable to become a cyclops, narrow-visioned, blundering and unfeeling.

I limited my photography to Utila's main street, just wide enough for one of the island's dozen or so cars to squeeze along on its own, the wooden houses on stilts, painted either green or white and each with a swinging sofa in its verandah, and to taking pictures of my tent for the manufacturer, Vango, who had given it to me for this purpose. Utila was the perfect pitch, and made a pleasing contrast to the last shots I had taken of it against a background of icebergs in Greenland. Then I put the camera away and absorbed the atmosphere of the island, from the beaches to the cheerful 'You all right, mister?' calls of the villagers.

It really was paradise. Humming birds flashed in the air and stopped abruptly in mid-flight to consider which way to go, poised as if motionless as delicate imitations of kingfishers which could comfortably sleep two to a matchbox. A long-faced pelican stood on a rock staring at the sea over his baggy bill, wondering how on earth to fill it. Ghost crabs scuttled on the sand from hole to hole and frigate birds swept down out of the sky, skimmed low over the ground and snapped up surprised crabs with flicks of their hooked beaks. Two boys went past with nine iguanas, four of which were stuffed head first into their trouser pockets. They had caught them with a dog and were taking them home to eat. Lying in the cool shade of my own palm tree, without any worries or predators, I felt a dream-like quality about my environment, a Bacardi commercial to perfection. It was enhanced when a local girl came along and offered me a coconut ready to drink. Her name was Nally.

'You live in paradise here,' I said.

'For you, maybe,' she replied, and explained that she was twenty-one years old. Her day was spent at home fetching water from the village well, cooking, and washing. Nally knew everyone and everyone knew her. There was no electricity on the island, although the 'Bucket of Blood' had its own generator and ran a disco to entertain the familiar faces. There was no work, barely any more opportunities on the Spanish-speaking mainland and even less for a girl who spoke Creole, and no escape. Passports were expensive and hard to acquire. She had been waiting two years for the necessary documents and was no nearer receiving them because of the stringent conditions laid down by the authorities and the sloth of officialdom. She wanted to go to the United States but wasn't prepared to achieve this by accepting the first traveller who proposed marriage ('That's not why I brought you the coconut!') as some of her friends had done. Nally would wait, and hope one day to leave.

And so I discovered the two faces of paradise. This girl would happily exchange a crowded shopping street in the rain and a nine-to-five job for unlimited use of sun, sand and the romance of the 'Bucket of Blood'. Paradise, it seems, can be anywhere we happen to be – as long as we don't stay too long; or anywhere we happen *not* to be. It never stays in one place for very long, it never lets us become well acquainted, and it always seems to set up camp on a horizon we have never visited, or the one we have just left.

The receding tide left the sand glassy and with the rosy sheen of evening light, coconut palms turned to sharp silhouettes against the lapping silvery vastness of the Caribbean, and the sun balanced on the horizon as a utopian beacon for me, as a great red sour grape for others.

Paradise dimmed for a while, until my self-indulgent pity faltered and the scene became bright again. They could be hard – these countries, this travelling – unless you retained the ability to detach yourself from what you hadn't caused and couldn't change. It was a brief, selfish triumph. I wallowed in blissful simplicity and refused to see beyond the tranquillity of my perfect moment.

*   *   *

'Are you going to Trinidad as well?' I asked.

'No. I am afraid that a second time it would not be so good,' Hans replied. 'I will go to Venezuela or Colombia instead.'

As we were both heading in the same direction over the next few days we agreed to travel together as far as the border of Nicaragua. Each of us was glad of some company as this border crossing was rumoured to be a 'difficult' one for backpackers. During the ferry trip from Utila to the mainland we passed massive freighters lying at anchor awaiting cargoes of bananas, self-contained worlds whose unlimited potential for travel was quietly provocative. The *Honolulu* from Holland was departing with 260,000 boxes, *Tropical Gold* from Brazil was manoeuvring towards the wharf, while other ships lay idly tugging at their bow chains, emanating an air of melancholy at the indignity of being restrained. These ocean tramps, Hans explained, had come to take away the produce of the two American commercial giants, United Brands of Boston (formerly United Fruit) and Standard Fruit, with the worst reputations in Central America for the exploitation of their workforces. Between them they controlled one-third of Honduran revenue. (And it was for them, at least for the interests of United Fruit, that the CIA engineered the 1954 coup in Guatemala. Behind bananas and the mines of Bolivia and Chile were stories to make the United States eagle go bald and blush.)

We reached the mainland port of La Ceiba and were waiting for some form of transport to leave the town when I discovered one of the drawbacks of having a German shadow. Hans had wandered off while I was in the process of photographing a genial old man wearing a straw tricorn in the fruit market, looking like Napoleon set in bananas with a monkey on his shoulder. When everything was just right, Hans returned at a run shouting that a *collectivo* taxi was about to leave. Before I could take the picture the monkey had panicked and fled and then Napoleon was chasing it, turning to shake his fist at me as he ran off down the street. This upset me and I swore at Hans before hurriedly putting away my camera.

Collectivos were cheaper taxis which collected as many fares as possible along the way, and whose drivers had an inflated notion of their capacity. This one was a pick-up and we sat in the open back with other passengers, our backpacks in the middle propped up by twelve pairs of knees. The road climbed into the hills through an avenue of palms whose clusters of fronds burst out above us like eruptions of green fireworks. The view was filled with the gentle gradations of tropical greens, but its enchantment was partially dispelled by my lingering annoyance over the Napoleon incident.

'It will rain soon,' said Hans suddenly. His manner was always dogmatic, even allowing for the fact that English was not his native tongue. '. . . *will* rain . . .' This was irritating. The clouds didn't look at all threatening to me.

'Nonsense,' I replied. 'At this time of year it doesn't rain until the evening. At a quarter to six, usually.'

An hour later I was trying to avoid his eyes while rain ('*Ja, ja*') drummed down on the tarpaulin we held over our heads.

'You know,' Hans offered some time later, 'in Lake Nicaragua they have migrating sharks. They go and come between the sweet and salt water.'

'Yes, I know the lake has sharks but I think you'll find they don't migrate. They have adapted to fresh water and live there permanently.'

'No, no. Look . . .' he rummaged in his pack and pulled out a German guidebook. 'I have it here. "*Wandernde Haie*' – migrating sharks.'

'What a relief,' I said. 'It's stopped raining.'

We broke our journey in Tegucigalpa. The name was worth repeating for it entertained the tonsils, but unfortunately this was the nicest thing about the capital. We found it impossible to move around unnoticed because children herded us through the slum streets chanting '*gringos, gringos*', and made us feel as popular as April Fools. We spent the night in a basic hotel and the following morning I had a haircut at Barberia Jerónimo. The name alone should have warned me but Jerónimo claimed another scalp and dismissed me with two hearty thumps between my shoulder blades, causing a few more severed curls to fall to the ground which looked like the aftermath of a cockfight. Hans had meanwhile arranged a lift to the border with a truck. As we bumped along with sacks of flour, I found some consolation in my near baldness with the knowledge that Nicaraguan officials did not like long hair.

'It is not good that you have a green kitbag,' proclaimed my mentor during the three-hour ride. 'Border guards are mistrustful of things that look military. Especially when you have a soldier's haircut.' But for once he was wrong. I passed through customs without any trouble while Hans was subjected to a long questioning and a detailed search.

'*Ja, ja,*' I gloated, when he was finally released, 'it'll probably rain today. At about 5.45, I should say.'

We parted company at the border to make hitching easier and I soon found a lift with Umberto Ramos, a member of a farming cooperative and a former Sandinista guerilla. The Sandinistas took their name from the folk hero General César Sandino who was tricked into giving up his arms and then killed in 1933, thereby ending five years of successful guerilla warfare against foreign control of the country and the occupying forces of United States marines. This brought the first Anastasio Somoza to power, the man who during an official visit to Costa Rica once said, 'I don't want educated people. I want oxen.' He began the Somoza family's forty-five-year domination of the country's affairs and treated the people as oxen until his assassination in 1956. His son, Anastasio Jr, maintained the same attitude, soon learnt the useful Latin American ruse of crying the threat of communism to swell his coffers with the generous US aid that financed his totalitarian rule, and increased his family's possessions to include Nicaragua's twenty-six biggest companies and land equal in size to El Salvador, five million acres. It was less than a year since the Sandinistas, the Frente Sandino Libertad Nicaragua, had ended the Somoza dynasty by ousting Anastasio Jr, who had fled to Paraguay after exacting the final vengeances of bombing his own cities and embezzling a $65-million loan from the IMF (as he had done with the international aid sent to Nicaragua after the 1972 earthquake). The Sandinistas had been elected to govern and were trying to repair their country. During the drive south towards Managua I asked Umberto what guerilla life had been like.

He was a small man, about thirty, wiry and with thin sinewy wrists – not how I had imagined a guerilla to be at all. He took his eyes off the road for a moment and turned to me, his face blank save for the hint of an ironical smile. 'Have you ever heard of Father Betancur?' he asked. I shook my head. 'No, of course not. He was a good man, in his fifties but full of energy. He worked at a mission in the remote Zelaya region. He started a school there and formed a workers' society to help the peasant farmers grow better crops and market them more profitably. No one had ever done that for them before and he was popular. When the neighbouring landowner knocked down the peasants' fences and put a road through their property, Father Betancur quietly helped them to put up new fences. The landowner was a member of the National Guard which owned ten per cent of non-Somoza land, ran a monopoly on prostitution and gambling, and exercised unquestioned authority in disposing of suspected communist insurgents' – the words *insurgentes comunistas* skipped daintily with sarcasm. 'Father Betancur's body was found 150 feet down a well. He had been whipped and castrated. His body had no eyes, teeth, tongue, fingernails or feet. Alongside were the remains of five peasants who had been roasted to death in a bread oven for refusing to disband the cooperative. That was what our enemy was like. That was what we had to live with as guerillas.'

Neither of us spoke for a long time. Our car was stopped at a military checkpoint where it was sprayed with disinfectant to prevent the spread of a coffee shrub disease. We drove on past a gigantic banner portraying Sandino, bordered by the half black, half red colours of the FSLN. Their flags were everywhere, tree trunks and church steps were painted in black and red bands, and a file of schoolchildren marched behind their teacher chanting national slogans. Umberto nodded with satisfaction. 'A new Nicaragua,' he smiled and I smiled back hoping he was right. A fever of nationalism was rife and the newspaper on the dashboard was full of the witchhunt for Somoza supporters. The pictures of twenty-three 'traitors' awaiting trial were displayed on the front page. He said the new government had implemented an intensive campaign against the fifty-per-cent rate of illiteracy, had reduced infant mortality and introduced drastic agrarian reform. But this was not enough, he added. As Mexico had demonstrated, a revolution might bring about idealistic changes but progress depended on these changes being supported by technological know-how, equipment and finance. It would all take time, and already food was scarce in the shops, prices had risen sharply and the black market was booming.

The pine trees so common in Honduras had all but vanished and the rolling hills were covered with low scrub, dry grass and some broad-leafed trees. There was a paucity of people and fields. The road inclines became more acute as we flanked a chain of volcanoes which might have been turned on a potter's wheel, and descended to León. This university city had borne the brunt of Somoza's anger; many buildings were piles of rubble below tangled frames of steel girders and bullet holes formed wiggly lines along streets of houses. Over the next few days I continued south and passed alongside Lake Nicaragua ('*wandernde Haie*') which was so vast it was like staring out to sea. It would have been host to some of the world's largest ships had the original proposal to build a Pacific–Atlantic canal here gone ahead in the 1850s, but instead Panama was chosen for ships and Lake Nicaragua has had to content itself with sharks.

On reaching Managua, the capital of the country, I asked a man to direct me to the city centre. He told me I was standing in it. I stood amongst what looked like neglected fields and abandoned building plots surrounded by the odd outcrop of buildings. Managua had apparently never recovered from the 1972 earthquake. When I came to the president's palace it seemed closed, run down and eschewed as if marked with the plague. Nearby stood a large square plinth of hewn stone. A Somoza had once erected a fine equestrian statue to himself on this spot but it had been destroyed by the Sandinistas and now the block supported nothing more than four horse's hooves cut off above the fetlocks.

Trinidad suddenly seemed especially inviting and yet so far away; 1,500 crow-flight miles and half as much again by my land route, allowing for a short flight over the roadless Darien Gap where Central and South America meet. Two weeks to carnival. I wanted a carnival, and even felt I *needed* one. Smiling faces were plentiful here but too often they appeared brave in the context of the lives behind them. An assortment of trucks and cars, including a convoy of crusading Seventh Day Adventists driving a fleet of luxury caravans shaped as huge silver bullets took me down the long, snaking road towards Panama. My last view of Nicaragua was nostalgic; fields of golden crops, cows swishing their tails in acres of rich green, the cobalt blue expanse of the lake with Ometepe Island's twin volcanoes sweeping up to bury their tops in the only cloud to be seen, and the moist smell of Yorkshire sedgeland. It was a momentary impression but I couldn't eradicate the Dent dales from my mind despite the exotic scenery before me and the memory of four horse's hooves on a colossal pedestal.

A week later I was leaving Panama City on a flight bound for South America. By chance, Hans had bought a ticket for the same flight. He didn't carry a camera but collected postcards instead, and he was still slightly upset because Nicaragua had only offered a choice of two views. Both were in black and white and one was out of focus.

Costa Rica had been a rush for me, but an enjoyable one for this country is strategically placed to give the traveller some respite from the novelty of Latin America. Apart from being relaxed and yet efficient, it is unusual in that it has a stable government, no army and citizens who are predominantly white and relatively affluent. (They use umbrellas when it rains and are able to cycle *for fun and fitness.*) Panama had surprised me when its northern foothills of jungle gave way to an expanse of veld studded with mango trees. I had kept on expecting to see a herd of African elephants milling around but there had been only some cattle and groups of funereal vultures too lethargic to fly. The sight of the canal had been totally captivating. My lingering memory was of an enormous flag fluttering on top of Ancon Hill, the Panamanian colours tugging eagerly at a mast like a rectangular spinnaker only partially secured. It seemed to represent the mood of excitement in the country at the thought of taking over the Canal Zone and (by the year 2000) full control of the canal itself. Hans offered a more pessimistic view, asserting that Panama's short-sighted policy of felling rain forest was now resulting in the canal's vital lakes silting up. By that year 2000 as much as forty per cent of the lake's storage capacity would have been lost, and only shallow-draught boats would be able to use the canal. There was already talk of constructing a new canal through Colombian territory, a sea-level canal which would obviate the need for time-consuming locks, and render the Panama Canal obsolete.

We had chosen the shortest flight across the Darien Gap and after an hour we landed at Cartagena, Colombia's gem of colonial architecture. Once again we shared a mutual goal, Caracas in Venezuela, and so we travelled together to the nasty border town of Maicao which we later heard was called the 'Texas of the south' on account of the frequent shoot-outs between rival drug-runners. A bus with long eyelashes hanging down over the windscreen as a fringe of tassels, perhaps shielding the driver from the sun but certainly reducing his field of vision by half, took us five miles out to the actual frontier. A Venezuelan guard came on board and looked at everyone's documents except ours. He then ordered us out with our luggage and directed us to a building. The kindly bus-driver said he would wait.

Inside the building was a pig. He was of a broad build and vastly overweight, his puffy skin bulged out of a khaki uniform, and small swinish eyes looked out over a bushy moustache neatly trimmed with the precision of topiary, contrasting with his black stubble of neglected chin growth. He rested his feet on a desk and lay back in his chair, balancing it on two flimsy legs by some unique Venezuelan law of equilibrium.

'Good morning, sir,' we said at respectful intervals. For a long while he said nothing, playing with his prerogative of time and deliberately letting his unblinking stare run from our boots to our heads before returning to linger on our more unusual features – the natural white streak in my beard and the crushed shape of Hans's straw hat. He grunted. 'Passaports.' As we handed them over I noticed he was sitting under a large picture of Dracula, and a chill crept over my flesh. (I was later informed that this was a portrait of President Mendez escalloped in a cloak.) He amused himself by looking at the variety of colourful stamps of other countries before examining my Venezuelan visa with a magnifying glass. Then he demanded to know why Hans had no visa. It took some time to satisfy him that West Germans did not require one. He stamped our passports and nodded.

The bus-driver was beckoning us to hurry as we left the building. The pig let us reach the bus before ordering a guard to stop us. He emerged from his office and looked formidable in the harsh reflected glare of concrete. 'Luggage check.' He pointed to the ground. 'Empty your bags here.' The nearest guard grabbed my pack and in one deft movement had deposited all my belongings as a heap on the ground. Hans managed to keep hold of his pack and handed over the articles one by one, whereupon the pig examined them and then tossed them aside so that they were soon strewn all over the place. The farrago became more chaotic as objects were thrown away, retrieved, picked up by guards or kicked back into the general disorder. The pig dropped some of Hans's belongings into my pile. I returned them to Hans and they were snatched back and reexamined. My tent was unwrapped and allowed to billow in the breeze, scattering pegs everywhere. I was beginning to collect them when my malarial tablets were spilt and sent rolling over the ground. While trying to recover some of them I failed to notice that my water sterilisation tablets, surgical dressings and other meagre medical supplies had been dumped into a waste bin. I was glad I had left my camera case in the bus but there were still some glass photographic filters wrapped in my clothes, and the pig held them up. What were they? I explained. He spat air between his teeth and lobbed them with a single flick of his wrist over his shoulder. They landed with a sickening clatter on the concrete behind him, their plastic cases somehow preventing them from shattering. I was incensed.

'Señor, you have no right to do this.'

He shifted his eyes to mine without moving his head, a hideous sneer creeping into his features and dissolving as he spoke. 'I–can–do–anything–I–like.' His words were spaced with vitriolic pauses. He put my penknife into his own pocket. A textbook *Teach Yourself Spanish* which belonged to Hans was read for a while and then tucked under his arm. The bus-driver came over and looked agitated, secretly tapping his watch. He had been waiting twenty minutes just for us, but we were helpless. All Hans's medicine (worth £40) was thrown away and a roll of lavatory paper was playfully unrolled and checked for heaven knows what. I managed to find my camping stove which a guard had hidden behind a chair and Hans regained a bundle of personal letters. The pig suddenly dismissed us and our carnage of belongings with a wave of his hand. We packed quickly and then waited for the missing items to be returned. He told us to go away. Hans protested and demanded to see his superior which made him give a flaccid smile. He took out my penknife and twiddled it through his fingers. 'All illegal,' he said. We threatened to report him to the authorities in Caracas. He opened my knife and began cleaning his fingernails with the point, and then grew bored and ordered us to leave. Two guards came and prodded us with their rifles and we had no option but to return to the bus.

'*Blöder Scheisskerl,*' Hans ranted. 'If they are looking for drugs, why do they put an *Arschloch* there who can't tell cocaine from a laxative?' We apologised to the driver and passengers for having held them back for forty minutes, and tried to swallow our anger. The driver was Venezuelan and said he felt so ashamed that he would not charge us for the journey to Maracaibo. We insisted on paying but he refused to take our money.

There were two more passport checks in the next ten miles, again just for Hans and myself. At the third we were ordered out with our packs. The passengers and driver assured the police that we had been searched but to no avail. Once more we had to empty our bags, this time on the main road, and we wondered what would now be deemed 'illegal'. Nothing was taken, but a car wanted to pass while our possessions were on the road and the police brushed everything over to the verge with their feet, kicking at the more obstinate articles. We passed through six checkpoints in the fifty miles between the pig and Maracaibo and were sick of this police state by the time we reached the city. Then things suddenly took a turn for the better. At the bus terminal our driver spoke to a friend, a small jovial man with the face of Harry Secombe, and our luggage was immediately transferred to a luxury bus for the eleven-hour journey through the night to Caracas, without charge.

The following morning we were let out in the most modern city in South America, rebuilt from the prodigious earnings of the derricks that have afforested Lake Maracaibo since the euphoric oil strike of 1917, and the one where the difference between rich and poor is perhaps most acute. The city covers the floor of a long valley as a pot-pourri of highrise buildings whose ranks become more orderly and concentrated in the centre of their ten-mile spread. Among these are residential areas enclosed by high fences, permanently guarded to restrict entry to the luxurious villas nestling behind their own walled fortifications and front doors like bank vaults, and containing patios roamed by tetchy dobermanns. Seen in the evening from the neighbouring hills, the whiteness of Caracas glows like the bark of silver birch by moonlight, but surrounding it, and here and there eating into make its purity ragged, the red fungus of shanties forms a broad swath. The 'low cost housing areas' – that charming euphemism of officialese which makes them sound tolerable – are built (if indeed they can be described so rigidly) of bare red stone, and their inhabitants account for the fear in those who own dobermanns and possibly also for the average of two bank robberies that take place within the city each day.

While Hans went off to the police headquarters to complain about our treatment at the border, I went to collect some mail at the post office. In Costa Rica I had received a letter from my parents saying that there would be two parcels awaiting my arrival in Caracas. They had wanted to send a small present for my birthday and, not wanting to encumber me with anything impractical, had decided to send a pair of sandals and a pair of socks. These had been sent in two separate parcels at intervals of one week (each parcel containing one sandal and one sock) as a shrewd measure to reduce the risk of theft. When I reached the poste restante section, the clerk handed me one intact parcel and the empty wrappings of the other with a gash neatly sealed with Sellotape. He said this was how it had arrived. My polite and then indignant reactions produced nothing but a curt and confident assurance that the contents of the parcel had slipped their wrappings in Britain. *Don't get aggravated – try to understand them.* I left carrying my useless birthday present.

Hans had fared little better. He said that several policemen, lounging around their office and performing the same balancing trick on chairs, had merely found his story amusing. The German embassy had been sympathetic but considered that we had got off lightly. They frequently complained on the highest diplomatic level about similar and worse incidents, but it usually took one and a half years before they received a reply.

Then Hans headed south and I continued east as far as Maturin where it was possible to fly the short hop to Trinidad.

4 · Carnival in Trinidad

Forged from the love of liberty, in the fires of hope and prayer
With boundless faith in our destiny, we solemnly declare;
Side by side we stand, Islands of the blue Caribbean Sea,
This our native land, we pledge our lives to thee,
Here every creed and race find an equal place
And may God bless our nation.

These words from Trinidad and Tobago's national anthem were written on the blackboard above my head as I sat writing my diary on a scarred wooden desk in the village school of La Brea. The schoolmaster had invited me to use the building when he saw me putting up my tent nearby, and had handed me the key of the main classroom. The top portion of each wall was nothing more than netting, allowing a pleasant breath of wind to pass over the encompassing tangles of purple bougainvillaea and enter the room, moving the warm air until the night was permeated by a sweet fragrance.

I wrote my diary into the early morning hours, catching up on the backlog of days from an assortment of rough notes which were as much as I had found time to write during the constant journeying. I finally had to give up, my task uncompleted through tiredness and the hurtful shadows which incessantly flickered around the room and across my page, caused by a vortex of moths and other flying contraptions swirling about the naked lightbulb. I lay awake for a short time trying to wriggle some comfort out of the hard floorboards and listening as frogs breeeeeeped and cicadas chattered. Fireflies burned in the dark (one landed on my nose and gave me a fright) and then I fell asleep with the sensations of floating on petals, thinking, God bless this nation.

The next morning I breakfasted on a small pineapple and left long before the schoolbell sounded, making my way to the north of the island through verdant sugar plantations which rose and fell on gentle hills and were occasionally interspersed with flooded fields of rice where figures waded and stooped. An oil and gas pipeline was being laid through a cutting in a dense tract of tropical vegetation to carry

Trinidad's most valuable raw commodities, while further on the less prestigious position of its principal crop was apparent from the queues of ox carts lined up by a rusty railway track as they waited for the train to come and take on their stacks of brown sugar cane. The road frequently ran through coconut groves which stretched for miles and allowed the sun to play with the tree trunks and cast bands of shadows across the road, creating endless zebra-crossings which were distracting and irksome to the eye. Houses were all built on stilts, and towns extended along the road so that everyone could live on 'Main Street'. Indian temples with punchy exterior murals outnumbered Catholic and Protestant churches exhorting 'REPENT' with notices in emphatic colours, and Chinese temples sporting writhing dragons were marginally more common than sporadic mosques. *Here every creed and race . . .* Trinidad is astounding for the diversity of peoples found within its shores. Almost half of them stem from African slaves and most of the remainder are descendants of the 150,000 immigrants from India, China and Madeira enticed over to replace the slaves as a workforce, or of the Dutch, French and British who variously ran the sugar plantations where all the others worked. The dominance of sugar in island life may also account for the statistic that twenty per cent of Trinidadians are diabetics.

A Hindu businessman – he would not be more specific than 'I operate a business' – gave me a long lift up the coast, once pointing to a burnt patch of ground beside a low sea-wall impaled by dozens of bamboo poles bearing multi-coloured flags, and he explained that funeral pyres were fired on that spot. I detected remorse in his voice, and wanted to offer him some sympathy and understanding. 'It's a long way from the Ganges,' I commented. He nodded wistfully, but added that of course it would not be possible for him to operate such a good business in India.

Few countries in the world have had their character affected by the oil barrel to the same extent as Trinidad, and no other culture produces music in US gallons. While a few government ministers are annually preoccupied with eighty million full barrels, one and a half million people are more concerned with the empties. The barrels are really metal drums which enterprising Trinidadians have converted into musical instruments called 'pans'. The range covers four types from the smallest ping-pong pan (which has the most notes – as many as thirty-two), the intermediate guitar-pan and cello-pan, to the largest bass or tune-boom pan which has a capacity of forty-four

US gallons. Pan music began shortly before 1940 when the West Indian's appetite for music went unsatisfied for a lack of instruments. Bands started improvising with percussion consisting of any available scrap metal, and oil drums proved particularly successful. Since then they have discovered that by heating and beating the tops of the cylinders into carefully tensioned and painstakingly tuned segments, a xylophone effect of pure notes can be obtained. Pans are struck with sticks tipped with a firm sponge or rubber from bicycle inner tubing in continuous rolls. Steel bands have perfected this vibrant shimmering music to be able to render such classics as Chopin's Nocturne in E flat.

It was mid-February and the island was gripped with the impetuous excitement of a child restrained from ripping open a present. Trinidad lives for its festivals and the biggest of these is the annual carnival which reaches a climax during the two days before Ash Wednesday. The first day is divided into three parts – J'ouvert, Ole Mas and Lil Mas ('mas' is short for masquerade) – which the outsider finds indistinguishable from the more important second day, an unnamed and glorious free-for-all. Carnival jargon is very simple; if you wear a costume in the procession you are 'playing mas' but if you are dancing along accompanying it, you are 'jumping up' ('Have you had a good jump-up?'). When one carnival ends preparations for the next begin, and some costumes are slowly prepared over the course of a full year. Crime rates drop during the preceding weeks because no one wants to risk being in jail for the climax of euphoria, and, as I discovered on my arrival in the capital town, hotels have been fully booked for months.

Port of Spain's streets were decrepit. I passed a flaking candy-pink Victorian mansion whose principal features were outlined in white, imprisoned within an undisciplined garden, a profusion of flowers and sculptured casualties which included a curvaceous nymph looking mournfully over her shoulder wondering where she had dropped her left hand, and another of Mercury, his cadaceus broken, leaping into the air trying to escape the vine which had snared his winged sandals. The central square took more pride in its appearance with modern offices and respectable administrative buildings, but the streets were largely composed of wooden houses, some clinker-built and with ornate jigsaw verandahs leaning out over the pavements on highrise posts of woodworm. The architecture gave a pleasing sense of spontaneous improvisation, though little balance, but whatever was lacking in paint was adequately replaced by the friendly spirit of the inhabitants. In one street a dinosaur foot with the legs of a small girl ran out from a doorway in front of me closely followed by another in the embrace of her smaller brother, and together they disappeared into the adjacent doorway where I assumed a disabled dinosaur was waiting.

The only room in town which I could find was in The Casbah – a four-tier banquet of dry-rot, invaded by cockroaches and, I suspected, a bordello. I accepted the room at once because there were no alternatives and because the owner was irresistable. Vivien was over six feet in height, and boasted a weight of eighteen stone which I had no reason to doubt. She led me to a room containing no more than a broken table and a metal-framed bed with a mattress whose shape suggested it must have had eighteen stones lying on it for most of its life. I had barely put down my pack, saying that I really ought to wash some clothes, when my shirt was grabbed from behind and whipped off over my head.

'Yeas-urr, what you'ze Moma tink if she saw's you'ze wearin' dat?' and the next moment Vivian was up to her elbows in soap suds, pummelling my shirt along a washboard. 'Ah'ze gonna make you'ze de talk o' de town, man!' and she broke into a little calypso, using the beat as sailors use shanties to add vigour to their drudgery.

"That's . . . that's very kind of you,' I said, tightening my trouser belt one notch. 'I think I'll manage the rest of the clothes myself.' Vivian's biceps bulged as she wrang out my shirt, twisting it into a slender length of rope, and I realised the choice was not mine but belonged entirely to six feet of muscular washing machine. Then the doorbell rang below and Vivian stomped off, leaving me to unfold my shirt. I hung it up and noticed it had only one button left, but it was certainly clean. I put on a spare shirt and quickly left by the back door.

That evening I queued for two hours to buy a ticket for the 'Panorama Finals' in a concert hall beside Savannah Park, where steel bands were competing for the highest honours. The competition lasted for five hours but much of this time was taken up by one band removing its instruments and the next installing itself. Bass players each had six full-size tune-boom pans which were fitted onto a frame with wheels and a canopy. There was no floor to the frame so the player stood in the middle and pushed it onto the stage with his feet appearing between the wheels like a Fred Flintstone car. Bands were distinguished by the combinations of bright colours which they had painted on their pans, and by their size – the largest had one hundred players (ie a tonal range and maximum output of approximately 4,800 US gallons).

The effect was electric. Metal being struck with hundreds of stick beats per second produced scintillating harmonies which swelled and faded above a compulsive rhythm, and charged the atmosphere with its energy. The quality of music from a collection of oil drums backed by percussions of car suspension springs, brake drum linings and large cheese graters rubbed with affro combs was truly flabbergasting. A compère introduced each band over a crackly loudspeaker with admirable brevity, and remained unruffled by the odd interruption. 'And the next band is the Ma'sters from San Fernando with seventy-eight members . . . What? . . . Right! . . . Would Mr Parks the plumber please come to the control box immediately as we have a blocked toilet which is flooding . . . The Ma'sters from San Fernando . . .'

I left early after the performance of the favourites, The Invaders (and a repeat call for Mr Parks), and made my way back to The Casbah. Night had fallen and yet the streets were still busy, especially in the less salubrious dry-rot section of the town. Lights were on in the windows of 'The Salvation Army Home for Working Lads' and the sign caused me to stop and amuse myself for a moment by rereading it in Geordie and Lancashire accents, finding the latter most apt. A figure slipped out of an unlit doorway behind me and talked business.

'Sixty dollars' – sixteen pounds – 'OK?' came a tacky voice, and a bared tit caught a stray beam of light and flashed in the darkness. Her price seemed fair in the shadows but when she stepped out under the street lamp, it was pure vanity.

'I don't think my landlady would approve,' I replied.

'Huh! You'ze scared, Mista. C'mon, my place, OK?' But I moved on, knowing I'd need to conserve my strength for my washing and for two days of jumping up.

For two days there are no half measures in Port of Spain. Carnival is a total commitment, demanding abstinence from worry, disregard for convention and an unreserved (albeit groggy) dedication to frolic. There are no bystanders and no divisions between those playing mas or jumping up, for everyone is dancing, sucked into the procession which fills the streets and absorbs the crowd, everyone dances on, coalesced into one endless flux of colour and movement which passes through the town, out into the park and over a judging stage, taking all day from dawn to dusk just to pass over this stage once without repeating itself, and then back into the saturated streets, a serpent eating its tail, a continual infusion of itself, a laughing dancing assimilation of humanity.

For two days . . .

The bedside alarm rings at four a.m. I still feel dog-tired, and this is just the start of day one. A mouse walks along a pipe in the kitchen while I eat some cereal and make coffee, and a gecko is doing inverted press-ups on the ceiling. This place is as much a zoo as it is a hotel. I lift up my camera case and prepare to leave but then take it back to my room. Hang it! I'll take pictures tomorrow but today it's just going to be me and five senses, and a flask of water and a bottle of rum.

The good thing about staying in a zoo is that there is never any shocking temperature change when you leave. The street is as cold as my room. I'm only wearing jeans and a shirt (very clean) because the heat will become oppressive after sunrise. My boots won't make it any cooler but if carnival is anything like an Icelandic shipyard annual dance, then I will be safer wearing boots. The night sky is clear and prickly with stars, appearing fresh and untainted compared to these jaundiced streets where wilting lampposts drop stingy yellow light onto vendors setting up stalls at intervals of a few paces. A small boy is buying a snow cone from one of them, looking up into what would be the face of a man planing off slivers from a huge block of ice and collecting them in a carton, were he not merely a sharp shadow against the glare of a hissing paraffin lamp. The shadow runs his hand along a row of bottles in prismatic colours. The boy nods when it touches the bottle of his favourite syrup, and he stomps in anticipation. The streets are more crowded near Independence Square and ultimately become acres of touching bodies. A dinosaur pushes past and I automatically look to see if it has both feet. Yes. I'm glad they arrived safely. Dismembered steel bands are setting up on the edge of the tumult and brightly coloured pans are held high above the sea of heads as their owners struggle through with more gallons of potential music.

Dawn is breaking. The babble of voices takes heart at this and increases, its monotony interrupted only by a periodic cackle of laughter or a jibe. Someone is ribbing a dragonfly which is trying to mince through the crush but the double wings of red lace held horizontally by a wire frame keep snagging and spoil the dainty gait. The smell of curry arrests my attention and makes me feel hungry. It is coming from a roti stall. Roti is an elastic pancake. The chef holds it by the upper edge and starts swirling it around to stretch it, using bold flourishes like a bullfighter being *macho*. It flips loops between his arms and grows effortlessly from a handkerchief into a dishcloth and just when I am spellbound and urging it to become a bath towel, it is dropped, filled with curry, wrapped up and handed over as a deflated haggis. I buy one (really to see him do it again) and it is delicious but each bite sends a dribble of curry down my chin. What will Vivien say if it marks my shirt? Still, this is carnival . . .

The sun begins to flood the streets and warmth seeps into the air. I open my bottle of rum and drink, but it's tasteless after the curry and it seems a sin to drink so early. Costumes of all descriptions are walking around now, and bands are tuning up. Trinidadian girls all seem to have their hair braided, each tassle ending in a coloured bead and taking on the appearance of squirming hydra when the girls dance. I am sinning again when a girl comes up to me. She says her name is Mary. I offer Mary a drink. She tosses her hydra in a captivating gesture as she knocks back the bottle. Liquid fizzes around her lips with the suction of deep gulps. She wanders off with 'Yes I do but not with you' printed on the back of her T-shirt. Mary drinks a lot of other people's rum, but she has style. She might not be so lucky if she approached in reverse. A man is standing on a stage speaking into a microphone which reacts to his words with apoplexy and prefers to hum instead. I ask the man dressed as a dandelion standing next to me what he's saying.

'Why! He is sayin', man,' replies the sunflower (my mistake) in a teasing sing-song voice, 'dat de carnival has gee-ust bee-gun . . .'

An almighty tremor shakes the air as sixty steel bands erupt into action, music ricocheting off every house and wall and bouncing all around, strumming the air with its quivering resonance. Port of Spain is suddenly trapped within a crystal goblet being hammered by a population of drumsticks. Energy pulses through the atmosphere and the transfer from music to dance is instantaneous, the crowd dissolves into a blizzard of colour and movement, the sunflower grabs me and we are flying through the air in a cross-armed spin until I am released and flung into the wings of a gyrating butterfly, we leap and prance, her wings are silver and blue and sparkle in the sun, her antennae bounce and flex and make me laugh, she laughs too, leaping, prancing, laughing and then suddenly she has gone, hands are reaching, clutching, pulling and off I go again, jiving and spinning through an endless chain of hands, deeper into a maelstrom of chromatic euphoria. The sun's heat is imperceptible, time has fled, energy is self-perpetuating and thought is hard.

A teenage boy springs by with a bulging watersack, squirting the contents into any open mouth. Mine is open and a warm liquid scorches my throat and I shake my head violently like an agitated duck while he breaks into a roguish grin and skips off to spike another stranger with neat gin. No one is walking or standing still. Those who aren't in the grip of a frenzied whirl are leaning back over their heels and oscillating in limbo, or resting by merely hopping. The music rapidly becomes louder and I'm amongst a band. Some members are bucking about and capering as they play but most are standing in their Fred Flintstone cars which now seem to have floors and are being pushed by a host of followers. The players' hands are a constant blur of motion, their necks are taut with stretched sinew and sweat trickles down from faces of intense concentration. The percussion players follow and the sound of hanging heavy metal being hammered at three beats per second is deafening. And I'm twenty feet away. How can they stand it for fourteen continuous hours? And then I'm leaping about more wildly. I never stop, I don't want to, and I can't. The music seizes my muscles and forces them to work. Each beat shoots adrenalin into my body and fires me with the thrill of movement. Steel bands hold the key. They power the carnival, their force is what stimulates, attracts and blends a crowd of strangers into carefree union. I know the secret but I am helpless against its hypnotic hold, and hope it never weakens. I am carried along in a trance of elation, unconscious of the hours, fatigue or the drops of sweat being shaken from my head with every jolting step.

Each band heads its retinue of supporters who are playing mas, dressed in identical costumes on a chosen theme. 'We'ze de biggest, man,' yells one of the Worshippers of the Cat, 'five t'ousand.' Suddenly I'm being spun around, weaving from figure to figure amongst five thousand hot-brick cats cavorting through the street. They last indefinitely and then I am going against the flow and am launched into the next host of playful strife, to be distributed in a furor of hugs and ejections like a slippery ball in the loose scrummage of Emotions in Motion. Iridescent costumes teem and tumble by, decorated in spectra passing from angry red, through cowardly yellow and the green of envy to heads crowned with gold spikes trailing wispy veils which sparkle with tinsel and sequins and wave rainbows in the air. These are followed by the Festival of Orchids, which turns the horizon into an inexhaustible expanse of tall green plumes nodding above three thousand bodies. They are speckled in lilac and white, and brandish floral standards cascading bouquets of paper petals.

My world is full of spinning shapes and colours, the smells of dust, blossom, sweat, roti and oranges, the sounds of laughter, squeals of delight, hysterical giggles, calypsos, infectious pan – music both provocative and balmy – and it extends above street level to balconies and open windows where more people are waving, jiving and throwing confetti and streamers. Then I find myself next to a woman who could be Vivien's double. She rolls her arms and dips at the knees, sending undulations through the flab of her voluminous body. I admire her gusto and that of her darling piccaninny, a tiny frail mite of a boy who can hardly walk and falls every few steps but he imitates her movements and is synchronised to the beat with that wonderful sense of rhythm inherent among his colour, and cultured from birth. 'How old?' I shout in passing, nodding at the child. ' 'most two,' she beams, catching her prodigy as he stumbles, and they are lost in the consuming revelry.

My bottle of rum is gone. I've only just noticed. I must have put it down when talking to the sunflower, but who needs it. I turn into a quieter side-street and find a woman selling coconuts to drink. Her feet are buried in empty shells. She opens each nut with three blows of a machete, holding the nut in one hand and sweeping the knife in two upward cuts to leave a point, and then executing a final horizontal slash to expose a hint of meat. She does it without concentrating, wielding the knife like a clumsy attempt at the sign of the cross. I hand her one dollar. 'Be careful of your fingers . . .' She glares at me. 'Listen, son' – *husk, husk, chook* (the last one always makes a different noise) – 'ah've been doin' dis since 'fore you'ze borned.'

I suck at the straw and the cool sweet liquid traces a path of pleasure to my stomach, and then I glimpse a distant peacock. I think it was a girl but she disappears round a corner and all I remember is

the radiance of her costume. I feel the impulse to run after her. I must
see her again. I'm running, the coconut is spilling milk over my hand
and less pleasant tracings are wobbling in my stomach. I round the
corner but a dense conglomeration of people has moved across to
form a wall in front of me, and the peacock has gone. She could have
gone into any one of three streets, each the start of a congested maze,
and I choose one of them. The Army for World Peace is blocking my
path with gigantic white feathers so I turn about and run in another
direction, lefts and rights until I'm disorientated, but this street looks
familiar – *husk, husk, clop* (it depends on how deep the knife goes) –
and I'm back where I started. I keep running and choose a new
direction. My run turns to dance as I pass through the bizarre
collection of Space Oddities dressed as Trinidadian Martians, only to
be engulfed by Red Indians and A Taste of Mexico. Could she be
amongst Vietnam Refugees? Possible. I plump for the hope that she
is beyond Autumn Leaves but beyond Autumn Leaves there are no
birds, just Danse Macabre which has embroiled an orphaned Tarzan,
sprayed with silver paint and somehow detached from Out of the
Jungle. Suddenly I am out of the streets and amongst Devils and
Demons, crossing Savannah Park. We are kicking up a cloud of dust
which rises above our heads. They turn and mount the judging stage
and their movements become violent spasms in their efforts to
minimise contact with the platform and stay airborne for the longest
time. Their boiling frenzy moves over the stage, bringing with it the
nebulous dust which sinks to their knees, and it is an awesome
spectacle, sinister and satanic, as hundreds of skeletons, white bones
painted on grey bodies and wearing leering skull masks, convulse in
that creeping dust. I look for the judges but they are hard to
distinguish for most of them are dancing too.

I want to find that peacock. My legs begin to run again and I pass
under a spider which is pushed along on a towering frame so that its
hairy appendages span a circle thirty feet across and are held in the
manner of a maypole by frisking girls dressed as juvenile arachnids.
It's hopeless. There's a lull in the music and my body feels drained,
leaving a desperate weariness which tries to drag me to the ground.
The music returns and gives me new strength. I'm trotting once
more, but it's hopeless. I'll never find one girl in this labyrinth of
congested streets and the pandemonium of a hundred thousand
people . . . and now the sun is going down . . . maybe tomorrow
. . . and then there she is.

She is moving away from me, along a street which leads into the setting sun. Her tail rises ten feet in the air and is fifteen feet wide where it trails on the ground. It is made of wire covered with plastic sheets in a dozen colours, each meticulously cut to shape and inset to form the perfect replica of a peacock's plumage. Real feathers fill the areas between the imitation spots and, against the light, the whole phosphoresces and glows in brilliant concentrations of purple, turquoise, lime, olive, ruby and all their permutations. The effect is overwhelming. I go round to look at her. She is pretty, maybe sixteen, with a generous smile and elfin eyes.

'*You* are the most beautiful in the whole carnival,' I say, and my words are spontaneous, without premeditation. She blushes and smiles. I stand back to let her pass and suddenly catch my breath and stand there, stunned. I can only see wheels on the ground. Her tail is a frame on wheels, and then I notice that her body is held too low and is too bulky, her costume ends where her legs are cut off at the knees, and her arms are pushing down to make her wheelchair move. My eyes move from her to the next, and then the next, and I see that this procession consists entirely of children who are crippled, deformed and cruelly distorted. They pivot on crutches above dangling, paralysed legs. They limp in calipers, swing useless arms and stare from palsied faces. But those who aren't able to show joy in their features, glitter life and gaiety in their eyes. Their loss of limbs is sometimes concealed under the exuberance of their costumes, fantasies of exotic birds and tropical fish, humping, jerking and hobbling through the streets. Helpers are there to guide and support them and to push the wheelchairs of the more severely handicapped, and they are singing and laughing and capering about. The crowd absorbs this procession too, lavishing the true spirit of carnival with characteristic extravagance, jiving and romping through the mass of maimed and paraplegic children dressed as the world's most beautiful creatures, holding their hands, hugging them, kissing their cheeks . . . Trinidad has not forgotten those who cannot dance.

My eyes are moist. My God, doesn't it make You feel just a touch of pride in mankind?

I counted the number of times I filled my water flask and each day I drank over two gallons of water alone. After the first day there were all-night parties and concerts and then the second day was the same, the pace never faltered and the sleepless festivities ran their course unabated. On the third morning the odd group of diehard merrymakers sang and stumbled through the wreckage of the streets piled deep with litter; empty bottles of Old Oak Rum and Johnnie Walker Black Label, coconut shells, fallen butterfly wings, discarded feathers of the Army for World Peace, intricately embroidered Autumn Leaves and other fragments of costumes which had been one year in the making, and had served their purpose. An old man with a scraggy beard and a crown of grey negroid curls lay in a gutter, his posture formed by the impact of his collapse, while two relics of When the Rains Came lay on the ground in tattered streamers of cheerfully coloured polythene, one spreadeagled and his stomach acting as a pillow for the other who still clutched the ravaged frame of a windswept umbrella. I nodded a greeting to a brood of Midsummer Night Fairies sitting forlornly on the pavement, but they appeared to be dazed. The desolation did not seem so because my mind was still full of the music, joviality and bewitching images that had caused it – the pleasant aftertaste while staring at the dregs in a silent crystal goblet.

Then I left Port of Spain. My clothes were clean ('You'ze call dat clean?' But carnival had given me courage and I refused to let Vivien improve on them), and I simply wanted to find a quiet place to recover lost sleep. A woman gave me a lift to Maracas Bay on a road that passed over hills covered in dense foliage and gave views into dells where the greenery was studded by the orange blossom of immortelle. She explained that the name of this plant is derived from the fact that its petals retain their colour when dried, and that according to legend, immortelle only flowers when it is dying.

This woman was middle-aged and came from a family who had lived in the area for generations. The decline in cocoa prices had forced them to sell their plantations to property speculators, and over the years since her birth even their orchards had been sold. Like so many, they now stood neglected and overgrown in the shadow of oil. She resented the mass intrusion of immigrants which had so radically changed the character of the islands. Most of the land and businesses were owned by Syrians and Lebanese, Indians dominated the country's politics, the placid native people had been swept aside and strong currents of ill-feeling and racialism ran through the cosmopolitan population.

'You can only love Trinidad now if you have never known it as it once was,' she said.

'But the carnival . . . ?' I argued. She smiled, but it was a patronising smile.

'Yes, the carnival . . .' Her words formed a sigh and I saw that for her, carnival was Trinidad in flower, a dying immortelle. But I could not forget the elfin eyes and the smile of a legless girl, and for me the colours of a resplendent peacock would never die.

God bless this nation.

5 · Down the Devil's Nose in Ecuador

Broadly speaking, the journey across the top of South America from Trinidad to Ecuador can be described as flat at first then bumpy (Andes); hot then cool and showery; scrubland cattle then highland subsistence plots or valley plantations of bananas, coffee, cocoa or cocaine. My destination was still Tierra del Fuego via Machu Picchu, and my immediate goal Riobamba, an important provincial town in Ecuador from which a train rolls steeply down the Andes on a corkscrew track to the Pacific.

This span of land, from his native Venezuela to Ecuador, was once held by the liberator Simón Bolívar as a vision of one nation called Gran Colombia. While travelling towards the limb of the Andes that extends into western Venezuela, I felt I was getting to know Bolívar quite well, having been rudely evicted from a small park by an irate policeman who considered me disrespectful for eating a sardine sandwich beside a statue of the country's hero. Bolívar has become monotonously prolific; Venezuelans have named a city, their currency and highest mountain after him, every village has a Plaza Bolívar where he is honoured by a mass-produced statue (blanched by irreverent pigeons), and he commands more veneration today than he did in 1812 when he was expelled from the land as a common outcast.

Surely the man who slept rough and led his energetic army on the successful march that ended Spanish domination in South America would not have objected to a sardine sandwich during the long tramp through the Andes? (Bolívar's dream was realised when he raised the standard of independence in the whole region consisting of modern Venezuela, Colombia and Ecuador, and later in Bolivia as well, but his success soon crumbled and after one decade Gran Colombia split into its smaller identities.) Venezuela's excessive Bolívarisms and Bolívar-olatry today are belated thank you's for independence and penitential apologies for having allowed him to die destitute in a Colombian street.

My route out of Venezuela followed that of Bolívar, and he could not have made a better choice. The road from Valera to Timotes was one of the most enchanting of my entire journey. I sat in the back of an open truck as we toiled up continuous zigzags to a pass at 13,500 feet. The valleys were steep, hamlets were built on shelves of level ground, and fields were narrow terraced ledges subdivided into many plots, mainly growing vegetables. Every so often a small field of carnations formed a pocket in the stony landscape and added a jolt of bright colours to the otherwise pastel hues.

The sun was rising when we began our ascent and men ploughing with yoked oxen where thrown into silhouette by the yellow glow, their legs hidden in a trundling cloud of dry earth, spotlit as they cut a furrow through the dust of an instant in time. Hens strutted onto the road and stopped, stupified into a moment's indecision and then they panicked, fleeing as our wheels were almost upon them, squawking pathetically, wings flapping, little yellow legs stabbing at the ground. Goats lay by squat stone houses adorned with pot-plants, women washed clothes in doorways or stood about gossiping, dressed in the different-sized garments of their entire wardrobe as protection against the mountain cold. An aged woman in black held flowers and talked to a man in a heavy poncho and the usual misshapen straw hat. Only the children playing on the many dry-stone dikes showed unreserved energy, everyone else looked old and statuesque, and even an unattended donkey walked with an exaggerated plod. The air smelt of damp farmyards and of those surprising carnations. Some plots were watered by roadside sprinklers and the breeze occasionally carried a shower of fine spray over me, but this only enhanced the magic.

This is the way to travel, I thought. The last thing I wanted at that moment was to be shut behind the luxury of glass, protected from the dirt but isolated from the drops of water, squawking hens and the smell of damp carnations which were as much a part of the land's character as the sights.

At the top of the pass stood a sculptured eagle, a monument to Bolívar, and then the road began the tortuous descent down the other side. When the truck made its final stop I had to transfer to a bus as there was no other traffic. After this it was impossible to be sure of the colours of the countryside because the bus had tinted windows which made everything appear nicotine brown. An adolescent girl wearing a patched dress and occupying the seat next

to mine was avidly reading a Bible with every line in the second half
of Luke, chapter 16, underlined in red. It was about Lazarus going to
heaven and the rich man suffering in hell. She seemed to be enjoying
the story.

'You are Protestant?' asked her mother, sitting on the far side and
noticing my curiosity. I hesitated, trying to put a simple label on my
decanted beliefs, and she took this to be an affirmation. 'Here you
will find we are not so much Protestant,' she continued, subcon-
sciously tracing an embellished cross on her breast, 'thanks to God.'
With her hands folded in her lap once more she turned to look out of
the window, and a short time later nodded to a roadside Madonna
surrounded by a deep pile of car headlights neatly stacked in veneration. In response to soft evening light and distorted vision, the
Madonna simply glowed non-denominational nicotine brown.

The image of Lazarus came back to me a few days later when I
found myself in a village thronged with crowds watching a religious
procession. It was the week before Easter and each evening gory
effigies of Christ, carved several centuries ago but whose blood had
recently been touched up, were carried through the dark streets
interspersed along a line of choirboys in red and white cassocks
holding flaming candles. I found it distressing to see feverish people
waving their arms and clamouring to touch the lacerated statues, and
left the street to enter a gilded mountain of a church. 'God does not
accept the bad,' stated a sign, below which stood a collection box
with ragged and torn Bolívar notes pinned to its sides.

If there can be degrees of distinction among utter poverty and
excessive wealth then Latin America has the most squalid slums on
earth, and her churches are the most opulent. This apparent hypoc-
risy and complacency shown by the Church was, to my mind,
irreconcilable with the Christian doctrine. The endless tabernacles of
riches, where everything that glittered usually was gold, tempted
me to believe that they were self-gratifying monuments of pomp,
and made me question the Church's attitude. People now came to
offer their prayers and worship to jewel-encrusted images. It seemed
to me that God had become secondary to the objects and rituals of
worship, lost among idolatry and ecclesiolatry. The House of God
was figuratively 'always open' but physically it was usually locked
because it contained too much of value to allow unsupervised sinners
to enter freely. I put my dilemma to a priest in this church.

'No, you are mistaken. You must remember that God and the

Church occupied much greater importance in people's lives when these churches were built than, regrettably, they do today. They built their church as big as possible and decorated it with their most precious possessions. The wealth in our churches is the worldly wealth that was renounced and it represents the offering of our greatest gifts to the glory of God.'

'But why do you continue to store this wealth? Why not give it back to those in need?'

'We could give it all away today and there would be just as many poor tomorrow.'

Didn't he think, I argued, that the Church had become too content to remain aloof from the underprivileged as a spangled object to be admired and feared by them, but all too often unwilling to assume responsibility and strive for their physical betterment?

'We are concerned only with the spiritual welfare of the people,' he replied. 'It is the job of a government to provide for their material condition. We must work within the confines of each political system if we are to be allowed to work at all. The supreme sacrifice has been made. Nothing more will be achieved if the Church ends up on its own Golgotha.'

I put it to him that the Church had become preoccupied with the horrors of hell and the death of Jesus rather than his love and kindness, for these people could identify more readily with an oppressed carpenter's son portrayed as a tortured bloody corpse than with his spirit of benevolence. Theirs was a consolation that robbed them of the incentive to help themselves and encouraged the belief that their lot was to suffer patiently for Lazarus's reward in heaven . . .

I was interrupted by the start of Mass, and the priest was called away.

'You are very confused, my son,' he said, and turned to go. 'I shall pray for you.' His footsteps sounded hollow on the bare stone slabs, and I caught the words of his muttering between two great pillars, an echo '. . . pray for you . . .' before the heavy smell of incense and burnt wax became too much and drove me out.

My thoughts returned to an abstract painting I had seen in Mexico City. The picture itself had been meaningless but the caption had read, 'Christ the Leader: "What have you Christians done with my doctrine in 2,000 years?" ' Pondering the question, I left Venezuela and took the road south, through the Colombian Andes to Ecuador.

★   ★   ★

Quito was normally seven hours away by public transport but unfortunately much longer by petrol tanker. It was the slowest lift of my life. As we crawled up one steep hill I spotted a drinks stall set back from the road and immediately felt thirsty. My driver also wanted a drink but considered it too difficult to stop on the hill so he kept on going with the rev-counter showing maximum. I jumped down from the cab, bought two bottles of orange and caught him up again without having to break into a run.

The length of time before kilometre markers became excruciating. After a while I happened to glance in the wing mirror and saw two buses approaching from behind. One was trying to overtake and, just as in Guatemala, they were neck and neck. We were almost upon a bend but both buses continued their race. The one in the overtaking lane had a clear run into the blind curve but our tanker was in the way of the other. Undaunted, its driver simply took to the rubble verge and the next moment we had rounded the corner and been overtaken simultaneously on both sides.

'Did you see that?' I asked my driver in disbelief.

'Bad driving,' he said.

The road passed through rolling valleys where outcrops of stratified rock formed narrow gorges amid sparse but green grazing and trees in brilliant yellow blossom. We dawdled along in our self-induced cacophony, and I would gladly have swapped these colours for a nicotine landscape and speed. A butterfly flopped leisurely up to my window, then went round and landed on our windscreen and finally flew off in front of us.

'Did you see that?' I asked, wondering if he was being deliberately slow.

'Very pretty.'

Very pretty! Ten thousand miles lay between me and Tierra del Fuego by my intended route and I was currently travelling at eight miles an hour and had just been overtaken by some jazzed-up moth. I was grateful for the lift but I got out at the next village and took a bus the rest of the way to Quito.

Ecuador's charm won me over at once. It is perhaps the most delightful country on the continent. Its land is a compact variety of jungle, astonishing panoramas of patchwork fields and haughty volcanoes, and its character is enlivened by Indians wearing a combination of pigtails, ponchos, spotlessly white shin-length trousers or half a dozen skirts and coils of necklaces as if a fakir's rope trick has backfired, and dented Charlie Chaplin bowlers (even the babies bound to their mothers' backs). Ecuador also has those laughably elongated sheep, llamas. Quito, its administrative centre and the old northern capital of the Incas, is second only to Rio de Janeiro for its beauty. The modern section is clean and efficient (unlike Bogotá where the bus system operates a permanent traffic jam), and here are banks, travel agents pushing London and New York, businessmen mingling with fashion shoppers and a street vendor, an interloper from the other Quito selling Jivaro shrunken heads, lips and eyes stitched shut, imitations made of goat hide. The old section is less spick but with grandiose architecture from which a conquistador might emerge at any moment, and contains eighty-six churches dating back four hundred years to impress even those jaded with (and confused by) opulence. Old Quito's streets are narrow and twisty, packed with Indian markets and exposed lives, crossed by alleys full of clockmakers, cobblers and cafés and liberally fronted with pompous buildings. The city is rumpled by three hills whose slopes always seem to be against the pedestrian but which nevertheless permit views of the higher hills encircling the urban area. On one of these stands the enormous figure of an angel painted in silver. Her halo is slightly askew but she devoutly gazes down on the scene, and her smile is wholly understandable.

Until as late as 1885 Quito was connected to the coast only by a mule track which was impassable for six months of the year. Then came the railway that established an all-weather link. I wanted to ride its steepest section, starting 125 miles down the line at Riobamba. While wondering how best to reach Riobamba I met Señora Sales, a housewife whose feet splayed out at ninety degrees to her direction of travel. She told me I would arrive too late for Saturday's train and that Sunday was the railway's day of rest. On an impulse I decided to accompany her by bus to her home village of Zumbahua, a cluster of mud, thatch and tin houses in the mountains halfway to Riobamba. Señora Sales had only two eyeteeth and smelt of *ahi*, burning hot peppers. Her family ate plenty of *ahi*, she said, and never fell sick as a result. I said even the thought of *ahi* made me sick, and she laughed infectiously from her belly upwards and revealed both her teeth for a full minute. She was a jolly woman but, as I was about to find out, she had less amusing neighbours.

The bus journey to Zumbahua was slow on account of the punishing climb and many stops for passengers greatly magnified by a quarter ton of luggage. On our arrival Señora Sales led me to a stream at the back of her hut for a drink of water. We walked along a slender path through deep grass and she said she had walked to this stream every day for forty years. The path was the exact width, from toe to toe, of her outsplayed feet.

Her children followed us and one was a boy of ten wearing striped dungarees. 'He's an orphan,' she said, tapping him on the head. 'His mama and papa don't want him.' The boy dropped his gaze to the ground and stood meekly with his hands behind his back. I felt her directness was hurtful although it was not intended to be and she was obviously fond of him. Despite having four children of her own she had taken in this extra one when his parents could no longer afford to feed all their family. I asked if I could take a photograph of him in the hope that it might cheer him up. He was shy but thrilled. Señora Sales told him to say '*chancha*' (it is a Spanish photographer's 'cheese', although it means 'sow'). Then she noticed something wrong.

'That's how a *woman* stands,' she chided, 'here, like this . . .' She pulled back her shoulders and stood stiffly with one foot placed slightly forwards, '. . . this is how a *man* stands.' So the little orphan changed his position and posed like a man, and his new mama beamed proudly. He was learning how to be *macho*.

I camped the night in Zumbahua and the following morning went for a walk among the tiny cultivated plots whose irregular fretted patterns shaded the hills in green, yellow or brown, and yielded only to crags and rocky summits. A minor track led me up a sharp incline and between a few houses with no signs of life. Then a stone struck the ground somewhere behind me and I turned to see the back of a woman disappearing behind a wall. The rock had been badly aimed, but the gesture was clear enough. I carried on cautiously and reached several more houses where I met an old man. He stared at me for some time before speaking.

'This is not a good place for strangers,' he said quietly, and was gone.

The track ran over a small ridge a short distance ahead of me and I continued towards the top in the hope that the view beyond might explain these ominous occurrences. Some men suddenly appeared higher up the slope to my left and set loose two dogs. They came racing down the hillside along with a volley of stones which I was forced to dodge, barking furiously and baring evil rabid fangs. Thoroughly alarmed, I stooped to pick up a stone in each hand and the action alone brought them to a halt at a safe distance where they continued to bark. The next moment at least thirty villagers – men, women and children armed with stones, cudgels of prickly cactus, cattle bones and sticks – came over the ridge fifty yards in front of me. I began to back away.

'Get away from here,' shouted a man, brandishing his club. I called out something about being a friend but a shower of stones landed around me and a wizened crone hissed abuse and mutterings about not wanting my accursed money. I retreated as quickly as possible, walking half-backwards and stumbling as I continually glanced up to dodge the stones. One caught me painfully on the ankle and another bruised my arm. The villagers could easily have caught me had they wanted to do so, but I was thankful that they were content to drive me away. The crowd soon stopped following but children chased me for five minutes. I returned to Zumbahua suffering from shock and with several cuts and aching bruises.

For some reason they had felt threatened. Had they suffered from a gringo's intrusion in the past? Or had they taken me for a government official who might disrupt their way of life? I never did discover the reason but I heard later that these communities had formed tight-knit cooperative farms and valued their insularity and traditional lifestyle. The local priest told me he had lived in Zumbahua for eight years before he had been allowed to visit these villages.

The ticket office of Riobamba's railway station was next to a travelling wax museum whose doorway showpiece was a figure in the third stage of syphilis. The effect was so harrowing that it was hard to imagine anyone being encouraged to enter the place, and I hurried past and bought a first-class train ticket to Guayaquil. This is one of the world's classic lines and has been hailed as a remarkable feat of engineering ever since its completion in 1908. The construction took twenty-seven years, mainly as a result of difficulties in financing the project, but the technical problems encountered by the Ecuadorian engineers were formidable. The track's giddy descent through the mountains incorporates a total curvature equivalent to forty-five full circles, one of which exists as a tight loop, a double zigzag with a V-switchback and gradients of 5.5 per cent, the maximum for an adhesion railway. The scenery was said to be unsurpassed and so I chose the most expensive seat to ensure trouble-free viewing. It is the only time I have bought a first-class train ticket and ended up sitting on the roof.

We skirted around the snow-capped Chimborazo Volcano (20,561 feet above sea level but the world's highest peak when measured from the Earth's core), passed between arid sandy hills, bald except for areas of stiff grass, and alongside a muddy river sloping gently through slender gorges. The excess padding of my luxury seat made it uncomfortable and the empty compartment gave me a feeling of having been ostracised. When we reached a station beyond a steaming lake and groves of plane trees with shredding orange and grey bark, three pigs were pulled by their back legs, wheelbarrow-fashion, along the platform. They were swung upside-down and hauled skywards, being aimed towards the roof until they proved too heavy, and they disappeared into a carriage once a fifth pair of hands had hoisted on the tail and provided sufficient uplift. There is something particularly piercing about the squeals of passengers forced to travel second-class.

It was at this point that I realised many people were sitting on the roof of the train. By the next station I was bored with first-class and clambered up a ladder with my luggage to join them. There were over sixty people, one dog, several hens in cages and considerable piles of vegetables spread along the tops of the coaches. The convex roof had a flat walkway along its crest and everyone sat on this with legs sloping down to a low rail on the edge. I approached a man wearing a straw deerstalker which was tied tightly under his chin and around his head. Each time he smiled his eyes bulged like those of a gargoyle. It seemed a ridiculous question but I asked if the sitting space next to him was taken. He shook his head, smiled and bulged.

We set off through poor wheatfields that had been stuck like felt cut-outs to the stony valley but these soon faded to lavender grey and pale mustard shrubs which clung to the bare rock of natural quarries. The track had developed a distinct downhill tilt and the sensation of the rumbling train and the wind in my face added exhilaration to our route, snaking through gorges and crossing and recrossing a river on countless invisible bridges so that at times we seemed to be flying fifty feet above what had become a turgid current. The track increased its tilt and then held it constant so that we slid with even and positive bloody-mindedness into a landscape that resented us, contriving our destruction by standing solidly in our way, leaping abruptly to one side and at times nearly disappearing altogether. The train, trapped in this canyon, turned from side to side, running first along one cliff ledge and then gliding over the void to try the other in an effort to find a way out. I was engrossed in the view behind when my neighbour, the deerstalker, suddenly knocked my arm and I turned just in time to duck for a tunnel – a lump of low-hanging rock rushed by and made me think I had missed having my head dashed by no more than an inch, but there must have been a clear six inches. I crouched in the darkness and felt the turbulent air bouncing off the ceiling of rock and buffeting my body. 'I could have been killed.' The thought kept racing through my mind but when we emerged from the tunnel, my bulging friend was grinning reassurance. He could have been killed too but he was used to the proximity of death and his margin for fear was narrower than a gringo's generous allowance.

I barely had time to thank him and recover when we had to flatten ourselves once more for the next tunnel of darkness and lethal stalactites. Tunnels, bridges and ledges were our precarious means of thwarting nature's traps and avoiding plunging into a gorge whose depth varied from several hundred feet to shallow, but always adequate for swallowing a train. We came upon the Alausi Loop without warning and were swept around a 360° turn in the tightest feasible circle that almost enabled the train's engine to pass underneath its last coach. After this, railwaymen appeared at the end of each wagon roof to operate large brake wheels for the impending steep section. The track turned bends sharper than I felt was possible and often we headed towards cliffs where it seemed there had to be a tunnel, but there would be none and with a violent lurch we would sheer to one side.

At one point a signal passed along the line of brakemen. We gradually lost speed and were ambling past a branch line which ran off downhill, angled back the way we had come, when I saw that there was no railway track on the hillside ahead of us. We had reached the Devil's Nose double zigzag. The Devil's Nose (Nariz del Diablo) was a thousand-foot perpendicular wall which protruded high above our river gorge, effectively blocking our progress. It had taken engineers two years to devise a way around this obstacle. We drew to a halt in the cul de sac, the points were changed behind us,

and then we rolled backwards down the branch line. This levelled
out in another cul de sac, more points were changed and we moved
forwards to descend a new section of the line, having completed a Z
manoeuvre on a slope too steep and narrow for a corner. This
railway ladder took us down once more and we got around the
Devil's Nose by passing underneath and running along what was
possibly his Upper Lip. The breathtaking views continued and I
revelled in this unique combination of natural beauty and fairground
thrills. Sometimes it felt as if we were out of control, accelerating
towards the next illusive barrier and wobbling on the edge of
precipice and chasm. Minor derailments are not uncommon on this
line – they were an accepted part of Latin American railways, and
usually involved a twenty-minute delay – but the thought of being
pitched into the plummeting surrounds was no longer frightening. I
could fly. I had already been flying for three hours.

A ticket inspector scrambled up at one end and made his way
along the roof. He knew the track well and had a paranormal sense
for judging when to collapse among the vegetables and passengers to
avoid a tunnel. The deerstalker didn't have a ticket and had to pay a
second-class fare. The inspector examined my ticket.

'This is first-class . . .'

'Yes. I think so too,' I replied but the retort obviously didn't work
in Spanish and he moved on with a mystified air that almost caused
him to forget about the next tunnel.

The air grew warmer and the vegetation greener as we exchanged
the temperate for the tropical and dropped 10,600 feet on 100 miles
of mountain track. At the lowland station of Bucay the diesel engine
was replaced by an old steam puffer of a type I thought had become
extinct, for the level haul to Guayaquil. I stood up to catch the full
effect of the breeze and to look out over the expanse of plantations;
bananas ripening in blue polythene tubes which tasselled the trees,
sugar cane, cocoa and coffee, all in lush abundance. The train
stopped at every village, the track running up the middle of main
streets without isolation or distinction, and our approach being
heralded by the loud blast of our whistle, falling and rising in a
conscious palindrome of POOoooooo–oooooOOP. People sat
about half-naked and even sweating seemed an effort. Mangy dogs
dozed in the dusty streets, opening one eye in bored precaution at the
train's noise and the yells of vendors who swarmed out to greet us.
They climbed onto the roof before the train had halted with trays of

sweets, drinks, sliced fruits, ice cream and savoury fritters balanced on their heads. The wooden houses looked poor, primitive and delicate with glassless niggardly windows and frail verandahs where heavy-bosomed women made banisters sag as they lent out, and just stared. To them the train recalled the time of day or some overdue chore and it was the thought of the chore that showed in their features, not the excitement of trains, new faces or distant destinations; they had no chance of knowing the inspiration of travel, the wonder of fresh experiences. Trains were no more than a short interruption in their routine, a whistle blast of activity in the apathetic heat, and their vacant stares absorbed my searching one into their emotional void.

With deep throaty puffs our engine tugged at its load and slowly moved off, forcing dogs to slink away grudgingly, and soon we were riding into the evening sun, passing ricefields and narrow canals where naked children splashed in mud-curdled water and dugouts laden with produce paddled towards the river Guayas. We reached the end of the thirteen-hour journey after dark and I took a small ferry across the river to the city proper, the boat's spotlight prodding at water hyacinths and oil slicks which choked the surface.

In order that Ecuadorians may enjoy the splendour of Quito, it seems they have to suffer the imposition of Guayaquil as retribution. It is the country's largest and most important city, being the leading industrial site and the port which handles almost all foreign trade (except Ecuador's lucrative oil exports which leave further north). Despite its slick, renovated centre, it has the usual ring of slums and is a soulless brooding place with a damnable climate. The air is hot and humid and sticks to the skin like a wet veil. But Guayaquil does have one attraction. It has an awesome cemetery. This comprises a minor city of several-roomed mausoleums and sepulchres styled as churches, palaces and fancy knick-knack boxes bearing the RIPs of VIPs and the super-rich, and overpopulated by larger than life statuary. A grand avenue of lofty palms runs through this ornamental hotchpotch of white marble which jabs the eye with dazzling brilliance. Compared to the shanty-dwellers nearby, the dead live better than the living.

The afternoon following my arrival I restocked with ten rolls of film and sat on a park bench near the city centre. The bag of films lay by my feet while I looked at a map of Peru and periodically lay back, flapping my open shirt to scare the sweat trickling down my chest and trying to think of all the times I had felt cold. My thoughts returned to the coolness of Quito with longing and then I was reliving the train journey, the fresh mountain air, the kind deer-stalker who had befriended me . . . When I next looked down at my feet, the bag had gone. Someone must have crept up behind me and stolen it by reaching under the bench. Anger welled up inside me and was readily converted to resentment against Guayaquil. I loathed the place. It was a hellhole. Clammy, callous and corrupt. No wonder its highlight was a cemetery.

Gradually I calmed down and accepted my loss more stoically. It was infuriating but unimportant. This was one of those ill days which would help to make the next favourable ones seem even better. It was all part of the ups and downs of a long bumpy journey. Sometimes one felt like an outcast, at other times one was fêted like a hero – it was a paradox of South American affection, leaping from inadequacy to excess – the unique experience of being bolivared.

6 · A Night with a Peruvian Witchdoctor

A special feature of travelling in the Andes is that an entire day can be spent at either an uphill or a downhill angle. In Peru trucks replace buses as the principal means of transport and they can climb steadily, but slowly, for over fifteen hours at a stretch on the high and steep mountain roads. Sometimes you look out on the same view for hours on end as the dirt road ascends in a thousand bends, but this is merely a bonus. Andean scenery is so spectacular that even the roads like to make the most of it.

After leaving Guayaquil I made my way to the Peruvian border in three days (up, down, up, respectively). It was in a truck during the next downhill day that a fellow passenger with eight sacks of ironmongery told me about *los curanderos*. He said they were witchdoctors who were descended from generations of mystical healers and they were famous throughout Peru because they could cure any ailment. They lived 13,000 feet up in the mountains around Black Lake, several hours walk from the northern town of Huancabamba. I bought a small mess tin from him, postponed Machu Picchu (still far away to the south) and decided to try and find *los curanderos*. It took two more days to reach Huancabamba. Half down, one and a half up and two punctures.

Huancabamba was an attractive town set amidst steep mountains which occasionally relaxed their gradients to allow meagre plots of crops to interrupt the stony ground and sporadic clumps of subtropical vegetation. The town's original plan, if one had ever existed, had been altered by frequent subsidences, leaving the houses crooked and the streets falling away at confused angles; Huancabamba's reputation to 'walk' was associated with the magical properties of the area. The local market sold *cuy*, roast guinea pig and a worthy Andean delicacy although indistinguishable from tough roast pork when vendors have kept it warm for a couple of days while waiting for customers.

It was raining when I set off for the Laguna Negra. The villagers had told me it was only a five-hour walk but I was carrying enough food for three days to allow the option of extending my stay. There was no way of knowing how the witchdoctors would receive me; perhaps favourably if my approach were sufficiently humble and respectful but more probably my arrival would be seen as an intrusion and these remote mountain folk would turn me away – at least I hoped this would be the worst that would happen. Señora Sales' neighbours were still fresh in my mind.

The path had been worn into the hill so that a bank ran along one side and the other fell away sharply towards a dirty river in spate. The irregular hillside forced the path to rise and fall and weave around in its effort to follow the river and avoid precipitous crags. Tall clumps of cacti lent out from the bank, their sword-shaped leaves edged with vicious hooks and tipped with a needle to catch the unwary. The way was greasy with well-trodden mud, and trickles of water ran down the middle and collected in puddles of challenging width and uncertain depth. When my socks became wet and mud began oozing between my toes, I realised my boots were in a worse state than I'd thought. I resolved to buy a new pair at the first opportunity but this did nothing to help my actual predicament and made the prospect of walking away from the nearest shop into a sloping quagmire appear all the more dreadful. Sixty pounds of luggage on my back only served to exaggerate the effect of each misplaced foot and each spine-wrenching loss of balance. Two miles further on the path left the river and rose up into the mountains in a series of devil's nose zigzags which sacrificed very little to the direct line.

After three hours of this relentless slope I was in a foul mood. The rain had soaked my clothes, my shirt was stuck to my back with sweat, my muscles ached and I felt exhausted. The altitude gave me only half a breath of thin air and the path continued to be so slippery that sometimes I had to take four small steps to cover the distance of one normal one. At other times my legs locked and I struggled to keep my balance as both feet slid slowly backwards, frequently failing with the result that my arms soon had mud up to the elbows from the many falls.

I met the odd downhill traveller, mostly men in dusky ponchos, bare legs and carrying a stave. In reply to my repeated question of how much further, the answers were wildly different but equally depressing. 'Five hours . . . eight hours . . . Oh! A long, long way . . . two days . . . twelve hours . . .' It seemed the nearer one came, the further one had to go. From these replies it was obvious that I was not being given any encouragement to reach my destination, but then I met a woman who pointed to somewhere on the horizon which was only visible when my head was bent back as far as it would go. She said the village of Cataleim was there, and Laguna Negra was eight hours beyond it, 'but you walk so fast, gringo, it'll be less for you.'

I plodded on up this spiralling track and came to Cataleim, a collection of mud huts bordering the path. The only water for drinking was in a small irrigation ditch carrying dark treacle which slurped and bubbled and made me think of beer. It passed through every field and beside every house. I cursed. Surely at 12,000 feet in the Andes I had the right to clean water? Obviously not. I filled my bottle, noticing that there were small worms in the murk, and dropped in some Ecuadorian sterilising tablets at triple the recommended strength. When I next opened the bottle after walking on during the two hours stipulated as being the minimum safe period, the worms were still swimming about vigorously. Damn that Venezuelan border pig for having taken my best sterilisation pills. Thirst made my throat feel full of thistles. I took off my shirt and poured the water through the fabric, catching the filtered liquid in my new mess tin. It tasted earthy and probably harboured all sorts of virulent bacteria but it was at least free of worms. It quenched my thirst, and left me with a cold patch on my shirt.

Two hours later the path became less steep and passed through a barren area of moorland grass and bogs. A girl herding six sheep told me it was still three hours walk to *los curanderos*, but there was one called Señor Cordoba in Cataleim. This news heartened me a little but I still wanted to reach the main group at Laguna Negra. The weather worsened. Rain came in sudden squawls, the mist lowered and it became very cold. I tried not to reflect on how many Peruvian hours of walking might still be ahead and concentrated on something which had been puzzling me for some time. Apart from the common and understandable five-toed footprints which shoeless walkers had left on the path, there were the unmistakable marks of car tyres. It was out of the question that anyone could drive a car up here, no one would own a scrambler motorbike and besides, the marks were always disjointed.

Then my mind began to wander. I felt chilled and exhausted, and recognised the advancing symptoms of hypothermia. I had experienced it once before in the Cairngorms and the memory of how rapidly it had reduced me to total apathy, and made me want no more than to lie down on the spot and go to sleep, returned with frightening clarity. I rested for a moment and swallowed three large spoonfuls of sugar, and within ten minutes a new surge of energy flowed into my muscles. Another peasant appeared coming down the track but he refused to tell me anything about the witchdoctors and tried to persuade me to turn back. His secrecy merely strengthened my resolve. As he went off I noticed that he left a trail of car tread impressions behind him – his sandals were foot-shaped soles cut from a car tyre and secured to his feet by rubber thongs!

My determination to find the witchdoctors stemmed from a personal encounter with a spiritualist healer several years earlier in Edinburgh, and a Venezuelan photographer's account of a *chongo bongo* ceremony (related to Haitain voodoo, and Brazilian macumba and candomblé) which he had recently attended. Before setting out on my travels I used to run regularly in the hills. One year a bad fall in the Ben Nevis race left me with torn ligaments in one ankle and although these mended fairly quickly and allowed me to resume training, the joint remained slightly stiff. Some time later I happened to meet a spiritualist healer who offered to see what he could do. He asked me to sit on a chair and hold out the affected leg. He did no more than pass his hands around my ankle, interlock his fingers and support the weight of my leg as he squatted there. His hands were relaxed and did not grip my ankle. The next moment it felt as if someone had fastened onto my ankle and was pulling forcefully at my leg. So intense was the sensation that I was about to be dragged from the chair that my hands automatically clutched the arm rests and my body braced itself against the strain. But this man was relaxed, leaning slightly forwards and looking down at his hands held open below my ankle. The stiffness did eventually disappear, whether through his help or time I was unable to say, but I couldn't deny that intense and inexplicable sensation.

The other incident concerned a Swiss friend who lived in Venezuela and was a respected professional photographer. He had been invited to a *chongo bongo* ceremony during a trip to a remote part of the north-east and had asked if he could photograph the event. He knew of several colleagues who had photographed ceremonies –

but their films had always developed as blanks. Permission was readily given. The participants were mainly black women that evening. What my friend had found most disturbing was the way the women became zombies, for hours gyrating captives to the hypnotic beat of the drums, and the sight of a huge obese woman froghopping across the floor continuously for twenty minutes – the exertion would have crippled a trained gymnast. Later he was bewildered to discover that all the films he had exposed before the *chongo bongo* ceremony developed normally, but the rest turned out to be blanks.

These two incidents had aroused my interest in similar aspects of the paranormal, a cautionary interest which appeared increasingly unhealthy the longer this particular quest continued. Eight hours of walking ended when the light began to fade and a new chill and weariness crept over me. The witchdoctors were certainly onto a good thing, I thought. Anyone who survived the strenuous journey up to see them must already be as agile as a llama and have the constitution of a yak. I put up my tent on the least marshy spot, washed my feet in a stream of gelid water and ate bread, corned beef, raw carrots, onions, and an orange with spoonfuls of sugar. It seemed quite palatable up there with rain drops exploding against the flysheet. Moisture soon seeped through from all sides. I wrapped myself in a blanket and purposely shivered to try to generate some warmth, hoping to be asleep before the dampness reached me.

It was depressing to wake up the next morning after an uncomfortable night, rain still beating hard against the tent, and having to face a pair of wet socks and deformed boots. Breakfast consisted of Quaker oats (an American brand converted to sawdust under Peruvian licence), milk reconstituted from powder with earthy water, and goat cheese. It was a diet that discouraged lingering before a storm. My tent was quickly bundled up and I set off into poor visibility with the rain in my face. After an hour my path split into six parallel minor tracks, each as slippery as the other. When a fall brought me to my knees at the point where all six tracks came together before diverging into different directions, it finally became too much. My clothes were drenched again, I was cold, covered in mud, no longer sure of the way and exasperated with the whole venture. I turned back.

Some distance down the track I was overtaken by a man who wore a large hat like that of the Quaker depicted on my packet of oatflakes, a mud-spattered poncho, trousers rolled up to his knees and tyre sandals. He carried a stave and a hen, and said his name was Alberto Meiral. He was going to Huancabamba to sell . . . (his eyes sparkled) . . . Would I like to buy a hen? He would let me have it for 600 soles (93 pence) because, although it was a very good hen, it was a bit small. He was disappointed when I declined his offer but on hearing of my intention to visit Señor Cordoba in Cataleim, he immediately said he would lead me to the house. I admired his sandals and heard that he had worn them every day for the last eight years. He proudly raised his foot to reveal the sole and the tread showed no sign of wear. Alberto set off and forced me to break into a trot to keep up with him. Any concern about the weight of my pack and my recent discomforts vanished as I half-ran, half-slithered down the path, following the wiggly lines of xyx radials. We reached Cataleim within the hour, and he pointed to a tin roof. Then he shook my hand and continued the 5,000-foot descent of his two-day quest to earn 93 pence. At least Peruvian shoes came with a 10,000-mile guarantee.

Most of the houses were made of mud and straw plaster over wattle, but Señor Cordoba's house was built of adobe bricks, somewhat similar to the ones I was carrying around each foot. I knocked on the door positively enough to disguise my apprehension. It was opened by a haggard grandmother who ushered me in without any fuss.

The witchdoctors were rumoured to be extremely rich but there was no evidence of wealth in this house. I entered a small dingy room full of smoke. The smoke drifted up and ran about the ceiling until it found one of the many holes in the roof which also provided the only source of light. The furniture consisted of a bench and table, some shelves, one chair and three tiny footstools, and a net of food suspended from a rafter. A modest fire was burning close to one wall with three rocks supporting a tureen of maize soup over its flames. Señora Cordoba was stirring the soup and peered at me through long clarty black hair which draped her shoulders and fell to her chest. The flickering flames gave her face a sorcerous glow and made her affable smile appear fiendish. She motioned me to sit on a footstool. A baby girl clinging to her skirt eyed me shyly while three other children sat on the ground along with a teenage girl, a man in his twenties, a woman weaving in one corner . . . ten guineapigs, two cats, one dog, five undersized but very good hens, and a sixth which came and went through a hole in the wall, fluttering its wings with more effort than achievement.

No one showed any surprise on seeing a gringo enter, and the young man's blank face, nodding, just nodding, was reassuring. After a suitable pause and an exchange of pleasantries, I explained my interest in the healing powers of the doctor and asked if it would be possible to attend a ceremony. The young man introduced himself as Alejandro, the doctor's son and himself an apprentice to the hereditary profession, and said he would have to ask his father. Señor Cordoba had evidently just returned from the Laguna Negra with some patients and was busy in another room. Initially Alejandro was reticent but after a while he spoke quite freely about the ceremony.

'Each healing session lasts two days. On the first day we go to the lake and the patients stand up to the waist in water and duck under three times. Then the doctor anoints their heads seven times with blessed water. It's very cold and the people have to run about afterwards to get warm again. This part is not obligatory but it's best to do it if they can. Then everyone comes back here. Tonight is the second and most important part. My father will arrive soon.'

The mountains here were evidently exceptional for their growth of herbs. The most important were *mischa blanca* (floripondium), black tobacco and the San Pedro cactus. Alejandro mentioned other names which meant nothing to me – *guarana* (used as a nerve tonic), *caapi, simora* and *huachuma* ('make you go dreamy') – and explained that these were sometimes used purely as medicine for organic ailments but could also be used in conjunction with specific rites and chants, *tajos*, which dated back 2,000 years. Such treatment was required when the sickness was caused by evil forces, usually curses, love magic or bad luck, which had been directed at the sufferer through the envy of a rival. Envy was seen as the root of most ills. Herbs cured the physical illness; the lake bath, hallucinogens, vomit-inducing drinks, a night without sleep, the *tajos*, the *curandero*'s power charms and the rites all purged the body, broke any evil spells and reunited it with good earth forces; finally the body was sprayed with perfumed herbal liquids (a mixture of holy water, white cornmeal, petals, sugar, sweet lime juice and powdered lime) to refreshen it and signify purification.

'Are you married?' asked Alejandro, suddenly changing the subject. This was one of the most frequent questions put to me and my answer usually made Latin Americans raise their eyebrows in surprise. Being in one's late twenties and unmarried was considered either neglectful or suspicious. I shook my head. He raised his eyebrows and pointed to the teenage girl.

'This is my sister, Isidra. What do you think of her?'

The bluntness of his question caught me off guard. I smiled at the girl and commented that Peru had many pretty girls. Then I shifted my eyes quickly to Alejandro because, unfortunately, Isidra was not one of them. She was a plump girl with a plain round face, the rosy brown cheeks of mountain folk, big honest eyes and a slightly deformed nose as if her skin had been burnt or grafted. I suddenly recognised her as the girl with six sheep who had first told me about Señor Cordoba the previous evening. Before I could remark on this and turn the subject away from marriage, her mother took up the cue.

'She cooks well and makes a good poncho.'

Everyone was staring at me except Isidra whose eyes were cast meekly towards her feet. My mind went back to another time when I had found myself similarly compromised in a small village of narwhal hunters in north-west Greenland. The criterion of a good wife in that region had been her ability to make a good kayak. I used the same excuse as on that occasion, saying I was sure she would make a fine wife but I was not ready to settle down yet.

'Isidra would like to travel . . .' continued her mother, not easily dissuaded, but she was interrupted by the arrival of the witchdoctor himself.

There was nothing extraordinary about Señor Cordoba's appearance. He was about forty years old, medium in stature and he wore a grey poncho, dirty blue trousers from a baggy suit and 10,000-mile sandals. His narrow face and heavily lined forehead displayed Mediterranean features rather than the broader, more Mongoloid characteristics of the Andean Indian, which was in keeping with the history of the Huancabamba area and its particularly long occupation by the Spanish in colonial times. His manner was one of detachment, as if he hadn't slept during the days of beard growth on his chin. He talked to Alejandro for a while in Quechua. When they fell silent the woman spinning in the corner put down her distaff and got up to go. She was not one of the family and I got the impression she was working to repay a debt as she was making a poncho for Alejandro. (He told me it would take her thirty-six days to spin enough wool and then twelve more to weave and sew it into a poncho.) Before leaving she said she felt slightly feverish. Señor Cordoba took a bottle from the nearest shelf and poured her a

measure of brown oily liquid. The woman drank and was pathetically grateful. She pressed him to accept a 1,000 soles (£1.60) note, not
expecting any change, but he muttered something about paying
another day. It seemed expensive medicine. (Fifteen per cent of
Peru's population exists outside the money economy, living off
subsistence farming and bartering. This makes the statistical value of
an average income less credible and usually inflated. I was told later
that the average man in that area earned 120,000 soles [£200] per
annum and that the average treatment cost 5–10,000 soles.) Señor
Cordoba turned to me before leaving and, without any enthusiasm,
said he had no objection if I wanted to attend the healing session that
night.

Señora Cordoba was poking at fish crackling in the fire's glowing
embers when a group of patients shrouded in ponchos entered the
room. We were all handed a bowl of maize soup and a portion of
fish. Isidra was giving me furtive glances while she chopped what
looked like a marrow into large segments and dropped them into a
cauldron. My legs were beginning to cramp on the low stool and my
field of vision had become claustrophobically restricted; I had to
avoid looking at the patients in case it seemed rude, and the area of
Isidra in case it was misunderstood. Eventually I excused myself to
go and wash my mud-caked boots, soon finding a stream which
contained little worms, was evidently the bathwater of the village,
its sewer and its irrigation canal, and which had been my drinking
water the previous day. On my return Alejandro lent me one of his
father's ponchos against the cold. I sat dressed like a witchdoctor
beside a fire where a cauldron of marrow was bubbling and with a cat
sitting at my feet, its tail curled round its paws and the tip twitching
over some dying embers. Their apparent acceptance of a stranger
amongst them and their hospitality was deeply touching, but my
gratitude was tempered by a faint suspicion that it had all been a little
too easy. Could they possibly have an ulterior motive? It was an
uncharitable thought and a disconcerting secret to possess in the
house of a wizard. I felt faintly insincere and entirely transparent.

Alejandro sat next to me and lowered his voice to a whisper so that
it was scarcely audible in the light hubbub of conversation, gesturing
towards the cauldron. 'That is the San Pedro. It makes you see
things. When my father drinks it he is able to see what illness a
person has, how bad it is, whether there is an evil force present and
what cure is needed.' Then he made what I thought was a brave

admission. 'We know which plants and herbs are best but the cure is also in the mind. The San Pedro helps a person believe it will work.'

He maintained that *curanderos* had the power of divination, could locate lost objects and cure all illnesses but the more severe ones took longer: epilepsy, blindness, infertility and making a couple sterile if they did not want any more children. The flow of patients was getting greater each year. Some came just to bathe, to 'raise' their luck, but most came because medicine and hospitals had failed to make them well. He pointed to one man and said he was very sick. His teeth bled and blood appeared from many parts of his body. Another had been here a year ago but he had been extremely ill and now needed 'just a little bit more medicine'. This showed me that the *curandos*' treatment did not always work or at least was not always totally successful.

I became drowsy and must have dozed off for some time. My next recollection was of being awakened at about nine p.m. by two men who had come to collect the cauldron of San Pedro. It was dark but one of them held a candle and I saw that the room was now empty. I followed them out and round the building to another door. The doctor sat crouched in the middle against the far wall, surrounded by about four dozen bottles ranging in size and shape from miniature samples to flagons. Alejandro sat next to him and the shapes of adults and even some children lying scattered around the floor were discernible amongst the aggregate bundles of clothing. I sat in a corner and watched as the cauldron was placed in front of the doctor.

Nothing happened for an hour. Then a bottle was filled with the cool hallucinogenic San Pedro. The doctor drank first, slowly and heartily, and then it was passed around. I wanted a clear head to observe what would happen and tried to refuse the drink but they insisted and a few jokes were muttered about my reluctance. The San Pedro smelt of blackcurrant but the taste was like bitter cucumber juice and unpleasant. Another bottle was then handed round the room and again I had to drink. This one contained strong alcohol which smelt yeasty like home-made wine but the taste was closer to gin and tonic. Both bottles did the rounds continuously for some time but after my initial taste I only pretended to drink, blocking the mouth of the bottle with my tongue each time I had to make a show of tilting it. People talked and each time they addressed the doctor, they called him *maestro*.

The maestro suddenly addressed one particular man, speaking

rapidly and drawling his words as he asked questions. The man rose and stood before the maestro, answering in a voice soft with respect. He talked about his home, how well certain crops grew there and generally about his life and background. From his account the maestro was diagnosing the problem and deciding whether an evil force was at work. A sickly sweet essence filled the room. The maestro had opened some bottles and he handed one to the man who crossed himself, took a swig and then disappeared outside into the darkness. Then came the sounds of sniffing and snorting. The patient returned and the maestro muttered a ten-second incantation before handing over another bottle for the same performance to be repeated.

The maestro drank more San Pedro and spat on the ground before next questioning a husband and wife. By this time his voice sometimes rose in pitch and betrayed long yawns but he carried on talking as if nothing had happened. The couple were each given different bottles and left the room. The same sounds followed: sniffing, snorting, spitting and then hollow flute noises caused by blowing into the neck of a bottle. This went on for hours. There was no sign of the maestro having to go outside and slice a sword violently through the air to fight off evil or of anyone having to leap three times over a fire to break a curse, as Alejandro had said sometimes occurred. Rituals were repeated three or seven times: for the Trinity and the seven joys and sorrows of Mary. The ceremonies were based on practices which went back to the Chimu culture but these had become interwoven with aspects of Catholicism. The atmosphere became soporific with the flickering candle, the mutterings, incantations and perfumes, and eventually I fell asleep.

I stirred as dawn was beginning to break. Through the open door I could make out a distant valley of green-brown patchwork fields and cottonwool clouds scudding over the hilltops. The atmosphere in the room seemed more boisterous than before. The San Pedro and gin had done their work. Figures continually came and went through the door but they disappeared out of my view to the source of the spitting, hooting noises. The activity gradually petered out and the ceremony appeared to be over. I began wondering how to extricate myself honourably from this situation when I heard murmurings of 'meester' and 'gringo', and became aware of the maestro's sideways glance in my direction. He rose to his feet and beckoned me to follow as he left the room. He stopped in the middle of the courtyard and turned to face me. The bright sunlight hurt my eyes, but he was in the shadow and his eyes were wide and alert. He seemed to have shaken off his weariness and wore a confident and determined half-smile.

He indicated I should remove my poncho. I asked what was happening and he replied that he was going to 'bless my journey'. I caught sight of a hen walking along the side of the building and when it was passing a doorway, a hand shot out and grabbed it around the neck. The witchdoctor suddenly hooked a finger in the V of my open-necked shirt and pulled down sharply, ripping some of the button-holes and removing two buttons. His aggression startled me. A man emerged from the room carrying five small bottles, and then I saw Alejandro in the background through the doorway – my breath caught and blood drained from my face with tingling need-ling sensations. He had stabbed an ornate machete into the dirt floor and was anointing it with oil and rubbing the blade with leaves. My mind held a horrific vision of ritual cardiectomy . . . They couldn't? . . . they wouldn't? But then this man was a witchdoc-tor . . . My body stiffened with fear. The witchdoctor was busy talking. I could run . . . and my eyes began searching for the best way out. As my panic was mounting I noticed that Alejandro had put the knife back into its sheath. This brought some relief but I was still deeply suspicious. I decided to question the witchdoctor about the knife when he stopped talking, and run if he showed any hesitation or malice.

'Why was Alejandro anointing a knife and speaking to it?'

He was surprised by my question but replied immediately. 'It is a blessing for a good harvest.' I didn't know whether to believe this or not. It was quite possible but it might have been a convenient cover. Perhaps I had overreacted but my distrust was not dispelled. The witchdoctor came up to me holding one bottle in his hand while his assistant stood alongside with the others, and folded back my shirt to expose my chest. He told me to make the sign of the cross. I did so but got it all wrong and gave up after three points. He blew a flute note into the first bottle, took a swig of the contents, gargled and then coughed a fine spray over my chest and into each ear. He mumbled a spell mixed with a prayer, alternating between Quetchua and Spanish. He did the same with the next bottle but this time aerosoled the salivary liquid into my face and over my shoulders before reciting different words which were incomprehensible except the phrase 'Holy Mother of Jesus'. This routine was repeated with each bottle, fifteen mouthfuls of powerful perfume being spattered across my head and upper torso. A bell was rung and he slapped my chest several times with the palms of his hands.

The ceremony was over. My fears had been unfounded and I hesitantly thanked Señor Cordoba, more for not doing what he might have done than in gratitude for anything he actually had done. The patients began to come out into the courtyard while I was trying to fasten what buttons were left on my shirt, and Alejandro invited me to stay for breakfast. I felt ravenous and followed the others to the kitchen where Isidra, who smiled at me, was preparing the meal. The hen lay in a wok-like pan over the fire, half-plucked and simmering in its own blood. I felt a strange twinge of guilt. 'There but for the grace of God . . .' ran through my mind and after that I had no stomach for the creature, or for my present company.

I made my excuses, declined the invitations to stay, insisted on several pressing reasons why I had to go and repeated my thanks. Patients were chatting and laughing freely, thankful that their own ordeal was over, the dog was barking, the witchdoctor had reverted to his bleary-eyed state, Alejandro was teasing a guineapig by pulling it along with a lead made of string, and Señora Cordoba was saying once more, 'Isidra would like to travel . . .' when I took my pack and waved goodbye.

I walked slowly at first until I was out of sight and then began jogging. It would only be four or five gringo hours back to Huanca-bamba and downhill all the way. Once more I slipped and fell but this no longer bothered me for my thoughts were on *los curanderos*. They had to have some power. They would not have existed for centuries if they could not effect convincing cures. People would not pay them so much hard-earned money or come back for more treatment unless their ailments disappeared or were at least relieved.

And could they possibly take possession of a gringo's soul, or exert control over his mind and force him to return, winding him back like a guineapig on a string to marry their unloved daughters? No! That was blatantly ridiculous! Nevertheless, I did stop and strip to the waist at the first stream and, still smelling like a Fabergé samp-ling counter, I eagerly washed off the last vestiges of their magic.

The shock of seeing that machete being anointed had not yet subsided and the residual nervous energy strengthened my legs and made my body and luggage seem weightless. I hurried on down to Huancabamba, and had never felt healthier in my life.

7 · The Incarcerated Incas of Machu Picchu

I first met Efrain when he was slanting downhill with six tons of flour and as much dried fish. He was a village schoolteacher (a content one but not rich, he said, which was why he had to travel by truck) and a passenger on one of many obstinate Dodges which carried me towards Cuzco and Machu Picchu on a road wriggling through the Andes for 700 miles. Efrain's passionate interest was history and during the three days we travelled together he became a Peruvian Sheherazade apparently delaying our arrival by recounting the intrigues of the Spanish conquest.

He related how Athualpa ruled a highly organised society as the last effective god-king of the Incas. They were a race of expert builders, innovative farmers, and efficient statisticians. Work and land were allocated according to the needs of the state, storehouses were kept stocked with food to offset future shortages, and relay posts housing runners at five-mile intervals along a comprehensive network of roads enabled the Incas to send messages 150 miles in a day. They are thought to have begun their rise to power towards the end of the eleventh century and by 1450 they controlled a vast territory and had created a state of political and economic stability far in advance of their time and strong enough to consolidate their military conquests. A simple pyramid of administrative channels united the empire, albeit at the cost of individual freedom, and made possible its successful expansion for almost 500 years. It was already outgrowing its efficiency when in 1531 Francisco Pizarro arrived in Peru.

A bastard swineherd-turned-soldier, Pizarro had passed his first sixty years without distinction, and he remained illiterate to the day of his murder by malcontent Spaniards in 1542. Having captured Athualpa by arranging a peaceable meeting and massacring his entourage of 6,000 unarmed Indians, Pizarro sentenced the god-king to a heretic's death by being burnt at the stake. Athualpa pleaded for another form of execution as this would have damned him irrevocably by his own beliefs. Pizarro was not a gifted leader but a ruthless soldier who possessed exceptional courage, determination and luck. He could also be 'lenient', however, and he allowed Athualpa to be baptised, christened and garotted.

Peru's latest political drama was evident during the journey south. The first general election had just been held after twelve years of rule by a military junta and the country was daubed with political slogans. Few of the population seemed to know what any of the parties stood for and election campaigns had been simplified into blunt orders and appealing symbols. 'Put your cross on the spade,' ran the words beside a stylised spade. 'Your vote is this, comrade,' offered a carrot top or a fleur-de-lis and three stars petitioned with much the same authority. Efrain shook his head sadly and said there was scant value in holding an election, except for the prestige of being a democracy, in a country where sixty per cent of the people were illiterate and voted on the basis of the nicest symbols. 'What we need is a good dictator,' he added. Fernando Belaúnde was chief Spade and the Spades had won. Efrain considered him a conscientious man but doubted that any radical reforms would be tolerated by his opponents. He asked the other passengers for their views.

'He is a good man,' said one.

'Huh!' scoffed another, 'a new government, a different set of thieves. But Belaúnde is . . .', he held one thumb horizontally and waggled it up and down, '. . . is more or less.'

'More or less what?' I asked, but he didn't answer, because of course *más o menos* and *mañana* were never to be taken literally. They were Latin American rhetoric, non-committal vagaries. The second man had voted Carrot Tops and didn't wish to contradict his friend, a Spade. Efrain told them that in Britain the president was a woman. They made him repeat this and then asked me what her symbol was. I tried to be evasive and said it wasn't as simple as or as nice as a spade, but they insisted on more details. I drew a Conservative arrow. They found British politics very amusing.

Over the next two weeks I came to understand the character of Peruvian truck-drivers. They displayed many of the attributes of Guatemalan bus-drivers but also possessed the determination of Pizarro, the arrogance of a long-necked sheep and, alas, the survival instinct of a lemming. They sometimes drove for twenty-four hours at a stretch and chewed coco leaves continuously as a mild drug to ease the strain. Their ancient Dodge trucks were frequently overloaded and running on bald disintegrating tyres without carrying any spares. The banking on the rubble roads often contradicted the bend and served to throw the truck onto the crumbling edge of a thousand-foot drop, and I understood why passengers all took off their hats and crossed themselves each time we passed a cemetery, a Madonna or a roadside cross marking the spot of a fatal accident. These crosses were everywhere and one bend displayed thirty-four of them built as a pyramid to show where a truck had left the road (we had a puncture there so I was able to count them). Truck-drivers were strangely fatalistic about the dangers and painted their aware-ness on the rear plate of their trailers: 'No one knows my destination', 'Lord, show me the way', 'Help me, Lord of Miracles' and 'It is the work of the Lord' (in flowery script on the back of one hauling beer).

I soon learnt how to change a heavy truck tyre with the minimum of effort, how to extract the inner tube, locate the hole, attach the magnesium-backed patch and light it so that it fused into place, how to reassemble the tyre (and how to dismantle it again when we missed out part of the valve), how to repair the hand pump with a pebble after we had pumped ourselves weary for half an hour to no avail – and when simply to pay my driver the full fare and abandon him without revealing my certainty that this time his Dodge really had died.

Efrain arranged a lift with tons of cement which took us down to the lowland expanses of sugar cane and through the deserts where slender tornados vacuumed the shimmering sand and danced through mirages in the blistering heat. A dust cloud followed the truck and overtook us each time we stopped. I prayed we wouldn't break down in Chongoyape. It was everything I feared; hot, water-less, dusty and life was slowly evaporating; starved dogs, dazed goats and fey humans baking to the colour of the mud houses that were gradually absorbing them. We paused there for a meal and I ate a bowl of chicken soup. It was an insipid liquid of fat globules and noodles but it was undoubtedly chicken because a hacked-off claw lay below the surface. Each mouthful helped to convince me that it was the lukewarm slops of live hepatitis, but it seemed a lesser evil than Chongoyape's languid fate of dehydration.

A new lift (mangoes – 'Help yourself!') took us up into the Cordillera Blanca where Efrain pointed to llamas with red and yellow tassels hanging from their ears. These were 'lady llamas', he explained, whose owners liked to distinguish them from 'the boys'.

And often condors flew high in the sky, spans of wings turning ceaseless circles without a wingbeat. Condors were Inca kites that had escaped. I loved the way they flew but wanted to pull them down for a closer look. After a while they became boring because they no longer responded to their strings.

That night was the coldest I had experienced since Greenland, a miserable collection of sleepless hours. My tropical blanket was useless against the cold but was perhaps envied by the Peruvians who had no more than their ponchos and bare feet in Goodyear sandals. Our travelling group became lively when a couple of men brought out *chicha*, a corn liquor. Another man produced a miniature wooden skittle-shaped bottle whose bulbous stopper was withdrawn to reveal a skewer protruding from it. Each person dipped the skewer into the bottle and licked off the adhering white powder. It was refined coco and had a slight tang which numbed my tongue, and eventually my discomfort. It also made the song they were singing, a wavering ditty which warbled down ten notes at the end of each line, seem pleasant in the moonlight as we passed under huge rock overhangs that were tunnels with one wall missing.

It was late at night and a week later when I reached Cuzco. Efrain had said the city's usual population (140,000) would be swollen with Indians from all over the country gathering for the annual Inti Rymi festival, a theatrical reenactment of an Inca rite in which a llama took the part of a bloodless sacrifice to the Sun God. The only room in Cuzco I could find was in Hotel Okey. (Never trust even modestly self-complimentary names.) I was awakened early in the morning by a hen which had walked in through a hole in the door and was pecking up cockroaches lying helplessly on their backs and waving their legs in the air. Then a young pig came through the hole (it was a large hole), chased the hen aside and ate the cockroaches itself. I took umbrage at this invasion and drove them both out into a courtyard where other pigs were pushing their snouts along the ground into everything in their trail.

The old Inca capital of Cuzco stands at an altitude of 11,200 feet and is an alluring town with many narrow cobblestone streets which become so steep that they dissolve into flights of worn steps. The Spanish colonists built many of their churches, houses and fine cloistered mansions on top of the chunky hewn rocks of old Inca walls which are visible in every street, and give an inkling of the Herculean splendour that Cuzco once vaunted. The streets were abuzz with activity and pickpockets and bag-slashers were rife. Efrain had warned me about this danger. 'The Incas were a proud and honest race,' he had said. 'In Quetchua we say of them, "*Ama sua, ama ccella, ama llulla*" – they did not steal, they were not lazy, they did not lie. But that was before the Spanish came. Now, my friend, you must be careful.' The cover of my camera case was cut on my first day but fortunately the thief found nothing but an inner wall of aluminium.

The festival took place three miles outside the town at the ruined fortress of Sacsahuamán whose walls of exquisitely masonried rocks (some weighing 300 tons) must rank as one of the world's greatest human accomplishments. The highlight of my afternoon came after the festival when I met the leading actor, the Sapa Inca, the god-king himself. He sprouted feathers like a psychedelic but savaged cockatoo and was going through a variety of poses for a photographer. I made the most of it and shot my pictures alongside. His bearing was noble, his forehead broad and his nose aquiline; he was just how I imagined Athualpa to have been. After several minutes of laudatory modelling the Sapa Inca suddenly turned to me

'Do you speak English?' His words came without an accent and with such coldness that I was momentarily disarmed. 'This is my private photographer,' he continued, 'and I don't want these shots duplicated. Please go away.'

I was stunned. I saw that my archetypal Inca, the ephemeral god-king of modern Peru, had lost his ties with the old way of life too. The Spaniards had severed all the strings, and Athualpa's twentieth-century equivalent was linked to royalty only through the copyright of his aquiline nose in print.

I left and took the train towards Machu Picchu.

The train was mobbed. I was crushed so tightly in one compartment that there was only room to take a breath when the person next to me exhaled. Eventually a window cracked under the pressure of bodies and several Indians missed their stop because they couldn't get out.

I left the train at Kilometre 88, a platform too insignificant for a name, its whole identity being the start of a footpath to the best known of the Inca lost cities. The way was blocked by a gorge containing a ferocious river but a man ferried me over on an elementary cable car, a small barn door suspended by four wires from a wheel which ran along a steel hawser. It was not until we stalled in the central dip of the hawser and he had to haul us up to the far side by hand that I realised how flimsy the contraption was. He said that a Canadian gringo had fallen off and drowned the previous day and he was worried that this service, his livelihood, would be banned by the authorities. I offered him sympathy and hurried away, not at all reassured by his concern for a lost customer and suspecting that the Incas would have replaced this flying trapeze with a simple bridge.

The walk took three days and involved a strenuous ascent to over 12,000 feet; it traversed deep cold valleys which sunlight seldom touched, groves of dark primeval forest where tangled leafy boughs suffocated under green moss or were bearded with blue lichens, a profusion of wild flowers bending under the weight of butterfly or humming bird, and led beside pellucid streams and tranquil tarns. The last part was a paved Inca trail which passed through ruined villages and incorporated steps, rickety tree-trunk bridges over alarming drops and one tunnel which had been chiselled through a rock blocking the most favourable route. My gaze frequently followed the line of the path ahead to distant icy peaks, or else slipped from my leading foot straight into densely wooded valleys. Camping each night was an endurance test (for these were also the coldest nights since Greenland) but one which was reduced to insignificance by the bottomless view from my tent door each morning and the simple pleasure of brushing my teeth in water made to gush from a rock by original Inca engineering.

On the afternoon of the third day I rounded a corner and found the crest of the mountain ran down before me and levelled out to form a delicate saddle, ending in a towering spear-headed hill. Beyond this and on both sides there was nothing save precipitous slopes which dropped 2,000 feet to the snaking Urubamba River. The ruins of Machu Picchu were perched on this saddle. The sight was breathtaking and I sat down to absorb the fulfilment of an ambition cherished since the start of my wanderings. Fragmented picture-book captions came back to me: '. . . archaeologists . . . perplexed at finding ten times more female skeletons than male . . . a complete city dating back to A D 800 . . . never found by the Spaniards . . . lost under jungle for centuries . . . 1911 . . . chance discovery by an American explorer, Hiram Bingham . . .'

I waited until dark before descending to the ruins, wanting to be alone so that this city would become mine for a while. The ruins covered an area of five square miles and were connected by over 3,000 steps. Most of this area was terraced fields; the main group of ruins occupied a smaller strip along the higher ground, being divided in half by a central avenue of carefully-tended grass. The section on the left was constructed on a hillock and consisted of the temples, palaces and public buildings; now just walls high enough to enclose doorways and windows, but solidly impregnable walls of massive rocks shaped and fitted together with belittling expertise, and the pleasing touch of neatly bevelled edges. The buildings on the right were long rows of houses separated by a narrow track until the level ground fell away and the subsequent rows were forced to descend the steep hillside in uniform steps. These dwellings were identical in construction to the ruined single-room cottages, chimneyless but with both gables intact, common in the Scottish Highlands, only they had been joined together end to end. Machu Picchu was a roofless ghost town, mysterious, majestic, and all mine.

A full moon lit up the stone walls in grey light, creating faint shadows to enhance the rough texture and oblique shape of each meticulously positioned rock, and adding a sinister element to the deathly quiet. It seemed to detach me from time and lead me into a surreal world without props for support. I felt caught in another dimension, floating between two panes of glass through the handiwork of fantastic industry but without any sign of its creators. Their presence was still in this place but they were invisible to me through my glass. It was a temporary and artful disappearance which enabled them to look at me while I was looking for them, and they were amusing themselves by seeing if their captive would find a way out. There was no impression of hostility, merely that of a game in which the observer is observed and his blindness is about to be jollied by the sudden reappearance of his playmates. I sat on a rock, still trapped, and my consciousness slowly sank into it until I became that rock. No sensations reached me other than sound. I thought I heard stone endlessly hitting stone. My awareness followed the regular beat and found a way through my isolation and into the lives of those who remained hidden from view and who were now unaware of my intrusion. The noises of activity projected pictures before me . . . shrieking laughter showed me a woman with braided black hair and a dirty red shawl leaning through the window of a ruin joking with a friend outside. The scrabbling of hooves on steps brought llamas being led by a man with a deformed leg, wearing a dull tunic and leather apron. He stepped over a fallen lintel and disappeared through a doorway, ducking as if the lintel had been in place. Grinding noises came from an old man sharpening a knife as he sat on a missing step, and chanting children ran by, followed by a toddler who hesitated before a walled-up entrance through which the others had disappeared . . . The sounds suddenly stopped and the pictures vanished. I grew out of my rock and back into myself. My senses returned and placed me solidly under the moonlight, amongst the grey stone walls of a ruined city high in the Andes.

The images had all been incomplete or irrational in some way. It would perhaps have been too obviously a dream had the houses and streets been able to restore themselves into a living city with roofs and repaired walls. Instead there had been an uncertain mixture of dream and reality, past and present, and illusive inhabitants who were not only aware of the discrepancies but also delighted in playing with them. I felt I was not alone in Machu Picchu. It was an uncanny perception but it passed and left me with a rare moment of total contentment.

The path to the top of the spearheaded hill Huayna Picchu which overlooked the city was a dizzy scramble, but the Incas had nevertheless built terraced fields close to the summit. Each field was a narrow strip of soil about six feet wide and flush with the top of the retaining wall that held it in place as it followed the contour of the hill. They descended the slope as steep steps until the last whose side fell away into the surrounding void. The soil would have been enriched with the guano of pelicans, gannets and cormorants that was transported with llamas from the coast and used to fertilise 240 varieties of potatoes. It was easy to imagine the farmers falling from these fields when distracted by the magnificent panorama, now tenebrous but unmistakable in its grandeur.

I returned to the main ruins and was sitting contemplating hens and omniverous pigs, and wondering if the Incas had kept either, when I was startled by an angry shout. A guard came running towards me and he became more abusive with the diminishing distance between us. He swore at me, yelled an incoherent verbiage about trespassing, locked gates and permits, threatened me with prosecution and then locked onto my wrist and led me off with my pack hanging from one shoulder. I had no alternative but to let him exhaust his fury before trying to apologise and explain that I had reached the ruins from the side without gates or fences. However he was not to be consoled and was convinced I had climbed over a barrier. Had he spoken English, I should have been persuaded that he was the Sapa Inca's ugly brother. When we reached his sentry-box he took out some paper and a pen.

'First name?' he snapped.

'Alastair.'

'In Spanish?'

'Alastair.'

He became even angrier at this and demanded to know the Spanish equivalent. I said it didn't have one. He said it must have. I argued that there was no reason for it to have one at all. He ordered me to produce my passport.

'Alejandro,' I relented, unwilling to show my passport in case it would be seized.

'Second name?'

'Scott.'

'In Spanish?'

'Oh Jesus . . .' I hadn't meant to say it but he was being so irksome that it slipped out. The name was quite common in Latin America and the guard did not catch my meaning. He wrote it down without further thought, said he would report me to the police if he ever saw me again, and then one Alejandro Jésus was rudely evicted from Machu Picchu.

It was not the reception I had anticipated amongst the Incas but at least the consequences had been mild – milder than others had experienced after their capture and christening.

8 · Bolivia's 189th Coup – and President Stroessner's Poor Cousins

History leaves some countries as its proud monuments while others are left as the detritus of its abuses. I had expected to find Bolivia a sad country because its history was one of injustice; it had lost considerable and often vital territory to all five neighbours; it had suffered 188 political coups in the last 155 years; its population was the poorest in South America and centred around the cold high Altiplano instead of the more productive lowlands; and its principal industry, tin mining (now equalled by petroleum), had long been of benefit to no more than three families – in 1952 the Patiño family's income exceeded that of the government and one of the sons received more pocket-money than the national budget for education. After four days in the country my expectation of a dispirited nation was being fulfilled as I journeyed by bus from La Paz to Cochabamba, the second largest city situated roughly in the centre of the country.

A soldier had given me a lift from the Peruvian border to La Paz four days earlier. 'Guaqui is the biggest port in Bolivia,' he had solemnly informed me, waving his hand back towards Lake Titicaca and the town we had just left. Ports have been a touchy subject here ever since Chile annexed Bolivia's coastline a century ago, so I did not consider it tactful to seek confirmation that Guaqui was also the only one. Politics is another risky subject in Latin America, particularly with a soldier, and so we avoided ports and politics, and conversation pivoted on my route. But even this was tricky ground. Most Latin Americans never have the opportunity to travel long distances, certainly not abroad, and travel has to have a specific purpose such as selling produce or buying an essential tool. Travelling for travel's sake is an unknown pleasure and an alienating concept. For this reason I didn't mention Tierra del Fuego or the fact that I was in Bolivia because it lay on a convenient route to Rio de Janeiro, but gave my destination as Cochabamba because mail was awaiting me there. It seemed a lame reason for travelling half-way round the world but fortunately my soldier-driver accepted it. The road east led first to La Paz and we reached the capital in three hours.

If history has deprived most Bolivians of stability and justice, then geography has deprived them of oxygen. The adaptable people of the high Andes and the Altiplano, which begins at Lake Titicaca, have a red corpuscle count of eight million (to a lowlander's five million), a greater lung capacity by one-third, and a much slower heartbeat. These characteristics are not inherited but develop after birth and assist these people to lead vigorous lives in the rarefied atmosphere. For those without these special assets, La Paz is an exhausting city. Its altitude of 12,000 feet makes it the world's highest capital and because the thin air results in such slow combustion, it was unique in having no fire brigade until twenty years ago when the increased use of modern and more inflammable materials made one necessary. The city lies in a trench in the Altiplano with the snowy Mt Illimani in the background. It appears as an anticlimax of adobe huts at first, but beyond them the plateau ends abruptly and you find the city proper a thousand feet below, filling the trench and running downhill, getting warmer and richer (for altitude dictates temperature and class) until it ends at an area of badlands – alternate sections of tin roofs, concentrated skyscrapers, villas and canyons.

I didn't stay long because the thought of mail 200 miles away in Cochabamba was an irresistible lure. So often letters from home had failed to arrive and left me with the loneliest of feelings, but these disappointments never dashed my hopes that next time it would be different. Soon I was bussing across the Altiplano and eagerly anticipating my first letters for two months. It was unusual to see such a quantity of sky after the restrictive Andes, but the Altiplano's fifty-fifty split between earth and heaven would soon have become dull if not for its copious life. Sheep abounded.

Cochabamba is an important agricultural area and enjoys a pleasantly warm climate in its surrounds of low green hills. Fruit and vegetables were certainly plentiful in the street market where the bus let me out. Oranges were scattered about the pavement and several looked unblemished. I picked one up but its underside was rotten and when a second turned out to have wormholes, I walked on without further interest in them. Then a woman came running after me. She pointed to the fruit on the ground. 'No good,' she said. 'Take these, go on, take, take . . .' and she held out six fresh oranges. Her concern was genuine. I tried to pay her for them but she refused my money and became offended at my insistence. It was only after a great deal of persuasion that she allowed her child to accept the money as a present. She had thought I was hungry. I recalled the hospitality I had received in Acapulco, and there had been many other occasions, but now this – to be given a present in the poorest country in the world by a woman who owned little besides the armful of fruit she held out each day for sale . . . never did 'thank you' sound so weak. Poverty hid many virtues, and I realised that not least amongst Latin American tragedies is for a generous people to have been provided with so little to give.

My letters had been sent to the British consulate which was closed by the time my bus arrived. According to the town information office it opened only in the afternoons, and so after lunch the following day I made my way there with an essential street plan. Cochabamba was laid out as a calendar of historical dates. The consulate was near 14th September Street and starting from 6th August it was best to go to 10th November Square. Then I went along 9th April, turned right into 16th July, then left into the one that led to 14th January and was intersected by 25th May, and duly reached 14th September. (Any modern map of the city will make this clear.) As I walked to the consul's office the interim president, Señora Lydia Gueiler (MNRI party: symbol, a hand giving a V-sign, for victory I think), had just been deposed *in absentia* by a military junta, and 10th November Square was being cordoned off by soldiers.

Despite her name the consul was a full-blooded Anglo-Saxon. Señora Charlotte de Tabaldo was elderly, plump and delightful, domineering but with the bubbling sweetness of an Agatha Christie aristocrat and radiating that comforting eccentricity of English unflappability. She was coming down the steps of her office after locking the door when I arrived and introduced myself. 'Ahh! Mr Scott!' Yes, she knew there were two envelopes for me inside the building. 'I've been *guarding* them for you,' she said with a conspiratorial air, but added that it was quite impossible to open the office and collect them. Her orders were to lock the doors until further notice.

'What a pity you didn't come this morning before we had the coup,' she said, looking up at the sky to see if it would rain. 'Of course you know there's been a coup?' and she began using her umbrella as a walking-stick because it looked fine. I didn't know anything about it, so she led me back to her house to hear about the coup over a cup.

Bolivia's recent election had been won by Hernan Siles ('a communist') who had vowed to disband the army. As his party had secured only 35 per cent of the votes he was being forced to form a coalition, and the army had been awaiting his choice and trying to woo his opponents – until today. The generals had finally tired of the uncertainty.

'They followed the usual pattern,' Señora de T. explained. 'The army simultaneously took over all communication networks and stormed the presidential palace. Gueiler won't be able to return now, but she was damn useless. Never knew anything. Soldiers have blocked off the main plazas in each city as a show of strength and Santa Cruz – the second political hub – has been placed under curfew.'

'What effect will military rule have on the country?'

'On the local Indians – none whatsoever. But the army will throw out all the students from university as they are all Left, and similarly those they suspect among the professionals. With the army's less able supporters as replacements, the economy will soon be ruined. The problem is that all these people, and the miners at Oruro and Uyuni, will fight against military rule, and there's no chance of the army stepping down. Three people have already been killed in La Paz, and one has been kidnapped – but he was a nasty man so that doesn't matter. Cochabamba is in the middle, between anti-military La Paz and pro-military Santa Cruz, and is always the last to be affected.' She leant towards me and resolutely tapped her saucer with her teaspoon. 'I think you should leave the country at once.'

'But my letters . . .' I began. She shook her head. It was no use. Consuls are inexorable. Her features hardened into an explanation of how Great Britain had ruled the waves for centuries. With a cup of tea, orders signed HM and Señora Charlotte de Tabaldo at the helm, we'd never have lost control. Her office would remain locked. 'If only you had come this morning,' she repeated. 'We're only open in the mornings anyhow.' I left her house, cursing the town's misinformation office, and skulked through the streets. (In the interests of any without a name, the date was 17th July.) Troops were now marching inoffensively but noisily about the town, and I glowered at them for having ruined my day. They looked so young, and I wondered if they knew what they were fighting for. A principle? Adventure? Or just pay? But some of them would have had a different reason. They were conscripts and had no choice. Uncertainty is little suited to khaki, and there were many soldiers who did not wear their uniforms well.

I was still unaware of the full significance of what was happening when a truck took me to Potosí nineteen hours to the south. I strolled the streets trying to buy white petrol for my camping cooker. At the first garage the attendant said he'd fetch some, and returned with a pink spirit. He said it was white petrol that had gone pink. I said I needed petrol without lead. Did this have lead in it? Yes, he admitted, but it was exactly the same as the leadless stuff. I moved on to the next garage and found a long queue of cars waiting at the pumps, and soon forgot about my leadless petrol when I heard the bad news.

'Soon there'll be no fuel. The *campesinos* are blocking the roads to stop all deliveries and transport as a protest against the army.' No fuel, no trucks, no buses. Everyone I met said the country would soon be paralysed – and it was a full day's journey to the nearest escape at Villazón on Argentina's border. I waited with a group of hopeful travellers also heading south but no buses came and the only two trucks that passed were fully loaded with passengers and wouldn't stop. I passed the time by reading a brochure which described the place we were trying to flee from as having been the largest town in the New World in 1670 with 160,000 inhabitants (one-third more than at present), and a rich source of tin and silver. It ended, 'God's faith is guarded in the thirty churches of Potosí but the Devil laughs in its 30,000 mineshafts.' At that moment I could hear his laughter quite clearly.

After four hours a truck did stop and we scrambled on, hardly able to believe our luck that he was going all the way to Villazón. It was a bitterly cold night but my travelling companions were a cheerful crowd. We had to stop twice to remove stones which had been laid across the road to disrupt traffic, but fortunately the *campesinos* were sleeping and there was no resistance.

'It's nothing to worry about,' said one passenger. 'We get used to this happening. Often I have to ask . . . "*Buenos, amigo*! Who is president today?"'

Everyone laughed. 'It's true,' agreed another. 'Our politics have become very popular. Many tourists come here now to see a real revolution . . .'

We passed through a violent thunderstorm with fork lightning splitting the darkness and one flash illuminated a graveyard whose adobe tombs were raised above the ground and shaped like solid tunnels with a window at one end displaying plastic flowers and a photograph of the deceased. Heavenly explosions shook the air, and I felt glad to be leaving this country and its troubled tourist attractions.

My relief lasted until we reached the sizeable but uninteresting town of Villazón, and there I heard that Argentina had closed its border with Bolivia. A dozen other gringos/as were waiting for it to open and each morning we all trooped along to the soldiers guarding the barrier, only to be told to come back later in case there had been a new development. On the fourth day Argentina decided to open its border for three hours. I found myself at the front of the queue to cross the international span of concrete over a thin flow of earthy water. The Argentine consul was waiting to greet the first arrivals on the far side, and he was beaming hot-doggishly.

'Welcome to Argentina,' he enthused, and he pumped my hand furiously and then did the same to all the others, working his way with unflagging zeal along the chaingang of foreigners who had been allowed through first. He hoped we were in good spirits after our 'ordeal' and talked about '*Libertad*'. His ebullient philanthropy was bewildering, but it had only just begun. The next moment he invited twelve complete strangers to a celebration in La Quiaca's best hotel that evening. 'Eight-thirty. Just come if you can', and he sauntered off.

The tables of Hotel Turista were laden with food and silver candelabra when our international assortment of ragamuffins arrived, and Jorge Brandtmann was there to meet us. His English was poor but he made a brave attempt with a brief address which ended '. . . and I am happy to be your . . . your guest.'

An Australian called Ron corrected him. 'No, you're the *host*. *We're* the guests.' The consul didn't understand and laughed. Ron turned to me with a wide-eyed expression and whispered, 'I hope!'

After several bottles of champagne had been emptied, glasses of both red and white wine were simultaneously placed before us (a wonderful custom) and continuously refilled while we ate pâté, pea soup with croûtons, vast steaks garnished with salad, and finally a selection of local cheeses. Señor Brandtmann made a short speech about '*Libertad*' and said there was nothing finer. He didn't draw comparisons with his government and neither did he allude to any nation who recognised or infringed human rights – he was only interested in the broad concept. We raised our glasses and drank to '*Libertad*'.

The consul left after the meal, urging us to continue our celebration. The hotel patron joined us, setting the pace and finally inviting us to unroll our sleeping blankets and spend what little remained of the night on the dining-room floor. It was about as far as most of us could have managed anyway.

As a welcome to a country, this occasion was unparalleled in my experience. Next morning I wrote a postcard home:

> Please send my kilt and sporran to the British Embassy, Casilla de Correos 2050, Buenos Aires, Argentina. On the customs declaration mark as being '*una falda escosesa*', and tick the boxes denoting a gift, used and of no value (they'll believe that). Tear your postage stamps – and hope for more luck than met with one sock and sandal!

Nine months later I was to recall with added nostalgia the taste of that wine, the ambiguous toast to '*Libertad*' and the handsome Argentine hospitality when I heard the gloomy news that Britain and Argentina were at war, both trying to liberate the Falkland Islands.

It frequently took me some time on awakening each morning to work out exactly where I was and how I had arrived there, but my somnolent awareness was never more confused than on the morning after the *Libertad* party. My hung-over eyes found no clues amongst a row of Scotch whisky bottles set on a bar shelf in front of a mirror which caused unfair double images of strange brands – 'Old Eight', 'Jolly Full' and, the most alarming, 'Old English' – and it was only after seeing '*Hecho en Argentina*' on a manufacturer's label above my head that I realised I was lying under a tablecloth in the luxury hotel dining-room of a country I hadn't intended visiting so soon. The Bolivian coup had forced a detour of 700 miles from my route but this was not immediately apparent as I lay on a deep pile carpet and replanned my route to Rio. The natural way east was to move 500 miles across the top of Argentina (skirting underneath Bolivia) and cut through Paraguay which now lay squarely in the middle. My map had a scale which was refreshingly small and made South America look manageable by compressing it into the size of a postcard. My actual route was to become extended into one of 5,000 Brazilian miles alone but at that moment, and under a white table-cloth, I merely laid a piece of string from Hotel Turista to the Paraguayan border at Clorinda and measured the next stage of my journey at half an inch.

The road first passed some of the poorest people in Argentina who were bundled up in so many layers of dark clothing that they were dehumanised and assumed the appearance and capabilities of scarecrows. They stood in the gnawing cold which had frozen Hotel Turista's fountain overnight, and watched their shaggy llamas graze in a geological showpiece of a landscape. Hills like striped humbugs had been squeezed up out of the Altiplano to display samples of the area's rock colours and patterns, growing into caramel mountains, scabrous with pinnacles, canyons and trails of scree, and streaked in tints of purple, ochre, rust and rouge. Argentina then ran downhill into the Chaco, a swath of scrubland where cattle chewed despondently at thorn bushes. My final lift was with a Lutheran minister from Germany, Pastor Klemens, returning to his home in Paraguay where he worked amongst a nomadic community of impoverished Germans. I accepted his invitation to accompany him and together we crossed the turgid River Paraguay by ferry at Clorinda. The border officials gave us a thorough search.

'That was because we have beards,' said the Pastor afterwards. 'Beards are considered subversive in Paraguay.'

In 1865 Paraguay was the most developed country in South America with an extensive railway and telegraph network and the first iron foundry. Jesuit missionaries had integrated the Indians into Paraguay's relatively balanced population of 550,000 by forming self-sufficient communities which, although autocratic, were unique in Latin America in preserving the native culture. Leading the country was the young caudillo Francisco López who had inherited this remarkably advanced and stable state from his overweight father, the 'Corpulent Despot'. Five years later it had all been destroyed and ninety per cent of the male population killed. López was well-educated and widely-travelled (he acquired his Irish mistress, the beautiful and flamboyant Madame Eliza Lynch, on a trip to

Paris) but he was also obstinate and impulsive, and unwisely extended Paraguay's borders into the territory of her neighbours. His blindness to the impending catastrophe was doubtless aided by 'La Lynch' who busily bore him five sons and, despite her unofficial status, used her open London and Paris accounts to create a world of *haute société* among the rustic Paraguayans. It took the combined forces of Argentina, Brazil and Uruguay five years to overcome gallant Paraguay and to leave only 28,000 of her men alive out of a population of 221,000. La Lynch was with her lover on his final retreat in 1870 when he and their eldest son were killed by Brazilian soldiers. She dug their graves with her own hands and buried them in the red mud banks of the Aquidabán River. (She was left with the largest landholding of any woman in the world, 22 million acres, but after the war this land was confiscated and she was deported. Sixteen years later La Lynch died in Jerusalem, penniless and largely forgotten.) Despite the national suicide he instigated, López remains the most revered of Paraguayan heroes.

As we drove to the pastor's community of Katuate, 250 miles away on a red dirt road through billowing green plantations (cotton and tobacco) and mighty forests, we passed numerous billboards extolling the virtues of President Stroessner's government. Stroessner was born in 1912 of a Paraguayan mother and German father, and worked his way up through the army until he was able to seize power. After twenty-five consecutive years as a dictator he was now a living legend, feared by many to be immortal, and an indefatigable billboard-erector to his own glory. Myopia was no excuse for disregarding the large letters which boasted how the leader had brought PEACE, PROGRESS, PROSPERITY and DEVELOPMENT to the country.

The pastor said Stroessner was the most ruthless dictator in the world today, enforcing a rule of terror by means of his favoured generals and police thugs in a land where nine-tenths of recorded deaths resulted from malnutrition. He had heard several first-hand accounts of torture and imprisonment among his parishioners, and unexplained disappearances showed that dissenters were not tolerated and added credence to the rumours that political undesirables were jettisoned from helicopters on execution flights over areas of dense forest. He found it completely in character that Stroessner had offered sanctuary to the desperado Somoza and his embezzled fortune from Nicaragua. Somoza was said to have recently 'won' a general's girlfriend in a bet and taken her off for a fun weekend in Bermuda. The general was a bad loser and he hired space in the national newspaper and began a smear campaign against Somoza. On his return Somoza retaliated with the same measures and the libellous attacks continued until Stroessner eventually had to intervene. For many days thereafter the newspapers carried blank pages which the two parties had bought but had been prevented from using. A few months later Somoza was murdered.

'Another school built by the government of STROESSNER,' read the next billboard.

The pastor stretched his neck to free part of the subversive beard caught in his clerical collar. 'And how many gallons of dissident blood did you mix into the mortar?' he muttered to the distant president.

The nomadic Germans of Paraguay make a strange tale. Katuate was just one of their many colonies, a town of 8,000 people with a wide red-earth main street bordered by wild west wooden buildings. Horses, mules and ox-carts outnumbered ramshackle vehicles. Eight years previously there had been six houses and dense forest here, and Katuate's population formed another community at Palotina, eighty miles to the east inside Brazil. These people were now the third- or fourth-generation descendants of the original immigrants who came from an area west of Bonn during the latter half of the last century and up until 1920, encouraged by Brazil's eagerness to populate the land near its borders. A regular cycle of economic misfortunes every five to ten years had forced them to leave their settlements and seek a land of plenty elsewhere. A total of 450,000 of them at the rate of 70,000 each year had come into Paraguay (population five million) trying to find cheap land now unavailable in Brazil. Pastor Klemens had come out ten years earlier and had moved with the community from Palotina.

'The saddest aspect is that they don't learn from their mistakes and each move leaves them worse off,' said Pastor Klemens. 'Uncleared forest was once given away but now it's expensive because of the value of timber. The only land they can afford has been stripped of timber but not cleared for agriculture. The most common tree here is the quebracho, the "axebreaker" – without heavy machinery they can never get rid of the stumps and so they have to plough small plots between them.' He said they had large families for the traditional purpose of a future labour source, and children worked the land instead of going to school. Most were illiterate, spoke German or Portuguese (when Spanish and Guarani are spoken in Paraguay), practised archaic farming techniques, had no idea of suitable crops or market trends, were too fiercely independent to form cooperatives and often squandered any profit on drinking or gambling. 'Then they go bankrupt and move somewhere else. I've started a school here and try to teach a more practical approach to farming – even though it's not the "shepherding" I studied! My wife teaches the girls sewing and cooking, and the older ones learn about nutrition, child care and contraception. We're having another attempt at forming a cooperative, and yet already the first few families have opted out and others have moved off. But I'm not moving again. This time we've got to make it work.'

I spent a few days with Pastor Klemens and his wife at their comfortable bungalow. They were both in their mid-thirties and both displayed altruistic zest far beyond that of vocational duty. One morning we visited Ralf Mühlen, one of the farmers who had moved here four years ago with his six children. This was the third home he had known in his forty-two years, and he had built the house himself. It was poor and primitive and yet homely in its simplicity and intensity of use. He had cleared by hand enough space in seventy acres of land to grow maize, soya beans, sugar cane and potatoes. Together with the proceeds from a small number of livestock, this produce was beginning to reduce his bank overdraft. His neighbour had been less fortunate and had already sold out and moved away after planting nothing but soya beans and suffering two years of unusual drought followed by two of catastrophically low market prices.

His children squabbled noisily outside over a game of football, and were wary of a stranger. Ralf sat down awkwardly as his leg had mysteriously become infected and was in bandages, and his wife, twice his size and cheerful in proportion, brought out glasses and a bottle of home-made schnapps.

'Come back in a few years and we'll give you a glass of our own wine. We've started our own vineyard,' he joked, pointing through the open door to a youthful vine growing up the verandah. 'Everything grows here . . . except money.' He was a tall gaunt man with a sallow complexion and deep-sunken eyes that gave him a desperate look. His lips were thin, and smiling stretched them till they almost disappeared, but he wasn't given to much smiling.

'It never will, Ralf, unless we all work together and teach our children how to face the future.' Klemens was addressing one of his lost black sheep.

'We've had this talk before, Pastor. I know you mean well but I'm not joining any cooperative. I've worked hard and things are looking good for me now. I'm not going to share it with everyone else. And I can't spare my children for school. They're needed here to work.'

'And if things take a turn for the worse . . . what then? You'll be alone.'

'We'll get by. We always have.'

The pastor gently tried to persuade him to reconsider. He repeated the benefits that a cooperative would bring and pointed out that more and more families were sending their children to school; twenty-two boys and nine girls were now in attendance. Katuate could only survive as a community, he maintained, by combining its resources and knowledge, and learning a new approach to farming. Ralf drank more schnapps and remained stubbornly uninterested. I felt uneasy in his company. There was a gloomy fatalism about him, perhaps only natural in a man who had lost two homes, but his inflexible reactionary stance was less understandable and in stark contrast to the positive attitude of the pastor. These two forces appeared distinct across the table, and the importance of which one prevailed was sharpened by the shouts outside of either six little Katuatans or six little nomads. They would have to fend for themselves sooner or later, and probably sooner, the pastor explained afterwards, because the relationship between parents and children was subject to a strange set of values. When a person left home and ceased to be a productive member of his or her family, they were treated purely on a business basis. The son of a relatively well-off family had married last year and had been obliged to rent land from his parents at a high cost even though they had plenty of land to spare. When his first child was born and he could no longer afford the rent, there was no question of its being reduced and he was forced to leave and take his wife and baby elsewhere.

We talked in German as it was our only common language, but I found Ralf's dialect and *Portudeutsch* hard to understand. He must have been drinking earlier and alcohol made him gloomier. Conversation turned to my travels and when Ralf heard I was heading for Rio he warned me that he had heard there was much violent crime there.

'*Viele Leute sterben in Rio*,' he said with an abrasive frown, and then he wanted to know how that translated into English.

'Many people die in Rio,' I replied. He repeated this several times as if to fix the phrase in his mind. For the rest of my visit every lull in the conversation was filled with a muted whisper of the part of the phrase he found hardest to remember, and a simple statement was transformed into a diabolical death wish. 'Die in Rio,' he said, holding his glass up in front of sightless eyes and then he would say it again and again and grin at me. His words began to assume ghastly proportions in my mind and I could only look on my host as an utterer of prophetic curses, toasting my death with his grin distorted into a sneer through the optical effect of the glass.

'Good luck with school, and with Katuate,' I said to the pastor when we left and I set off towards Brazil.

'Good luck to you too,' he answered. 'And do be careful in Rio. It does have a bad name.'

In a continent where the European has long been ranked with the social élite, it was an astonishing and incongruous sight to see a family of Arian peasants travelling along rutted tracks at four mph in an ox-cart, or standing bare-legged in red mud with their white skin and blond hair visible from afar as they worked their plots by hand. For those born of a dream of El Dorado and now nomads running out of places to go, this alien jungle soil had become a harsh and possessive master, and a struggle in the López spirit of misguided heroism.

PEACE AND PROGRESS WITH STROESSNER . . . THE COUN-TRY GOES FORWARD WITH STROESSNER . . . PROSPERITY AND DEVELOPMENT WITH STROESSNER . . . The billboards continued to the border. I wondered if Stroessner had visited his fellow Germans at Katuate.

9 · Mugged in Rio, Jugged in Uruguay

The devil's dismembered body is scattered around the world. His elbow is in Scotland, his nose is in Ecuador and if his laugh is in Bolivia, then this is ventriloquism for his throat is at Iguazú. Twenty miles away from the only point where the borders of Paraguay, Brazil and Argentina touch, the River Iguazú throws the main body of its water into a deep canyon and allows its broader reaches to divide around a host of luxuriant islands and find their own way down in 275 distinct cascades. Iguazú Falls are unmatched by any other stretch of water in the world. A cloud of spray hangs over the central fall, the Devil's Throat, and here the gargantuan force of peat-coloured water turns white and seems momentarily to linger in alluring slow motion before plummeting with helpless inevitability into the unseen roaring depths of some satanic digestive system. Flocks of swallows play among 275 shimmering rainbows, swooping in and out of the spray clouds, while canny darting lizards endeavour to blend into the vines and leaves of thick jungle, and squadrons of flashy butterflies follow the meandering scent of orchids.

The falls are shared by Argentina and Brazil, the first claiming to own the best part of them and the second maintaining that they own the best view of them. I wandered over bridges and a series of island-hopping catwalks on the Argentine side, marvelling at the deadly serious 'No Swimming' notice beside a near-vertical torrent, and then having to take the thirty-mile road round to the other side before I could judge the Brazilian case. There was nothing to differentiate between the degrees of extraordinary beauty but Argentina was superior in unconscious humour. Its prestigious Hotel Cataratas had automatic double doors activated by a mechanism under a small central doormat. The doors opened outwards, hitting me on the toes and forcing me to jump back off the mat, whereupon they instantly closed. I spent ten sportive minutes watching the same thing happen to other arriving visitors, all of whom eventually devised the necessary technique of a toe stab at the mat, a slight pause and an expedient hop forwards.

The memory of this kept me smiling while I took the long route to Rio, around three sides of a square formed by Brasília and Salvador. Brazil had replaced Argentina as the dominant influence in South America, and yet to me it appeared the secretive giant. Its name was seldom mentioned except in association with coffee, sambas and carnival in Rio, and its exploitation of Amazonian rain forest. I had nurtured a quiet hope that Brazil would still be full of wonderfully interwoven, plotting jungle; and this three-inch diversion across my map was intended to prove it. But there had been nothing except token clumps of jungle, like monuments, amongst the scrubland as far as Brasília. (This city was worth the trip alone. Brazil's leading architect, Oscar Niemeyer, had concocted tongue-in-cheek designs for a totally planned capital, and gone home laughing when they were accepted. Built in just three years, Brasília was a triumph not only for those who had created its bizarre examples of abstract art, but also for those who had persuaded government ministers and civil servants to live in them.) And there had been none before or after Salvador. A jungleless 3,000 miles. The immensity of the land had thrilled me but my misplaced expectations left me with a feeling of loss. As I bumped towards Rio on a road whose occasional disappearance was advertised with masterful understatement (*'Pista with defects'*), the truck-driver, João Castro, was adding to my disillusionment.

He said he came from Nova Iguaçu, a *favela* (slum) suburb of Rio where over one million people lived without running water, schools or a single hospital. Racketeers extorted protection money and police ran their own vice rings, and their death squads had recently received publicity in the papers by a defiant widow of one of their victims. João added casually that there were seventeen murders each week in Nova Iguaçu. It was a relief to stop for petrol and a free coffee, for Brazilian garages gave free coffee to the occupants of each vehicle that purchased fuel. João bought a picture from a stall, and during the last stage of our journey I passed the time counting the constituents. It was a colourful pattern made entirely of butterfly wings.

'This is criminal,' I said. 'Someone killed 124 butterflies to make this.'

He looked hurt. 'It's very beautiful. We have so many butterflies here anyway.'

'But soon you won't . . .' It was typical of the Brazilian attitude and the government's policy towards natural resources; exploitation and profit today, and to hell with tomorrow. The world's fifth largest country thrives on a history of affordable waste and a traditional belief in limitless resources. The figures of Amazonia's destruction come in millions: 250 million acres of jungle cleared for cattle pasture; 7.5 million trees burnt by Volkswagen to clear land for its ranch. No wonder the Brazilian economist Vianna believes Amazonia could become a desert within forty years. It was a grim prospect, framed into a pretty picture of 124 slaughtered butterflies.

But Rio allowed me to forget this aspect of the country, at least for a while. Brazil's African/native Indian/European genealogy is a success of striking good looks, politeness and friendliness, and few cities can offer them a more suitable background. Rio de Janeiro, for over a century the capital until Brasília was hastily contrived to adopt the role and to populate the interior, may have some hideous *favelas* and a chilling record of crime, but it is still one of the most attractive and exciting cities in the world. It is flanked by long beaches curling tightly around irregular bays and then sprawling out into the open, and by the extremities of the Tijuca Forest whose trees add strident green to the slopes sweeping down from towering grey rock faces and into the radiant white squares and rectangles of the streets. It is scarcely surprising to hear Brazilians assert that God made the world in six days and left the last day free to concentrate exclusively on Rio. The seventh-day citizens revel in noisy street cafés; enjoy the rich architecture of palaces with all the frills of colonial confectionary and high-rises with chessboard patterns converging towards the sky (though not, if they share my view, of the new cathedral which is easily confused with a conical multi-storey car park); and relax in abundant parks where statues of fierce national dignitaries loiter darkly at the bases of palm trees, and fountains gurgle around modern works of art which are variously soothing, provocative or unidentified mistakes.

The suburb of Copacabana, which could be construed as a prefab replacement for what is being lost in Amazonia, is one of the most concentrated areas of humanity on Earth with (on the day of my arrival) 62,001 people per square kilometre. It was in a restaurant here that I discovered *churrasco*. I ordered it thinking it was just one dish. The waiter put an empty plate before me and then returned with seven bowls containing beans, rice, meat in gravy, salad, beetroot, potatoes and a spicy sauce.

'Is all this for me?' I asked incredulously. He nodded, and I immediately loaded my plate in case his Portuguese-tuned ears had misunderstood Scottish-Spanish. I was half-way through and coping admirably, determined to finish everything on my plate, when he brought me a spit of barbecued sausages and knocked two off onto my plate. I quickly reread the menu to see if I had missed any small print but most of the print was unintelligible so I continued feasting with renewed gluttony. Next he came with roast chicken legs. Spit-roasted beef followed soon after, then hunks of pork, charcoal-grilled fish and ribs of veal. All my side dishes were promptly refilled and back came the sausages to restart the cycle once more. I finally admitted defeat, paid 220 cruceros (£1.50) and felt delightfully obese while I set off to look for Christ the Redeemer.

He wasn't evident on Copacabana's famous beach, a sandy obstacle course of resting bodies and beach games in which the lithesome physiques of youth played volleyball and the stiff frames of the aged were involved in agonising badminton knockabouts – creaking serves and gasping swipes with never enough coordination for a return. I suspected He would have avoided the wavy lines of tessellated pavements which were being trampled by multitudinous shapes of bare flesh, some perambulating in generous swimsuits which wobbled and bulged and highlighted the effects of excessive *churrascos*, others mincing in scant coverings of string and triangles which stretched and creased and teased.

Rio provided plenty of hills as viewpoints for anyone who wished to admire her beauty, and so I sought Him on the hills. Cable cars dangled from a wire attached to the Sugar Loaf and raised me high enough to see a marine suburb of luxury yachts lying at anchor. (The cable cars were made in Italy, a fact which worried my neighbour during the journey, a Mrs Higgins from Bradford, according to the label on her shoulder bag. 'Ah 'ope it's bluddy well better made than yon Italian washing machine we wunce 'ad.') Street trams carried me into the hills of the old colonial area of Santa Theresa, but He wasn't there, just the train robber Ronald Biggs living in a typical small house; the locals were said to be proud of him.

I found Him, or rather His likeness, on top of the highest hill, the Corcovado, a sharp peak crowned with a gigantic sculpture. I had spotted this figure soon after my arrival in Rio but had dismissed it as some colossal garden gnome being prepared for 250 million newly-acquired acres, and had failed to recognise it as the image – first seen as an aerial photograph taken from behind and showing a sweeping panorama of the city and coastline – that had inspired me to come here. Christ the Redeemer is one of the most imposing sights in South America, a charismatic statue in white stone, 120 feet tall and weighing 1,145 tons. The people of Rio paid for it by donation in 1931 and the Frenchman Paul Landowski masterminded every detail, including each eight-ton hand. The arms are held out in the posture of crucifixion and the face, though lacking the serenity of a sculptured Buddha, evokes great feeling. When seen in passing wisps of low cloud, the features soften and the expression becomes deceptively changeable. Most impressive of all, however, apart from the magnificent views down to the deep blue ocean, are Christ's huge toes. They are just visible to anyone looking up from the base, bulging above the edge of the podium. Somehow they make him seem very human. Together we looked down on the city, and I for one felt satisfied. 'Many people die in Rio' – the warning had slipped into my subconscious.

The following morning I was returning from Flamengo Beach, one of the nearest to the city centre, by way of a park and stopped to photograph an unidentified mistake artistically set in a fountain. While putting the camera back in my case I sensed someone very close and turned to see a youth of about seventeen peering over my shoulder at the spare lenses. He ambled off, frequently glancing back to stare at me and soon disappeared. I finished rearranging the contents of the case and then leisurely set off along the path without thinking further on the incident.

The path wove in and out of some bushes and I had almost reached a clearing when I heard a movement in the shadows behind me. I turned as a hand grabbed the shoulder strap of my camera case and a black youth was crouching before me, leaning away so that his weight strained against my stance as he tried to pull me off the path.

'*Paré . . . Paré . . .*' ('*Stop . . . Don't move . . .*') His face puckered as he spat out the words and his eyes bored into me with a desperate corrosive hatred. He continued to pull on my strap with his left hand, while his right hand held a pointed object hidden under a towel which he shook in an angry threatening gesture, and aimed at my face. Another figure brushed past and stood five yards away as a look-out and when he glanced in my direction, I saw he was the youth who had been staring at my lenses.

At first surprise dulled my reaction but almost immediately it turned to resentment. I instinctively braced myself against his pull and thought, with ridiculous simplicity, how I just wanted to shake him off and be on my own again. For a moment the object he brandished transfixed my attention and my resistance faltered as thoughts of injury, not of pain or death but of mutilation and an end to travelling, flashed through my mind. Then I found myself looking at him critically, my resentment fusing to anger on noticing how much the veins stood out on his scrawny forearms, how the sinews of his neck were taut as he continued to hiss '*Paré*', and although the look of lunatic desperation in his piercing eyes still terrified me, I felt he looked puny. This strengthened my resistance and I pulled against him. The look-out kept his distance. Each passing moment without a shot gave me confidence, and seemed to agitate my assailant.

'I'll shoot . . .' he snapped, and he looked more evil than ever.

Our tug-of-war lasted about ten seconds. I gained ground with nightmarish slowness. Soon we were on the grass, separated from the edge of a four-lane highway by a row of tall shrubs. At this point he raised the gun, and with one panic-stricken tug I wrenched the strap out of his grip and stumbled backwards through branches and leaves, finding myself on the main road and turning to run blindly towards the far side. Car wheels shrieked on my left and I was conscious of a shape rushing at me but when its impact seemed inevitable, it swerved and flashed behind me, so close I felt the suction of its slipstream. Then one foot gave way. A shoe had broken and suddenly gave no support. The flapping sole tripped me as another car braked and slewed to one side, and I fell onto the tarmac beside the kerb of the central reservation. I dragged myself onto the grass and glanced back in terror, dreading seeing the muggers pursuing me, but they were running into the distance. My knees and arms had been cut in the fall and blood was seeping through my shirt and jeans but being in the middle of a constant stream of traffic gave me a feeling of security. I began walking along the central reservation, scuffing my broken shoe, and managed to reach the safety of the streets before the effects of delayed shock hit me. My breathing became shallow and fast, my heartbeat accelerated to an incessant pounding, my muscles trembled and I was overcome by an oppressive lassitude. I sat in a busy café for over an hour drinking *aguardente*, staring nervously out into the street and feeling pathetically fragile.

For several days after this experience I was still deeply shaken. I recovered from the physical shock but inwardly it had left a scar. It was my pride that had been most seriously damaged. I had come to Brazil with an open, sympathetic mind. I was trying to travel in the shadows, blending in, looking, learning, hoping to share a bit of life and laughter with those of another world. I came without malice and my intentions were peaceful and amicable. My mistake was to believe that these salutary qualities would accordingly be returned to me; that I had become immune to misfortune and that misfortune only happened to others because they, in some way, always invited it; that I could breeze into the unfamiliar and transcend hostility with naked cheerfulness. Now it had become clear that the needs of poverty and greed do not discriminate between the just and the unjust victim in requiring satisfaction. I, with the best will in the world, was fair game. It was a bitter lesson to learn.

The thought of my kilt waiting in Buenos Aires spurred me on over the thousand odd miles to Brazil's southern border. The night before crossing it I enjoyed a final *churrasco*, an eat-all-you-can (and-I-did), and slept in a *burracharia*, but this was not as pleasurable as it sounded, being the tyre-mending department of a garage. Then my postcard-sized map of Brazil was exchanged for a wallposter-sized map of the little country officially named 'The Republic East of the River Uruguay'. Like postage and rubber stamps, the size of each country's map was usually inversely related to the size of its territory. It was already evening when I crossed the border, glad to be back amongst Spanish-speakers again, and found a lift with off-duty bakers who eventually let me out to camp in a quiet field. They said the weather forecast was rain.

Rain! It was one of the wildest nights imaginable. I awoke in the early hours to the sound of ear-shattering explosions. Countless times they seemed to come from directly above me and my heart leapt in shock at their suddenness and intensity. Thunder shook the air so ferociously that the ground trembled, and lightning repeatedly flashed in multiple forks, cracking the night with lines of dynamic energy which glowed brilliantly for up to one second. Then rain fell in torrents, blattering hard against the fabric of the flysheet – and I lay cowering in a Uruguayan field at the centre of Armageddon. When my tent began filling with water I finally abandoned camp and spent the rest of the night in a bus shelter.

Seen after a thunderstorm, bumpy buccolic Uruguay appeared instantly and continuously engaging. Cattle and sheep grazed within the bounds of rigidly straight fences rising and falling across the docile contours of the land, and there seemed to be a distinct will to get fat in the way the animals tore at the grass. Avenues of eucalyptus trees led the eye beyond the rank greenery to white *estancias* set amongst blossoming orchards, and even the towns of brick and adobe houses exuded the fecund smell of manure and pasture. The most astonishing aspect of this country, however, jammed like a bung in the nozzle of Brazil to stop it leaking into Argentina (and deliberately created to act as a buffer between the two), is that it is a living museum. Steam trains still pant across the landscape exhaling steam and smoke and carry a cowcatcher at the front, and vintage cars are parked in the streets as everyday bangers rather than carefully nursed restorations.

Hitching soon proved problematical. This was partly because, so I was told, it was associated with the Tupamaro guerillas whose robberies and kidnappings were rampant in the late sixties and early seventies, and also because of a hiker's form of Sod's Law: long waits but long, fast lifts in large countries – short waits but short, slow lifts in small countries. It took the same time and number of lifts to cover twenty-four inches in poster-sized Uruguay as it did to cover the equivalent half an inch in postcard-sized Brazil. I rode in a 1940 Bedford truck, passed a Baby Austin and two Model A Fords (the first in immaculate condition, the second held together by insulated wire) and as I transferred to a more modern 1962 Land-Rover, I noticed that Ford Populars were all the rage. The Land-Rover was owned by an estate agent and weekend pig farmer, middle-aged and married, he said earnestly, to the black Madame of Maldonaldo brothel ('the best in Uruguay'). He could have had the physique of a ten-foot Tarzan if the proportions hadn't gone wrong and restricted him to a height of six foot six, but he occupied the same volume. When he heard about my disturbed night he drove me the few miles back to his home for breakfast, even though he had just finished his own. His wife had not returned yet and so he did the cooking himself, in a house that lacked no comforts and had framed rugby teams from a Buenos Aires English public school on one wall. Breakfast consisted of fruit juice, cereal, toast, spreads, coffee and a single fried egg, one yellow and white island in the middle of a steak which ran off the dinner plate and touched the table on three sides.

'It's what I normally have,' Carlos explained. 'Sometimes I don't have any lunch so I need a good breakfast.'

His wife returned as we were setting off to visit his pig farm but unfortunately she didn't seem to require any explanation of my identity. She was tall, sleek and arrestingly beautiful.

'How was work?' Carlos called out as we drove away.

'Fine,' she replied, and waved goodbye with a smile. She might have been referring to meals-on-wheels.

The pigs were neglected that day and I saw little of the farm while my sodden belongings dried in the sun, because a barbecued lunch (ten pounds of steak, two pounds of sausages and ten litres of red wine) shared with his three farmhands took up most of the time. They sometimes ate steaks three times in a day, and they all drank their wine diluted with Coca-Cola.

'We work hard so we need a lot of liquid,' Carlos commented, and the farmhands nodded. 'Wine is a necessity, it's the coke that's the luxury.'

We talked about the abundance of antique cars and he said this resulted from all vehicles being so expensive here that people held on to them for as long as possible. His twenty-year-old Land-Rover would fetch £6,000 even though spare parts were impossible to get and it was largely composed of odds and ends ransacked from wrecks of all descriptions, including old buses and a wardrobe. Then conversation turned to the Tupamaro guerillas and I heard how Uruguay was another severe South American dictatorship with a gruesome side to its pastoral tranquillity. The size of England and Wales, it has a total population (three and a half million) a quarter of London's. In 1979 fully one per cent of Uruguayans were political prisoners and half a million former inhabitants were in exile. Carlos related how his country had been a bastion of democracy in the fifties but this had become eroded by inefficiency and a drastic fall in demand for its agricultural products. The Tupamaros (the Movement for National Liberation) rose from the agrarian classes to oppose the government and became an increasingly violent force. Then the army seized control in 1973 and had since effectively suppressed the Tupamaros in a brutal purge. The Tupamaros were still active, Carlos assured me, and he believed they would get stronger again.

'And yet Uruguay looks so relaxed and free,' I observed.

'Yes. The army has always been good at camouflage,' he replied. 'Here, have another steak.' He handed me one, adding that life wasn't too bad here.

A week later, what seemed to be my two-hundredth lift (a pre-war Chevrolet) dropped me off shortly before a border post at the start of a straggling bridge which ran for several miles over a confusion of river, islands and marshes into Argentina. It was pitch dark and I had little option but to camp where I had been deposited. I began erecting my tent on a patch of ground quickly chosen in the sweeping beam of headlights as the driver turned the car to head back down the road. The insects sounded particularly noisy that evening and my mind was concentrating on the routine of setting up camp by touch, unsuspecting that a group of soldiers were already bearing down on me out of the night. They had been alerted by the sight of a car approaching the border and hesitating, figures crossing in front of the headlights and the car then driving away. They lived in constant suspicion of a Tupamaro resurgence.

I was adjusting a guyline when a blinding light illuminated my campsite. A voice ordered me not to move. I shielded my eyes and in the peripheral brightness I saw two rifle muzzles and two pairs of army boots advancing towards me, walking into the beam held by a third soldier. My identification papers were called for and I handed them to one of the dark outlines whose weapon was levelled in my direction. A short pause followed and then an order was given for my tent to be collapsed, and I was led back to the guard-house.

They were polite and considerate as they asked questions in a drab room of bare plaster lit by an unshaded lightbulb and decorated with a map of the country, sheets of regulations and curled pictures torn from a modest girlie magazine. My luggage was given a critical search and every object's origin and purpose had to be explained in minute detail. My universal bath plug (unused) caused the longest delay. They found nothing to support their suspicions of Tupamaro involvement but still considered me a threat. When I attempted to collect my luggage and leave, the senior officer shook his head and waggled a reprimanding finger. A guard nudged me down a corridor and indicated the open door of a cell. 'For your own safety,' he said, meaning the opposite. In the background the senior officer

stood gloating over my luggage. I tried to protest, asking, demanding and finally pleading to be allowed to keep my camera case, but
to no avail. They let me keep nothing but my blanket. I entered the
cell convinced that I should never see the contents of that case again –
saved from the blackmarket hands of Rio only to fall into those of
Uruguay.

The cell was built around a foam mattress, with a small extension
at one end to accommodate a hole-and-footprints loo. There were
two windows, each the size of a cheap jokebook, without glass and
barred with a steel cross embedded in the thick walls. A small light
glowing deep within a tubular recess was also behind bars and even
the basin, which was fed a constant trickle of water by an end of pipe
blotchy with fungus, had been sunk into a restrictive alcove. (The
universal bath plug would have enabled me to fill the basin and have
a decent wash. The irony that this was an ideal opportunity to use the
damn thing did not escape me, but it brought me no amusement.)
The smooth walls and the lack of protrusions, breakable objects and
electrical terminals denied all but the most dejected of prisoners the
means of self-injury. The place had the fetid smell of its open sewer.
The guard wished me '*Buenas noches*' – whether with sincerity or
sarcasm, I couldn't tell – and the solid steel door slammed shut
behind me, making the air ring with its dull lingering resonance.

I lay on the mattress and stared at the dim light which refused to go
out, until my eyes no longer focused. I thought of the contents of my
pack and camera case being divided out as spoil among my captors;
of my disappointment at having found no mail awaiting me in Rio,
nothing forwarded from Cochabamba; of my family and how
long it was since I had last received news of them. Where were they
now and what were they doing while I lay locked in this godforsaken
cell in this rotting maggoty continent? Where were my friends,
lovers from the past and those of the future, still no more than the
heroines of idle dreams? Whom were they thinking and dreaming of
now? Not of me. I was too distant.

Why had I chosen to be alone?

I sank to the lowest ebb of my trip. My appetite for travel had
gone. I was sick of being homeless, of carrying my world in a canvas
bag and suspecting everyone was going to steal it, of always
counting the cost to eke out my fixed funds, of the same clothes, of
dirt, of stares, the delays, the inevitable bureaucratic brick walls, the
inconceivable complexity of even the simplest undertaking, the

demeaning frustrations of communicating on an infantile level, and the pettiness of my daily decisions. I wanted security, four walls of my own to decorate with the things that were meaningful to me, a job, a routine, a regular income and, most of all, friends. Suddenly I craved friends with a hopeless longing, people who would not ask me my name, my country, the name of my wife, and then delve into the whys and hows of my being. People with whom I could talk on an equal standing, exchange the pleasures of anticipated and spontaneous giving and sharing, and in whose company I could rest at ease in the moments of silence that weigh heavily on the minds of strangers.

The most difficult part of travelling alone is that it is up to you, and only you, to pull yourself out of a low patch. No one else will tell you to lift your chin up, help you to look on the bright side and raise your flagging spirits. You have to teach youself how to smile again, and it is the hardest discipline of all to learn. I felt lonely, isolated and hurt. I detested these soldiers, not because they had locked me up, but because they had broken my will. I wanted to give in and go home. Yet somehow I knew I would carry on. I couldn't explain exactly why. Perhaps the urge to continue dominated because after three years on the road it actually took more courage to throw aside a dream, however sour it had become, than it did to plod on in blind ambition and fulfil it.

Tomorrow would be different. I let my eyes focus on the dim light. I would carry on because today was an exception. I didn't regard this setback as being my Destiny. It was merely another episode in the saga of being bolivared.

This, at any rate, made a heartening argument on the eve of my kilt's return.

10 · English Tea on the Road to Tierra del Fuego

I was woken at six a.m. My luggage was returned to me intact and two guards led me outside to a waiting truck. As it was not permitted to walk over the international bridge, they had stopped this civilian truck and asked, or ordered, the driver to take me with him. The senior officer waved me aboard, then rapped his knuckles on the cab door and dispatched one suspected Tupamaro guerilla off to Buenos Aires with a consignment of dressed timber. I had thanked him for arranging the lift before remembering that it was on his orders that I had been locked up.

A few hours later the wide fast avenues that speed all traffic (even dressed timber) through the outer sectors of industrial estates and ranks of residential highrises and into the centre of Buenos Aires were not reducing my impression of immense urbanisation. In terms of city superlatives, Buenos Aires ranks second in the world to Mexico City for holding the most Spanish-speakers, and second to São Paulo in the Southern Hemisphere for size with over eight million inhabitants. In terms of character, São Paulo is South America's New York, Rio its San Francisco and Buenos Aires its London–Paris–Milan. Argentina's late-nineteenth-century history was one of European influence and phenomenal economic growth. The British were the dominant force, exploiting the vast pampas production of grain and beef, for which railways, deep water ports and refrigerator ships had created an insatiable demand, and owning all the public utilities in Buenos Aires. By 1914 half the city's population was foreign-born, French and Italian architects had designed the buildings to reflect their native cities, and the general prosperity, Girl Guides and British Saturday Football Leagues flourished. English was the language of high society – or, as an acceptable second, Spanish with an Oxford accent – and 50,000 Britons were already buried in Argentine cemeteries. The First World War marked the start of the decline of British influence but Buenos Aires still had a warm homely feel, as I discovered. Tartan skirts were abundant in the windows of the more fashionable shops and not uncommon in the many elegant streets. This was encouraging as I knew my kilt would soon number among them (by Spanish definition, at any rate). What had yet to be tested was my assumption that because Argentinians felt *macho* enough without having to prove it by fighting bulls, the same would apply to deriding Scotsmen.

The city centre was clean and confident, built too late to have become soiled with age and too early to have been scarred with shoddy styles and faceless concrete. Only an obelisk bearing the founding date 1536 showed the city to be old, for it had been rebuilt later through the benefaction of grain and beef. Buenos Aires appeared faultlessly symmetrical in its square mesh design, and 9th July Avenue was broad enough to represent metropolitan pampas. The avenue's name made me suspect an impending coup, so I hurried to find the tourist information office and a map marking the British Embassy. A young girl spoke eloquently, but for too long, about the cathedral's dozen Herculean columns and the city's forty-two theatres, 150 parks, 200 cinemas, British polo ground, and rococo race-track . . .

'A *what* race-track?' I interrupted. She repeated the information but uncertainly, as if rococos perhaps had life and four legs.

The British Embassy did not have my kilt but gave me a receipt which would enable it to be claimed at the postal customs office. I rushed along several blocks and reached the customs office shortly before it closed, and three days before my parcel was due to be returned to the sender as unclaimed. The official tore a hole in one corner to see the contents but had to remove all the wrappings before he could identify them.

'This is for your wife or girlfriend?' he asked. I said it was for me. He scowled, taking my reply as sarcasm but on realising I was serious, he became tickled.

'Ho! Ho! Ho!' – his laugh was Santa Clausish – 'it must be very cold inside!' I denied this and hoped he wouldn't laugh again. 'Are you going to Patagonia?' he prompted.

Patagonia, the great windswept plain occupying the lower half of the country, was ill-defined in my mind but I knew it would form most of my route to Tierra del Fuego. I explained this ('Ho! Ho!') and he charged me ten dollars for the number of days the parcel had been in his possession. Then he afforded himself another chuckle instead of charging the import duty which was normally payable on clothing, because he felt sorry for anyone going to Patagonia and particularly for anyone without trousers. He handed over the kilt and sporran but suddenly withdrew them and held them back, above his shoulder, so that they were as far from my reach as possible.

'You are from Britain, yes?' His face sharpened. 'Then you can have this if you give us back *las Islas Malvinas.*'

I looked blank. He nodded to a wall map which showed the Falkland Islands in enlarged scale. The name meant no more to me than the recollection of once meeting a merchant seaman who had been there to collect penguins for a British circus.

'That seems a fair exchange,' I replied. 'As far as I'm concerned, they are all yours.' He gave me my parcel. (I have regretted these words ever since. Let me now take this opportunity of apologising in case I was in any way responsible for what happened later.)

My initial and very hesitant trial-run of the kilt was planned as a short sortie that evening, but it turned into a protracted test. I had returned to my hostel much later than intended, having met with no hostility (partly because few people recognised it in the darkness), only to find I had been locked out. The owner responded to the bell by speaking to me through a grid in the brick doorway, but he refused to open the door outside the times stated on his regulations. Perhaps the real reason was fear of abduction by government forces, who had been responsible for the disappearance of over 20,000 people since the military coup of 1976. I found it impossible to argue with a brick wall and was forced to sit out the long night in Plaza Britannia. It was the 17th of September – no more coups, but late winter and extremely cold. My only consolation was the six-storey replica of Big Ben, presented to the country by Britain and British expats, and its familiar quarterly chimes.

'That's a beautiful tartan you're wearing,' commented the first woman passer-by early the next morning. 'What is it?' I tried to hide the patches in my pedigree and named its colours. She smiled and walked off . . . *a beautiful tartan* . . .! She had removed a great burden. Her words reunited an old partnership, and I set off eagerly to show my kilt Buenos Aires. We passed the 'Toil 'n Chat' school for learning English, and received one more compliment, some jokes and a few ribald comments. We soon grew used to being surrounded by surprised looks and withered conversations, and delighted in the way so many strangers were moved to approach and make our acquaintance. By the time we reached the pink Presidential Palace our confidence was fully restored and we were able to relax and enjoy watching a legion of soldiers and bandsmen changing the guard, shuffling along in their regalia with a peculiar foot-dragging slow-hop like the courtship dance of a lame turkey. They looked very odd.

Argentina is shaped like a leg of beef. The broad haunch at the top, with Buenos Aires on the side of the ocean and the lake district 700 miles away and almost opposite on the side of the Andes, tapers to Tierra del Fuego, the dislocated hoof at the bottom. The capital made me feel claustrophobic within a few days and so I headed west towards the lake district and the prospect of taking a long walk in the landscapes Argentina wraps around its boxes of chocolates. Hitching proved to be so effortless that, in effect, the kilt enabled me to borrow any vehicle on the road. The great pampas opened up beyond the city's limits, endless flat grassland tediously identical in every direction. There were black or brown specks of cattle, an occasional matchbox house with a small copse of trees which looked false on account of their bold upright profile in a world of wind-pumps and telephone posts where horizontal was natural and vertical was man-made or bovine. Everything appeared in miniature when set against this devastating slash of green, itself cringing below the more mighty expanse of sky, and running level, its distant edge seldom daring to rise above the top strand of barbed wire which flanked the road with monotonous loyalty. A breeze ruffled occasional fields of winter wheat and its progress was marked by shivering patches of lighter colours, but otherwise the pampas was a revolving view of the same still life. The farms here averaged 1,200 acres in an area of prime pasture for beef, where 120 acres were enough for an adequate living.

Later the terrain became arid and began to undulate, increasing its rises and falls until they fitted the whining cadence of the wind in a semi-desert of thorn bushes, dust and friable rock of a dull comfortless hue. Paltry herds of cattle and sheep roamed this wilderness nipping at the frugal growth, and sometimes a lone gaucho could be seen cantering across the scene with inexplicable haste, a low trail of dust billowing out behind the flying hooves and his black poncho fluttering in the wind and floating up and down with the soothing regularity of the horse's rhythm. My last borrowed vehicle let me out as the land was changing once more to ice-crusted mountains and pine forests. The driver knew the area and recommended a walk along the Ruta de los Sete Lagos, a dirt road little used in winter which ran for 130 miles into the heart of the lake district. 'If we meet again,' Señor Videla added, 'you will thank me for this walk.' Then he gave me his address and pressed me to accept a bag of apples and *yerba maté*, the tea of the gaucho – 'For your good health. Maté takes away hunger and gives you strength.' This was to become typical of Argentina's extraordinary hospitality. In this exorbitantly expensive country seldom a day went by without several invitations to stay and presents of food.

The walk started at San Martín de los Andes, a small place notable for the length of its name and its army barracks. The entire southern tail of the Andes, forming the border between Chile and Argentina, is a militarily sensitive region on account of a long-standing dispute between the two countries which almost culminated in open war in 1978. It concerns the ownership of three islands in the Beagle Channel to the south of Tierra del Fuego (only one island is inhabited, by a precarious Chileno family), although the real issues at stake are the rights to territorial waters, potentially lucrative offshore oil reserves, strategic control of shipping traffic between the two great oceans and the basis for allocation of Antarctic territory. I quickly slipped past the barracks, trying to look neither Tupamaro nor Chileno, and set off into lightly falling snow.

After five slushy miles an army truck approached from behind and stopped beside me. The driver explained he was taking supplies to a bothy and offered me a lift. I accepted and soon we arrived at a simple stone cottage where ten recruits, one officer and, nearby, 200 mules were either eating grass or mulling over their boredom. The recruits greeted me with a grapeshot volley of salutations and questions. By then it was evening and I readily yielded to their persuasion to stay the night. The officer was not keen but he relented to the popular opinion of his subordinates. Before long my wet socks were steaming with the others arranged before an open fire where rows of steaks were hissing and blistering. We sat around the hearth, our conversation and curiosity exhausted, raising mugs of ruby red wine to faces glowing with the flickering radiance of the flames. Through a window the sun's pink glow was tinting the crystalline coating on rocky hillsides and exaggerating scattered pine trees by projecting them as large soft shadows. The feeling of peace and harmony was almost tangible.

The silence was broken by my neighbour. 'Do you have national service in Scotland?' he asked. I explained that it had been abolished many years ago. He glanced askance at his officer. 'It must be a nice country then,' he remarked.

We were eating our steaks, and only steaks ('vegetables are too expensive'), when a radio was turned on. It was tuned to a station in Chile as these conscripts preferred the enemy's choice of music. I stopped eating in surprise when *Amazing Grace* was the first tune to be heard. I felt sorry for these youths, waiting for a war with Chile when they just wanted to return to their farms, friends, discos and colleges, and I felt divorced from time and place, in a juxtaposition of the strange and familiar; listening to the sounds of a pipeband with part of the Argentine army in a bothy whose view might have been sliced from my homeland. For our own particular reasons, we all drank a lot of wine that night.

The next morning I left early and continued along the Road of the Seven Lakes. No cars passed and no houses appeared until mid-afternoon when an avenue of poplar trees loomed up and revealed a drive with an attractive entrance arch. '*Hacienda Los Notros*', read the sign creaking in the breeze, and I decided to call in and ask for some information on the road ahead. A little further on was a clump of *notros*, a species of red-flowering shrub, and from this glared a more threatening notice, '*Entrada particula*'. It made me stop to consider the situation for a moment but then I carried on. If I in a kilt was not *particulo*, then who was?

The house was set on a hillock overlooking stables and a steading, and commanded a superb view to an inky-black lake teaseled into whitecaps, and to the distant perfect cone of the extinct Lanin volcano. The door was opened on my first knock by a man of retirement age with wavy hair, a ruddy complexion, and wearing an old RAF jersey.

'Well, well, a Scotsman!' He held out his hand. 'James Crighton. Do come in. We're just about to have tea and I hope you'll join us.' He led the way through a porch lined with riding and wellington boots, through a hall hung with oil paintings of horses and into a cosy drawing-room of antique furniture; an oak cabinet displaying silverware, a bookcase of English books ranging from leatherbound classics to modern hardbacks, family portraits and brass harness trappings decorating the walls, and chintz-covered armchairs drawn up before a blazing fire. His wife Stella, daughter Marlene and son-in-law Richard rose to greet me and I was astonished to find myself amongst an English family. Crumpets, scones and home-made cakes were passed around and we drank tea out of Royal Doulton china while I explained my chance arrival. They were visibly pleased to see a new face and yet showed no surprise at the way mine had suddenly appeared. Their manner was calm and reserved. It was just another quiet afternoon tea and I might have been Baxter's jam for a change. This matter-of-fact acceptance touched deeply, and for the second day running I felt very close to home.

It took time to steer the conversation away from my travels because the family took a great interest in the outside world, and it was only after they had eagerly followed my route on an atlas that I learnt something about my kind hosts. James Crighton was an alert, worldly-wise man who had been born in Argentina of English parents. During his career as a civil engineer he had been based in this country but foreign projects had taken him around the globe. When his wife inherited Los Notros he had retired and they had both come to live here. He took little part in running the farm and spent hours each day in a heated shed at his hobby of carpentry. Stella Crighton was a slight woman with short dark hair gracefully whitening. Such was her drive that I could imagine her at her happiest when having three things to do at once, particularly if one of them was riding. Horses had always been a part of her life and she still worked in the saddle with her gauchos; she also managed the farm, picked wild berries, cooked, entertained, taught evening classes and filled her idle moments with sewing, reading or gardening. She said she had inherited this energetic and practical nature from her Chilean mother but in most respects it was her father who had influenced her – and he had certainly been no ordinary man.

'That's my father's portrait over there,' Stella explained. She pointed to a picture of a broad-shouldered man, nearly bald, with penetrating blue eyes and a warm smile which was exaggerated by a splendid fair moustache. I could see the similarity in her features and most especially the shared expression of determination. 'He was born in Cornwall in 1882 and died not long ago aged ninety-two. Every morning he rubbed Bay Rum on his head and dusted his white linen handkerchief with lavender. He always wore a silk tie even when breaking in a horse or parting cattle. But the story really started with grandfather.' She paused to replenish my cup and went on to relate how her grandfather had been a Harley Street doctor, his wife a concert pianist and how they had lived in Kensington Gardens with their six children, a butler and several maids. On the death of his father her grandfather inherited a considerable fortune and decided to give up his practice and travel. He bought a 75,000-acre property in Argentina and in 1888 he hired a ship and sailed to South America with his family, two servants, two greyhounds, two terriers, two bulldogs, a monkey and a collection of fighting cocks.

The journey from Buenos Aires to their new home at the foot of the Andes was made by bullock-carts and lasted six years. The family stopped at intervals to gain experience of farm work on estancias, and Stella Crighton's grandfather bought and sold horses – sometimes a thousand at a time for they were two a penny on the pampas. The Rio Colorado flooded and washed away some of their possessions (they spent months trying to cross it by dismantling the carts and using the wood to make a boat), suffered severe water shortages in deserts and had to hack a route through the roadless scrub.

The family were delighted with the mountains, forests, lakes and pasture which had been their 'blind' purchase. They soon built a house, their first roof for many years, and amassed a stock of 10,000 cattle and 1,000 horses. The children all helped to run the hacienda, taking over when both their parents died in 1906 and adding to their landholding by purchasing Los Notros in the south several years later.

When it was planned the southern railway would pass through the property, the family agreed to donate land for a settlement, and Arthur and his brother drew up the first plans for the township of Zapala, now a city of 20,000 inhabitants. 'I remember it as one office, one shop and houses belonging to some Turks and Arabs who grew rich by getting the Indians drunk and cheating them. They never planted a single tree or made a pavement.' Then Spanish, Italian and British immigrants moved in and the town became an important trading post.

'Arthur, my father, married a Chilena and I was the second of their three children. We grew up at the Zapala hacienda where my father had assembled a huge library of English books. He only spoke English to us and mother always used Spanish, so we were bilingual. Mother made all our clothes, cooked English recipes which the railway engineers gave her and helped in every aspect of farm life.

Father patiently taught us all he knew and to love and care for this land. He was greatly respected as a tough, honest, hard-working Englishman. All the surrounding farms were started by either English, French, Spanish, German, Welsh, Irish, Swiss or latterly Belgian immigrants. Each year in mid-July many of these settlers, including my parents, would travel to Buenos Aires for a month's holiday. They stayed in the best hotels, went shopping at Harrods, Aulds and Mappin & Webb, visited the theatre, cinema and horse races, and chatted with friends at the livestock markets.'

In those days, Stella recalled, they always had to dress up whenever they took their little Belgian car (Fabricación Nacional) into the village. She wore a dress, white socks, black shoes, white gloves and a bonnet while her mother wore a long dress, buttoned-up boots and a wide-brimmed hat tied on with a silk scarf. All this even though the times were rough and dangerous. Her father often used to tell the story of the time he met an American friend near Bariloche. They were both on horseback, and the American had a dead man over his saddle. Her father greeted him.

'Hola, John. How are you?'

'I am well, Arturo.' He always spoke slowly in a soft deliberate voice. 'What brings you this way?'

'Buying cattle. But tell me, John . . . what have you across your saddle?'

'Ah, this is Pachaco. He would not pay me. I squeezed his neck, slowly, but he refused to pay. I squeezed a little harder . . . nothing doing. Well, I pressed a little harder . . .'

'And what are you going to do now?'

'Throw him in front of the police station.'

'But they'll put you under lock and key.'

'Hmm-m.' He scratched his head under his large Texan hat, and then his beard, and finally gave a shove and dropped the man to the ground. 'Ah well, Arturo. Thank you for the advice. Let's go down to the farm and have some *maté*.'

In 1942, after Stella and her brother had finished their schooling (at the best boarding schools in Buenos Aires, Quilmes High school and St George's), Stella stayed on in Buenos Aires where she met her husband. Now she was glad, and proud, to be back at Los Notros and running the estate with her daughter and son-in-law.

Afternoon tea merged into dinner and an invitation to stay for a few days. I was glad to accept. This family still saw themselves as predominantly English despite their long absence from the country of their roots. They thought in English, talked in English, and read English books. They were accustomed to five o'clock tea, plum puddings, birthday fruit cakes, Sunday roasts, and Christmas stockings, trees and decorations. Although Argentines ranked as their close friends, the majority of their friends were English, French or American families. They were Anglicans in a Catholic country, were all members of the once very-British Hurlingham Club in Buenos Aires (now true-British membership was in decline and currently stood at about forty per cent), and would send the youngest Crighton generation to the same traditional English schools. Stella gave monthly lessons in flower-arranging to the Ladies' Garden Club she had founded and her garden at Los Notros, planted with seeds sent directly from Thompson & Morgan in Ipswich, was renowned in the district. 'We love Argentina,' she emphasised, 'but find there is too much talk about its problems and never any concerted effort at solving them. If only the Argentine mentality were different it would so improve this beautiful country.'

The following afternoon I experienced another side of this beauty as, accompanying Richard, I bumped unhappily round part of the estancia on one of the family's thirty-eight horses. Richard was a tough thirty-year-old, instantly likable and moulded in the family tradition although he had previously been a city accountant. At first I had thought he looked the part of a country squire with his cravat and suave air, but this image was too sedate for him and when seen unshaven, roguishly grinning and riding in a heavy black cape, he was Dick Turpin to a T. Dressed in my borrowed black cape I also saw myself as a dashing highwayman, only I kept falling off my horse.

'We're very close to Chile and when the "nearly war" blew up, things were worrying. It could flare up at any time,' he explained, speaking normally when we were shoulder to shoulder and raising his voice whenever I disappeared. 'We've got 12,000 acres here, 700 head of cattle and 170 sheep. But we're a long way from our markets . . .' Farm machinery was prohibitively expensive, and to bring in some extra income they ran shooting parties for Europeans who came to hunt pumas, wild pigs and red deer. The hunters were mainly wealthy Belgians and Frenchmen having a holiday from castle life, and the family looked forward to these visitors as a source of new conversation.

We bumped a little faster and made it back to the house in time for tea. History seemed to spin in a slow tight eddy around Los Notros, the farm being run by the grandchildren of the same family and the same gauchos who had worked it three-quarters of a century earlier, the same problems of isolation being confronted with undiminished pioneering grit, and a reserve of English life being faithfully maintained in a backwater of South America.†

It was snowing again, this time heavily and not melting, when I left the Crighton family and continued my rambling westwards towards the seventh lake. There my route would turn south, directly towards Tierra del Fuego. I visualised this region as being like Iceland, a primeval land of fire and ice that had never really grown up, only its South Atlantic horizon would be dominated by the permanent storms of Cape Horn. My thoughts whipped up flames and made the ground bubble and hiss but it was impossible to maintain this deception in a kilt that was only marginally winterproof. A formidable forest of tall pines darkened the road for long stretches and their branches dipped under the weight of snow held precariously above my head. A deer once tiptoed out of the trees as a ray of sunshine broke through the clouds, and it stood richly illuminated, poised with one foot held in the air as it tested the breeze, motionless in a scene contrived to mimic the perfection of a Christmas card. Then

† After the Falklands War I wrote to the Crightons to see how they had fared, and received the following reply.

'We were on the "doubtful" list and kept out of sight and out of the way, shutting ourselves off for months. We have British friends who farm south of here and during the hostilities their old family cemetery was desecrated. Children's graves were dug up and marble headstones were destroyed by shots from a military training camp. It was all very sad as their grandparents, like mine, had sacrificed their lives to open up that part of the world and created a beautiful farm in what is now an important agricultural area. They did not deserve the hatred that was shown.

'We felt very bad that we went to war with Britain and that we had such fools to kill off so many of our youngsters, many under eighteen years old who did not know they were going to war, had never even held a gun before, and all lads from the warm climates of the north being sent to the coldest part of the world – it was all madness and a great shock. We shed tears for those killed and felt sadness, shame and despair. We lost so much and are still paying for it, and will do so for years to come.'

the pines thinned and views of some of the seven lakes could be glimpsed between the silhouettes of trunks and branches. Only the willows could see beyond winter as they stood flanking whitewater rivulets, their leafless limbs decorated with lightly scented yellow catkins which dangled like Chinese lanterns. I thanked Señor Videla for this walk.

But no one appeared and the stillness was broken by no more than the muffled discomfort of the snow and the regular rattle of the leather tassels of my sporran. They had worn bare patches in the sealskin base and now beat noisily leather on leather, bouncing with the spring of my stride and maintaining a rhythm which produced such a forceful incentive to keep going that I wondered if they had been designed for this very purpose.

About twenty miles fell away underfoot that day and then a further thirty under the wheels of a forester's truck. Darkness had fallen by the time I reached a small hotel. The forester had said it was closed for the winter but a caretaker lived there, and the cheerful glow of an outside light encouraged me to go and ask if I could sleep in a barn. An old man came to the door and stood there staring at my kilt, completely baffled. I explained about myself but I think it was only my imperfect Spanish that offered him any understanding, for folk dressed in kilts were outside his experience or comprehension. It therefore spoke all the more for his kindness when he offered me a bed in the empty staff quarters, and for his politeness when he never enquired about my clothes or background during the hour we sat beside his wood stove in the kitchen.

He said the hotel was owned by a German and this led him on to the subject of the last world war. It had been a bad war for Europe, he asserted. He had heard about it. He had seen terrible pictures. Did I know that millions had died in that war? Millions! And there had been death camps – the prisoners were just skin and bones. Skeletons! And all because of one man. Unbelievable!

Yes, I replied, I knew. In this distant land the Second World War was a story from overseas, a bad, fantastic story reduced to gossip, a source of hearsay horror snippets thrown between comments on the weather. Perhaps people here looked on us Europeans as a barbaric race? We regarded them as revelling in bloody revolutions, brutal régimes and a general lack of that something called civilisation, but what must they think of us in the light of our war atrocities?

I wanted to tell him more, to put it in perspective for him, but he moved on to how much snow had fallen that winter. The simplicity of his lifestyle and thoughts was touching. They'd had a bad winter, we'd had a bad war. I felt perhaps it was best to leave it at that.

On the fifth day of the walk I finally reached the seventh lake, Nahuel Huapi, and made my way along a peninsula to visit some of the world's rarest trees. Bosque Los Arrayanes was proclaimed to be unique in the world after the only other known wood was destroyed along with the city of Hiroshima during a bad war in Japan. The most remarkable feature of *los arrayanes* is their coldness to the touch, evidently due to the fact that they absorb eighty per cent more water than any other species of tree. Their trunks grow in twisted knotted shapes and the cinnamon-orange bark is constantly flaking.

Three fat gypsies were standing begging for money at one end of the wood. They stared at me from a distance. I changed direction to circle around them. One suddenly let out a peal of salacious laughter which was copied by the others and they moved across to intercept. There may not have been many of them but there was a lot of them, and these mountains of flesh shook horribly with laughter. One of the smaller ones, who still had an inch of height over me, asked where I came from. Her eyes betrayed an arsenal of mockery and a hint of carnal appetite.

'*Escocia*,' I replied. She nodded thoughtfully, and I realised my answer would have been equally meaningful in Urdu. The biggest, a colossal figure in a ragged jacket and a dress of red and candy pink stripes, squeezed between the others and looked sternly down the length of her nose towards me.

'RUSIA,' she exhaled with slow deliberate emphasis. The other two switched their gaze from me to their leader, impressed with her perception and understanding.

'*No! No es Rusia. Soy de* ESCOCIA,' I contradicted.

The smaller two, who had turned to me while I was speaking, now looked back to their leader to see how she would cope with this new complication. She said nothing for a while and simply expanded.

'*Rusia*,' she breathed. The word was pathetic and came as a complete anticlimax, but her prestige was saved by the smallest who gasped all of a sudden. One hand was partially concealing her mouth and the other was pointing at my bare knees, slightly red from the effort of walking. Her eyes closed below a brow of wrinkles, her jaw fell open and for a moment there was silence while she rocked forwards. A terrible scream shattered the air and her open palms hit her thighs in a gesture of helplessness; and her laughter was picked up by the second. Their leader flung an arm over each of her companions on realising this was a convenient diversion, and collapsed in hysterical shrieks.

I left them like this and walked quickly away feeling deeply offended and embarrassed. The burden of guilt and shame lasted for the next mile because it always hurt me whenever I failed to leave behind feelings of accord and goodwill. By the second mile I had reasoned things out more carefully and the incident didn't seem so damaging. I was not always a good ambassador for Scotland, but in this case I had been a disastrous one for Russia.

Over the next ten days my journey took me to a small village in the heart of Patagonia called Perito Moreno, which I now look back on with a vision of utter desolation and boredom, and a dog called Macanudo. But first I went south from Bariloche through barren land until Esquel, a town in a fertile valley. It was dark by the time I set up my tent in a field and unable to see any river nearby, I went to a house to ask for water. A middle-aged woman opened the door and although she stood against the light, I could make out a puritanical formality in her costume; she wore a black bow-tie and a frilly white blouse whose ruffles bulged above the modestly sunk neckline of a slate blue-grey dress which came down to her ankles. A dainty lace apron was tied around her waist, and on a peg behind her I noticed a brimmed witch's hat, black with a blunt end. She stood there in the Welsh national costume and I stood opposite her in kilt and sporran. The coincidence appeared beyond belief and the element of farce in this sudden meeting between two traditionally dressed and equally displaced Gaels struck me as being extremely comical. Perhaps because it was late, or dark, or because I was smiling more boldly than befits the first encounter between two Britons, she did not return my amusement or interest. A more detailed explanation about myself also failed to produce a response and in the end I just asked for some water, and Scotland and Wales retired to their respective hermitages, 200 yards apart and 7,000 miles from home.

A colony of Welsh settlers first came to Argentina in 1865 from Liverpool aboard the *Mimosa* (the passage cost £45) and various groups continued to arrive up until 1911. They turned desert into productive fields and created many farming communities of which the ones here at Esquel and neighbouring Trevelin were the most distant from the main areas of habitation on the coast at Puerto Madryn and Gaimán. (When I later visited Gaimán I found no children in the street who could speak Welsh and although the houses were untypical of Argentina – red brick two-up, two-downs – and the shop names were frequently Davies, Owens, Williams or Jones, the Welsh culture seemed ordained for tourism.)

My vision of Wales, cracked as it was, soon faded on a gravel road south which offered few distractions and fewer alternatives. From then on everything appeared cracked because all vehicles either had shattered windscreens or wore a visor of small-mesh netting. Perito Moreno village lay mid-way down the one thousand miles to Tierra del Fuego and as a testimony to the emptiness of the bottom half of the country, it was labelled in large letters on all maps. From top to bottom the landscape was identical, pure Patagonia, a land whose fascination is in its uniformity, its surprising lack of surprises, its haunting preponderance of unloved plainness. The vegetation is olive hedgehogs which are curled up into balls, never growing more than two feet tall and greedily claiming large territories so that their shallow roots can suck at more of the surface without competition for the rationed moisture. Darwin's rhea, called *nandu* in Spanish, is common. It hates being outrun. It will race cars for considerable distances, panicking at the stiff competition as it sprints alongside the roads, kicking up little clouds of dust from powerful legs which are said to be excellent eating, until finally admitting defeat and sheering away, avoiding the car's trailing plume of dust, gliding over the green hedgehogs with faultless footwork and disappearing into the undulating vagueness of perfect nandu country.

In Perito Moreno I discovered the eternal wind of Patagonia. It blew as a constant breeze at its kindest and rose to a howling gale at its cruellest. It tugged at the pleats of my kilt, it scooped upwards and inflated the material until it rose, the lower edges dancing around my thighs. But the wind was to prove the least of my problems as I walked away from the village, intent on hitching east through 200 barren miles to the coast and the main road south.

A shaggy collie appeared and began following me. I stopped several times to chase him back to the village but he always returned. Eventually I found a relatively sheltered spot to wait and the dog waited with me, keeping his distance at first and then gradually creeping closer until he allowed me to stroke him. I called him Macanudo, an Argentine colloquialism I had recently learnt meaning 'excellent', and it shortened conveniently to Mac. I watched the sun rise and shared some cheese with Mac for breakfast. I watched the sun pass overhead, and we had more cheese for lunch. I watched the sun sink down to the opposite horizon, making the gravel cast long shadows on the road, and I was glad of Mac's company. In thirteen hours a total of three cars passed and all were locals on local errands. Feeling deflated and numbed by boredom, I trudged back to the village. Mac followed but suddenly vanished as miraculously as he had appeared. I went to the town's only bar. The patron was sympathetic but shook his head mournfully.

'I'm afraid tomorrow will be worse. Once every ten years Argentina has a national census when everyone must stay at home to be counted. Tomorrow is National Census Day.'

Mateo Turano Vineyards had a nerve to label the previous year's produce as wine, but after receiving this news from a victualler who sold little else, I finished off one bottle and was almost through a second when I felt composed enough to go and camp in preparation for another setback in the snakes and ladders of a world safari.

There was to be plenty of time to write my diary.

22nd October, Perito Moreno. National Census Day. There's an extra one sitting by the road. Bloody hell. I think I'm here till I rot.

Was up at 6.30 a.m. Walked out along the road east for a mile, and Macanudo came bounding after me. I had secretly been hoping he would come. That damn wind buffeted my kilt and whined dismally through the telephone wires. We stopped near a herd of ponies. I sat on my pack and Macanudo curled up at my feet. I envied him his ability to find comfort and oblivion anywhere, and felt touched by his trust.

The ponies graze a little then wander on, tails billowing in the breeze, their heads held low as if too heavy for them and their footsteps small and weary. They look sad and lonely and merely add to my despondency. I see my life as a big clock with the minutes ticking away and I'm stuck in a void called Patagonia. My dog is snoring, his legs occasionally twitch. He must be chasing rabbits. Thanks, Mac. You bring a sense of proportion and cheer to a humourless land. Sand is being blown around me. I've reread all my letters from friends and family a dozen times but I turn to one with some bluebells sellotaped to a page.

The same three cars as yesterday tootled about. Then a fourth came. I leapt up but saw it was a Land-Rover of soldiers. They drew up alongside me and the driver asked for my passport and then snatched the pile of documents, including all my money, from my hands. The back door opened and I was ordered in with my luggage. Mac sat up and looked agitated, and this upset me more than anything. I was driven five miles to an army camp where my papers were taken off to one room, my luggage to another and I was led to a third. I was strip-searched and then questioned. They accused me of being a Chileno spy. More questions. My personal letters were put before me. One contained the sentence 'I hope you won't have any problems in Chile.' They could only understand the words 'Chile' and 'problems' and they wove these elements into a farcical spy plot. They interrogated me further. Eventually they softened. They didn't understand Scotsmen but they knew Chilenos – and they were not capable of such monstrous deception. An hour later everything was returned to me and they told me to leave. The bastards left me the five miles to walk back.

Was amazed to find Mac still waiting for me at the same spot. He came bounding towards me and we had a grand reunion. It's good to have a companion, but a deep attachment is irresponsible. What about tomorrow? I may be gone and Mac will feel deserted. Considerate travellers should remain detached, unloved, unlovable. What a grim thought . . .

Twenty-six hours by the road. I'm tired of waiting. Surely my life has more purpose than this? Tomorrow, maybe mañana. The sun is a gory orange on the horizon and sinking fast. Soon it will be cold for it freezes at night. I'd better go and camp. Three nights here – it's the longest I've camped on one spot since Alaska. Come on, Macanudo, we've got to make a mile to reach the village. Are you fit, old boy? So am I.

For some reason Macanudo did not appear the next morning as I walked away from Perito Moreno at the usual time. Maybe some dog-sense warned him of treachery, but I was glad for it avoided an unpleasant parting. There was something else strange that morning but it took some time for me to identify it. No wind. My kilt hung unstirred. Patagonia was calm and still, and seemed morose and brooding. The first car to come by gave me an early lift all the way to the coast, far from my dog and a wilderness slighted by silence.

The 'Land of Fire' was given its name by Magellan on seeing the fires lit by the semi-naked Indians who were inhabiting the island when he sailed by in 1520. The hardy Indians were still there when the *Beagle* with Darwin aboard came in 1832 and returned one of them, Jemmy Buttons, whom the *Beagle* had kidnapped two years earlier and taken to boarding school in England to learn to bowl underarm and become a Fuegan gentleman (the experiment was unsuccessful – he later arranged the massacre of eight missionaries). But the Indians soon died out after 1880 as a result of the diseases brought by immigrants coming to farm and exploit the newly discovered gold seams. Today the fires of Tierra del Fuego are alight once more only this time they burn on top of the flare stacks which mark the rich reserves of oil. The recent census revealed that the island's population has increased by eighty-eight per cent in ten years, mainly as a result of this expanding industry.

The island is divided by a vertical axis designating half to Chile and half to Argentina, and geographically by a horizontal axis formed by the mountain line of the southern coast. Rio Grande, the dull oil town in the upper-right Argentine section, is set in an extension of the Patagonian barrens, and here the wind continues its relentless labour of sweeping a region where each sheep needs twelve acres of grazing to survive, and where sheep poaching on a massive scale is still rife. This was the problem tormenting the farmer who took me south of Rio Grande and into another world. After eighty miles the road reached a lake and began twisting up slopes of pine forest towards distant white mountains. The scenery grew better by the mile, from the pleasant to the majestic. It wasn't at all like Iceland but something much closer to home. We drove ever upwards and reached a plateau where a black river with bubbling amber cascades cut through the crust of snow cloaking the land, and crystals of ice sparkled under the bare branches of silver birch. We dropped off the far end and descended into a Great Glen where a sinuous lake slunk through a forest intent on choking it; through a moorland of peatbog and beaver-felled trees, a Glencoe of towering rock walls which gave glimpses of sawtooth peaks, sharp, frosted and severe, and the rims of corries offering the hint of placid lochans cupped inside. I had come to Tierra del Fuego for no other reason than because it was at the very bottom of the world, but it provided me with the traveller's supreme reward, when two days of frustration and dusty solitude were dismissed in an instant – the unexpected discovery of enchantment.

I camped that night in what I at once decided was one of my favourite parts of the world. It conformed to my notion of an explorer's Elysium; the perfect blend of mountains, lochs, forests and rivers, where wildness and beauty did not hold their inspiration aloof but left it easily accessible. I smoked my pipe beside a lively fire and was staring at the waxing moon which cast a vitreous sheen on the frozen peaks, when a voice startled me. A drunk staggered into the glow of my fire and announced that he was a roadmender and that he had wine. He swung round at once and disappeared. He returned some time later carrying a stool and two containers. *This* was a roadmender's stool, he explained, and dropped his heavy frame onto it. His roadmending caravan was evidently nearby and he had seen my fire. *This* was a flagon of wine, he continued, and we had to drink it all because he had more for tomorrow, and *this* – he waved a can of petrol – was for my lousy fire. He flung it onto the flames and screwed up his face in surprise when they rose twenty feet into the air, obliterating the moon and the lights of the Southern Cross. Then he turned to me with a smug grin and he didn't have to say a thing. His eyes said it all. 'Now *that*, my friend, is what a roadmender calls a fire.' He could not have provided a more appropriate welcome to Tierra del Fuego.

My contentment made the days go quickly. I spent a week walking in the hills and by the sea, and felt, in many ways, that my journey had come to an end. Why travel on when you've found a land you like and friendly people? The inclination to remain in a place which appeared to have enough ingredients to satisfy the needs of comfort and ambition was tempting, but it had become my custom to resist this temptation and the basic force of wanderlust made the task less daunting. I had to resist. After all, I'd never have got as far as this if I had adopted a weaker approach. And yet it was never easy. It was a part of the ambivalent nature of the game, the traveller's paradox – he travels to find his chosen element and when he has found it, he needs to travel on to see if there is any other quite like it. I regarded myself as a dedicated traveller but not an insatiable one, and so the rift between staying and moving on was often felt more acutely by me than by inveterate gentlemen and ladies of the road. Diehard vagabonds suffer no dilemma for their element is not to be found in their final choice, but in the continual act of choosing. I decided to spend a few days in the world's most southerly town before moving on, heading north to . . . to wherever dedicated travellers finally come to rest.

Ushuaia lay breezily on the sea below its stately hills. The prestige of its position made it careless about its appearance; it lacked paint, and sheep inhabited derelict houses on the long main street but the town's old wood and corrugated iron buildings produced an air of simple charm which some modern edifices and two fish factories contrived unsuccessfully to emulate. The editor of the local newspaper seized on my arrival (the story made page eight) and I was asked to give a talk about my travels to a school class which seemed to achieve little except to allow the teacher to disappear for an hour.

It was while I was alone in a corridor waiting to give this talk that I picked up a child's collection of cigarette cards on the subject of Argentina's history. The first card showed a picture of islands with the white and two blue stripes of Argentina's flag above them. I had time to note the caption. It translated as: 'In January 1833, Great Britain, without deeds of sovereignty, claimed our Falkland Islands through an abuse of power. With just reason the people of Argentina maintain the hope of recovering the islands in the future and, by legitimate means which comply with international law, of securing them irreversibly for our government. Unjust power must never be allowed to corrupt or terrify our people.' The wording was strong for an entry in a schoolchild's scrapbook but this was the attitude fostered in the young. The Falklands issue was close to the heart of every Argentinian that I met and yet it was never allowed to affect their astonishing degree of friendliness.

One morning I went to cash a cheque at Hotel Albatross, the most esteemed in town.

'Hi! You Scottish?'

I turned from the reception counter to see a middle-aged woman approaching like a galleon under full sail with her arms held out in affection even though she was still twenty paces away. She had luxurious auburn hair, an attractive smile and high cheekbones but her elegant features were smudged by the bruise of a black eye, and excess makeup rendered her face as a soulless landscape of ill-assorted colours. She was as inebriated as the roadmender. Her arms closed before reaching me and my hand was grabbed in a ten-digit grip and pumped as a substitute embrace. She introduced herself as Madelena and proposed we should have some coffee. I declined but Madelena was insistent and her commotion was causing everyone to stare at us. I relented, wondering what the kilt had prepared for me this time.

We sat down at a table and Madelena ordered the coffees. The waiter looked impregnable as he walked past. She lit a cigarette, inhaled a large portion of it in one pull and refused to release the smoke until her eyes had completed a revolution of the ceiling.

'I'm a prostitute,' she said. 'By the way, do you like yours black or white?' Her forehead creased, almost cracked, and she touched a fingernail to one cheek until it created a dimple, then slowly gave an enlightened grin. 'The coffee, I mean. You have to order white specially.'

'Either way's fine,' I replied. 'Is business a bit thin at the moment, then?'

She shook her head. No, on the contrary. There were plenty of sailors, and camps packed with construction workers. Sailors were all right but the camp workers were vile, 'too rough'. She loathed Ushuaia and the job. She only stayed because of her daughter who was married to a fisherman, because her daughter was her world, and also because the money was good. She boasted that she was rich, had studied law, and would travel to Europe next year, maybe even to Scotland, and Madelena winked through her black eye while I wondered where our coffees were. Another waiter came and received our order impassively. Who was I? What about the Falkland Islands? She didn't like Arabs. Look! Here was her bank manager coming. He was a friend . . . She skipped from subject to subject like rocking stepping-stones to one afraid of water. She rose to greet the bank manager but he just nodded and dodged her outstretched hand.

There was still no sign of coffee. Our table was obviously being ignored. Despite her protested wealth, here at the Hotel Albatross her credit was bad. I got up to leave but she came too and clung to my arm, her grip acting as a tourniquet. I wanted to detach myself but she clung more tightly with the desperation of her loneliness and her expression evinced a tacit plea for support. She said she knew a café where we could go for a quick coffee but I knew she was only killing time until the bars opened at ten.

I felt sorry for her, fumbling through a life clouded by hangovers, plastering on cosmetics to conceal the lines of age and the blows of competition dealt by some rival bitch, selling her body to those she loathed and in a place she loathed for the unashamed love of money, nodding friendship to everyone and yet never knowing who cared, who were merely business associates and who were malicious gossipers, clamping onto strangers for honest companionship, and living for a moment the lies of release. She was down and almost out, lying on the bottom rung at the bottom of the world and fooling nobody but herself. Yes, I thought I'd want a whisky or two before ten a.m. if I had to face a life like that.

It was not the finale I had expected after a journey of some 35,000 miles from Thule in Greenland, but we gave the gossip-mongers a ball; two figures arm-in-arm walked the length of the world's most southerly street; one of them was a vagabond from the world's most northerly town and the other was the world's most southerly whore; he wore Highland dress, patched and faded, while she wore leather trousers, skin-tight and black.

The last mile always seems the longest.

11 · A Sad Song in Chile

'Defunct,' said Mr MacKenzie with heavy resignation, 'almost defunct. And it used to be such a busy place.'

He was talking about the British Club in Punta Arenas where we were sitting over drinks amongst the neglected lavishness of 1905 décor; a floral-patterned cornice around the ceiling, here and there broken and without petals, pine-pannelled walls, a library of exquisitely bound English books, three snooker tables laid out for a match, deep leather armchairs, stained and perished, and framed photographs of visiting Royal Navy ships which narrowly outnumbered those of Queen Elizabeth II. Mr MacKenzie's father had been one of many Scottish shepherds who had come out with their dogs to work the large flocks of the estancias. He had spent some time in the Falkland Islands before coming to Punta Arenas with a group of hardy Scots who subsequently became known as 'The Forty Thieves'. They had been a wild bunch and squatted on the land until they were eventually granted ownership. The last of them had died a few years previously at the age of ninety-six.

'There were many British here once,' continued Mr MacKenzie, 'but most never came back after the last war and then, what with the state taking over some of the estancias and other things, we've been in decline ever since. We've only got five members in the club now and the rent hasn't been paid for three years. I'm afraid it's almost defunct.'

Two days earlier I had crossed into Chile's half of Tierra del Fuego and then taken a ferry from Porvenir to Punta Arenas (Sandy Point) on mainland Chile. A notice on the ferry had stated the official fares for the two-hour crossing: trucks carrying explosives, 13,000 pesos; passengers, 61 (70p); pigs, 67. Punta Arenas was a bustling little town surrounded by grassland and hills which, a passenger informed me, boasted the only ski slope in the world with a view of the sea. If the Scottish shepherds felt the same way about wild scenery as I did then it was perfectly understandable to me why they had settled here, for Punta Arenas lay half-way between the mountain idylls of Ushuaia and the Paine National Park to the north. The original settlement had been not far away at Port Hunger. Spain had tried to start a farming community there but the crops had failed because of the poor land and harsh climate, and the people had died of starvation without discovering the rich offshore fishing grounds. Francis Drake found this so amusing when he arrived in 1572 that he shipped the only survivor back to England, not for a public school education but as an example of Spanish stupidity in colonising a fishing port with farmers.

Chile, 'the shoestring republic', is 2,600 miles long and an average of 110 miles wide. I was at the bottom, hoping to find a boat up the next 800 miles of roadless coastline before making my way to Valparaíso, one of the world's great ports, to hunt for a ship to New Zealand. Even thinking about the name made me sigh, and I hadn't thought about it very much. My time in South America had been so occupied with its vast array of stimuli and its problems and frustrations that I hadn't indulged myself in long-term plans. There still seemed too many difficulties to overcome before leaving this continent appeared feasible. I tended to look no more than one week ahead, gave my destination as being the next town, and sighed when the words 'New Zealand' came to mind snared inside the symbol for infinity.

The shipping agents in Punta Arenas were uninterested and uncooperative. Mr MacKenzie kindly accompanied me but not even his influence swayed them. 'They're a pretty chaotic bunch,' he whispered in one office, 'especially the domestic companies. Their ships never stick to schedules and no one knows if they're coming or going. I think they may soon become defunct.'

The next three days were full of negatives, doubtfuls and timeless maybe's. Punta Arenas was appearing to be a traveller's cul-de-sac when I discovered that the sum of six consecutive Latin American *no's* is *yes*. Three of them came from the naval office, two from the harbourmaster who didn't know anything about the gunboat *Aquilies* being in port, and one from a junior officer disembarking. The steward by the gangway simply said, 'You can have bunk thirty-eight. 1,000 pesos (£11.50). We sail at ten tonight.'

We sailed at eleven that night.

The voyage from Punta Arenas to Puerto Montt, following a narrow passage between thousands of islands which huddle close to the mainland's tattered edge, is alleged to be one of the world's most beautiful sea journeys when the view is not lost behind a curtain of low cloud. *Aquilies* motored steadily through the dreary weather and the English names of a chart plotted by James Fitzroy, the kidnapper of Jemmy Buttons and the captain of the *Beagle*.

Chile has split itself symmetrically into three geographical zones: the cold and stormy fjordland of the south through which *Aquilies* was passing, the central fertile region of pasture and agriculture which begins at Puerto Montt and ends in the scorched third of desert which stretches to the border with Peru. We reached Puerto Montt on the third morning at sea. The uncertainty of finding a ship to New Zealand made me feel unsettled and eager to reach Santiago and Valparaíso. I travelled by kilt faster than the scenery merited. The way passed below a chain of snow-capped volcanoes – Osorno, Choshuenco, Villarrica and Llaima – and was flanked by messy palettes of wild flowers and dazzling smudges of gorse in yellow bloom. Beyond the volcanoes was a forgotten region, the pride of South America, a paradise for Scottish shepherds and vagabonds; a tall ragged horizon, lakes, forests and verdant pasture framed by chunky log fences. Moving slowly on rutted tracks across this cheese label land were ox-carts whose creaking wheels were cross-section slices of tree trunks, and mounted herdsmen whose boots carried the Chileno spur (a circle of long closely-packed spikes) and fitted into stirrups shaped like the front half of Dutch clogs. The men nodded and touched their hats on passing, and I was reminded that even the Argentinians had said to the Chilenos were the friendliest people on earth. For a few days I forgot about New Zealand and bought milk from a cow called Clavella, and camped in her field. Few campsites have been so perfect and the setting appeared all the more poetic when seen above a log fire and the steam of Clavella milk rice pudding. Rice pudding became a dietary fad that lasted until Santiago.

It was here that I had the address of a friend of a friend, one of those 'If you're ever in Timbuktu, do go and visit so-and-so' contacts, comforting to have even if you never found time to visit them. I knew little about this person except that she was an elderly woman who had been forced to leave her home and flee from Chile during the brave, benevolent but un-US and therefore ill-fated experiment (1970–73) led by Allende. I didn't know why except that Señora Helena was said to prefer privacy to politics. She had evidently returned to Chile after the coup which brought to power the current ruler. General Pinochet, even though she didn't like him. No one liked Pinochet. He had a natty moustache, a sweet smile and bloodied hands. There was nothing extraordinary about him except that his name rhymed with ricochet.

Señora Helena sounded an intriguing character, and I had written a postcard several weeks earlier to introduce myself and express the hope that we could meet. As I walked along the street which was given as her address my inclination to continue diminished on seeing the unbroken row of derelict houses that had suffered a fire. Fortunately this ended by the time I reached number 1665 and entered the grounds of a spacious modern bungalow. A woman stood at the door of an outbuilding stirring a large pot and after a short conversation, during which I could have sworn she said she cooked dogs, she explained that this was the back door and directed me round to the front of the building. Two basset-hounds spotted me as I was crossing a lawn set up for a game of croquet. They began barking and came running towards me, tossing back their heads with each stride and skilfully jerking their long ears out of the way of their feet as they undulated along. Dogs suddenly appeared from all over the hinterland of shrubs and herbaceous flowers. I started running, trying to avoid the croquet hoops and silently imploring the powers that be to help by immediately extending all basset ears by a couple of feet. It wouldn't have done any good for the bassets were soon overtaken by a dalmatian, two labradors, several terriers, a mass of schnautzers and a rearguard of small shaggy objects that showed no signs of feet but skimmed effectively over the grass as furry hovercraft with snapping jaws. I managed to scramble through a gate and slam it shut before the dalmatian could reach the trailing edge of my kilt.

The sound of the gate made a chauffeur look up and pause in his task of polishing six vehicles which included a Bentley, a Cadillac and a Land-Rover, and he nodded me past a gardener towards the front door. I rang the bell before noticing my reflection in a polished brass panel. Footsteps were already approaching and there was no time to straighten my sporran, comb my tousled hair or hide a hole in one sock. A butler opened the door. I gave my name and requested to see Señora Helena.

'The Señora is in North America at present, but I am instructed that you are to be made welcome and may stay here for as long as you wish.' He gave me a bow which was fluent until he caught sight of my socks on the upward arc and then he faltered and quickly ushered me inside. I felt two feet tall as we crossed a highly polished parquet

floor and passed gigantic Chinese vases with dragon handles, delicate oriental wood carvings, antique clocks, European period furniture on an acre of Persian carpets, walls laden with paintings
including a small one of two children by Constable and another by
Zurbarán (both with certificates of authenticity alongside), a boulder
of onyx on a pedestal, on and on through what might have been a
field day at Sotheby's.

'We will prepare a bed in the gymnasium. It is next to the sauna in
a separate building and will afford you more freedom.' The butler
indicated a seat in the living-room and disappeared behind an
ivory-inlaid purdah to make coffee. He left me sitting there, only
recently emerged from a tent, the sole blemished object in a world of
embroidered silk, crystal, mahogany, ormolu, marble and the cer-
tifiably authentic. He returned shortly afterwards with a tray of
silverware. Through a French window the pack of dogs was visible
prowling around a swimming pool.

'The Señora has a lot of dogs,' I commented, stating the obvious as
a conciliatory gesture and wondering how to touch on the subject of
cooking them.

'She likes all types of dogs,' the butler replied with apparent
disapproval. 'We've between eighteen and twenty-five at the moment. I don't count them myself. They keep on having puppies and
now a lady is employed specifically to cook for them. Don't worry,
none of them will harm you.'

Seeing Santiago by Cadillac was not the best way (the old problem
of nicotine windows), but the chauffeur had kindly offered to show
me the city. It was obviously not the first time he had shown visitors
around this city, '2,000 feet high, founded in 1541, inhabited by 3.5
million people', and he knew when to stop and point out evidence of
the fires, floods and earthquakes that had plagued its history. I
scribbled these things down in a notebook alongside a reminder to
buy a new pair of socks, and added my impression that apart from
the plentiful parks and flower-beds, Santiago was undistinguished
beyond being a modern orderly city. It was only when we left the car
and took the funicular railway up the wooded San Cristóbal Hill
dominating the flat capital that I appreciated its imposing background of snowy Andean sentinels.

Later we drove down a main street. 'Look!' I cried, 'Bolivar!'

'No, Señor. That is a statue of our liberator and leader, 1818,
Bernardo O'Higgins.'

After this I began to look for more memorials to this half-Irish, half-Chileno scourge of the Spanish. And yet there was no currency O'Higgins or mountain, Pico O'Higgins. Admittedly we were driving along Avenida Bernardo O'Higgins but Chile had shown sensible restraint in the O'Higginsification of the country. My curiosity turned to Señora Helena and during the journey home the chauffeur told me what he knew, although his knowledge of her past was sketchy.

He said she was in her late seventies but still energetic and charming. She was generous, jolly and at times slightly absent-minded, a trait that had caused her friends concern when she took up flying. Either through marriage or blood (he was unsure), she was related to a Welsh doctor who had landed at the northern port of Iquique in the 1820s and set up a practice there. His patients had mainly been miners from the heights and as their respect for him grew, many entrusted their money to him for safekeeping. This led to the founding of Banco Edwards and eventually a move to Santiago, and fortune. His grandson had become the richest man in South America. The family's income was still derived from banking and an interest in the leading newspaper, *El Mercurio*. The house where I was staying was evidently the small one, a retreat for when the social life became too hectic at the main residence.

From then on Santiago represented the lap of luxury; the days were spent making forays into the city, relaxing in my swimming pool and sauna and being served the best in cuisine by a solemn silver-service butler. The contrast to my usual lifestyle was so acute, and amenable to it, that it was hard to return to the future reality of rice-pudding and the need for a ship to New Zealand, but five days after my arrival, I, scooping-the-fly-out-of-his-Salvation-Army-mug Alastair, wore my new socks and freshly laundered kilt to the port of Valparaíso. I never met the kind Señora whose servants and twenty-five dogs had given me a new insight into this sub-continent.

The days when tramping on ships was easy have long since passed. It is still possible if you are in an isolated port and meet the owner of the ship or are able to chat up an influential member of the crew, but otherwise the chances of obtaining a working passage are slim. Ships flying their own national flag are generally bound by union regulations to employ only their own nationals who are accredited seamen. A New Zealand ship which finds itself a man

Cups of kindness were abundant in Mexico, except for those in
kilts

100,000 costumes frolic through the streets of Port of Spain during the Trinidad Carnival

The Bard knows best – a temperance sign in Trinidad

Open Class on the Quito–Guayaquil line, rolling down the Ecuadorian Andes at the maximum gradient of 5.5 per cent

Indians at Zumbahua Market, the day after I encountered their hostile neighbours

The tail of the Andes at Paine National Park, Chile; a favourite spot for the condors

The genius of the Inca mason: stones weighing up to 200 tons fit together perfectly at Sacsyhuamán fortress, near Cuzco

short for the return journey from Chile will fly a New Zealand sailor
out to join the crew rather than employ an eager Scotsman. The best
hopes lie with those ships flying flags of convenience, registered for
financial reasons in (most commonly) Greece, Cyprus, Liberia,
Panama or Singapore, for they are theoretically free to employ
anyone at their own discretion. In practice, however, many of them
have binding contracts to use the cheap labour of such countries as
China and the Philippines and they too will fly out accredited seamen
in preference to employing casual hands.

The guard at the entrance to the docks refused to let me enter
without a special permit which, he said, was obtainable from the
police. The police denied this. Permits, they said, came from
shipping agents. The nearest shipping agent shook his head. He
could only issue a permit to visit a ship which he represented and
none of his ships was in port at present. But he gave me the formula:
discover the name of a ship currently in Valparaíso, find the oper-
ator's agent (there were dozens in the city), obtain a permit, take it to
the police station to be stamped, and then you would be free to board
the ship. I returned to the dock, peered round the guardhouse and
saw the name *Union Sunrise* on a tall bow. The guard consulted a list
which gave the agent's name and this enabled me to set off and
complete the obligatory mile of bureaucracy. The crew of the *Union
Sunrise* were Chinese and spoke no English but eventually they made
me understand that the captain was away and would be back in three
hours. My permit, of course, was valid for one hour.

I repeated this soul-destroying procedure twice for two other
ships, and two immediate refusals, and became thoroughly de-
moralised. Chile's marine reputation lay in tatters. Then the dock-
guard called me over. He told me to visit the ships freely. He would
not ask for any more permits. He winked. His grandfather had come
from Scotland. 'From Birmingham,' he added proudly.

The rest of the afternoon consisted of more refusals and an almost
incessant chorus of dockworkers' catcalls and wolfwhistles at my
kilt. I felt bleak. The alternative was to fly to New Zealand and if it
came to that, I would undertake the long haul back up to Ecuador
where I knew a travel agent who could offer me the cheapest fare.
But there was still the *Union Sunrise* to try again. The guard had told
me its destination. The *Union Sunrise* was bound for Fiji and
Auckland.

A little Chinese sailor led me to the captain's cabin. His legs seemed to bend at a point somewhere between his knees and ankles but it was impossible to judge through his baggy trousers. We passed other members of the crew who appeared as frail dwarfs busily painting and polishing lest idleness should make them shrink still further into the enormity of their surrounds. The ship was one of the largest I had seen, and the captain was even smaller than the diminutive sailor. I had no idea how he communicated with any of the ports as it was only after talking for a considerable time in Spanish, and then English, that I realised he was letting me speak freely because he barely understood either.

'Embolsible,' he said finally, and gave a broad toothy grin.

I tried again and this time he began to nod.

'Yo-go toe hen-gin,' he said.

'To the engine?' He nodded. My mind grappled with the possibilities. He didn't expect me to know what to do with a spanner, did he? Then I didn't care. 'You mean I can come?'

'Embolsible. Yo-go toe shee-ping hen-gin.' Slowly it dawned on me that he was sending me back to the agent. I apologised for having troubled him. He gave a slight bow.

'Velly solly,' he called after me, and I thought again how far away New Zealand was and what a long dusty road it would be to Ecuador.

'Arica 2,050 km,' stated the sign on the outskirts of Santiago, and that was only to the top end of Chile. The kilt, however, worked a treat and I hitched the distance in three days. The vegetation gradually became thinner and browner during this journey until all other colours had been bleached out leaving nothing but sepia tones. The sand, gravel and rocks of this southern desert lying some 2,500 miles from the Equator would extend almost unbroken to Ecuador's border, changing only their proportions, nationalities and collective names. At one point the road climbed continuously for ten miles and overlooked a misplaced valley whose level floor was filled from side to side with irrigated fields. Barley, vines and what cows might have recognised as alfafa formed a strip of concentrated green, touched but not infringed by the bald slopes of sand and stone which rose up on all sides from its sharply defined edges. After this came 600 miles of the Atacama Desert containing areas where rain has never been known to fall, and rich deposits of copper and nitrates. Chile had won this region in war, depriving Bolivia of land and allied Peru of ironclads. In the evenings the featureless desert took on character, the low angle of sunlight accentuating the creases, folds and humps of smooth sand dunes and exaggerating the roughness of littered stones. The desert assumed the texture of velvet speckled with crumbs, and distance and scale became confused. I wanted to run my hands over the vista, brush off the crumbs and pull out the creases in this crumpled land.

One night I slept in a desert guest-house and awoke at first light to the sound of birds singing. It came as a surprise for the desert had been silent, completely silent, the evening before. At breakfast I asked the hotelier if the birds were wild.

'No,' she said, 'they are my canaries in a cage. We don't get birds like that here – no birds that sing. We have no seasons, so no migrating birds come either. Singing birds don't like deserts.'

The canaries sang on and for the first time I listened to how beautifully they could sing. They sang with such energy, but their expression was sad and haunting. They sang for the love of singing but not for the love of living, and not for the love of cages or deserts. They were generous. Edith Piafs of the desert, I thought.

That evening I crossed into Peru with a busload of Peruvian women and children who were returning home. Shortly before the border the women unwrapped parcels and gave their children skateboards, wa-wa siren police cars and other fancy toys. It was mystifying as these women were poor and twelve days still remained until Christmas. We all had to disembark at the customs office and there were fearsome arguments and tears as Peruvian officials confiscated some of the toys. It annoyed me to see these officials effectively robbing such deprived families, doubtless to line their own pockets, and I asked one why they were doing this. He laughed at how naïve I was. These women were smugglers, he said. They were running toys.

'It is very expensive to buy these toys in Peru and few shops sell them. Each adult is allowed one new toy but these women try to bring in more by pretending the toys are used and belong to their children. They will sell the toys at a good profit.'

The women got back onto the bus grumbling. A small boy had managed to retain his police car and was wa-waing merrily along the aisle. His toy-running mama ripped the car from his hands and carefully returned it to the original wrappings. Christmas had come and gone for this wee boy, and he cried for an hour. It wouldn't be much of a better one for his mama.

The deserts and semi-deserts continued. I had changed out of my kilt before the border. Like the modern Aztecs, today's Incas didn't exactly go a bundle on kilts. It was truck transport again. The lifts slowed, the dust increased. One day I looked out of the back of a truck and stared down a hillside which was a tangle of hairpin bends. I wondered how many hundreds of thousands of bends I had passed around in the last three years, and marvelled at Peru's apparent ability to represent them in a single view. That lift ended in the middle of the night at a police checkpoint. A group of young policemen invited me to rest in their office and said they would find a truck to take me on early the next morning. I awoke to the music of pan-pipes. Mosquitoes hovered and whined above my face, and strangers were arguing in another room. I couldn't think where I was but it didn't bother me, lying on a dirty floor in what was recognisably a police station. Suddenly it felt as if I had been travelling all my life. I found myself unexpectedly in this strange setting, and it felt natural. A comfortable room with silver service or a dirty police station floor; both seemed perfectly acceptable. I loved the variety and adventure of this lifestyle, though I disliked the dirt. Unfortunately dirt and adventure often went together.

The policemen transferred me to another truck which was heading through the plains of the Nazca Desert with an assortment of locals and goats. We stopped innumerable times to take on and offload passengers. It is one of the most astonishing phenomena of South American life that in some of this planet's most forlorn and inhospitable places, a bus will stop and a woman with a baby slung across her back will get out clutching a hen, an armful of vegetables and a bulging sack, and she will walk off to her home in an empty landscape trailing a string of three children from her skirts.

And we stopped once to fill up with diesel. In a hotel adjacent to the garage was a porcelain lavatory – here in the Nazca Desert – with the brandmark 'Best Niagara'. Earlier we had passed three trees begging by the roadside. They depended on motorists for survival. 'Please give me water,' read their pathetic signs, and a driver stood beside one with his back to us, his legs apart and his hands at his flies. It was a token of the long-awaited flush and a fitting mark of desert humour.

Plant life returned with the proximity of Ecuador's border. Then I added another thousand bends to my name and reached Quito with my thirtieth lift, having hitched the 3,000 miles from Santiago in eight long dusty days.

My travel agent friend sold me a discounted ticket to Sydney, permitting an open stopover in New Zealand, and booked me on the first available flight which was to leave two days after Christmas. This left me one week to contemplate the full significance of the drastic change approaching. Now that New Zealand was an impending reality, South America seemed very precious to me and its rawness even more alluring. I'd miss the vitality of its people, the staggering diversity of its physical features, and its ever-changing moods.

Sleet was falling on the streets as I walked to the airport in my kilt on the day of departure. My appearance provoked chants of 'gringo, gringo' from some children, and laughter from Indians who had put their Charlie Chaplin bowlers into plastic bags to protect the material from the weather, and had then placed them on their heads. I stopped in a market to photograph two girls with cherubic smiles sitting on the ground in their plastic-wrapped bowlers. The next moment vegetables were being thrown at me and an angry woman came running out from her stall.

'Why do you photograph our children in misery?' she demanded. 'Go away,' she shouted, flinging out her arm, 'go back into the city – you'll find plenty pretty churches and nice things to photograph there.'

I tried to explain what had appealed to me about their features but to no effect. We were a world apart. The mother appeared at a trot and together the two women drove the children away from me, a foreigner who had come to terms with their poverty but failed to recognise their additional affliction, the shame of being poor.

I wandered on wondering to what extent I had become a thick-skinned traveller, one who now knew the price of bananas in eighteen Latin American currencies and deluded himself on his understanding of this region because he had glimpsed its sights and lived with its people. One who could bump along happily, or at least in self-satisfied discomfort, with a truckload of those who had to live in a godforsaken wilderness because he knew that within a few weeks he would have paid £270, almost the estimated annual income of a Bolivian, and would be in New Zealand.

When Bulari the Earth-Mother gave birth to the great land mass between the Rio Grande on the North American border and the town of the same name on Tierra del Fuego, her maternal pride was justified. Underneath the mantle of jungle, desert, pasture and snow she saw her Dream Child's loveliness, strength and fertility, and recognised her potential for greatness. She did not realise the ambivalent nature of this daughter, her capriciousness, her ability to be both uplifting and humiliating, ebullient and drowsy and as severe with her hardship as she could be generous with her kindness. Nor that the desire to possess her would excite so much passion.

Latin America is beautiful, haunting, but tinged with sadness. Her image lingers long in the mind, like a daring pass in a bullfight, like the sound of canaries singing in the desert.

12 · New Zealand – the Half-Gallon Half-Acre Pavlova Paradise

'Where did that bugger come from?' asked Miss Denholm, who guessed her own age at about eighty, when a car suddenly overtook us as she drove along at 25 mph in her old Ford Anglia which had no rear-view mirror. She was driving her equally elderly friend Mrs Woodruff from Kaukapakapa, near Auckland, to Waipapakauri in the northern tip of the North Island, and had stopped to give me a lift. I was finding the journey unnerving, constantly alarmed at the novelty of being driven on the left-hand side again although this was not always apparent from Miss Denholm's preference for the centre of the twisty highway. Mrs Woodruff was about to respond to her friend's rhetorical question when she noticed an enormously fat Maori roadmender enjoying a break ('smoke-ho', they called it) on the grass verge. His face peered through a bushy wreath of black curls and he was stripped to the waist, revealing an overhanging belly and swarthy skin which sparkled with sweat.

'Cor blimey!' she exclaimed, 'The sights you see when you don't have a gun.' She turned to me. 'We eat far too much in New Zealand.'

'Yes,' added Miss Denholm (still doing 25 mph and still about eighty). 'Dig our graves with our bloody teeth, we do.'

A short time later, after passing a country lane with a sign solemnly stating 'Cemetery Rd (no exit)', we came to a tractor blocking the road while the driver talked to a man in a field. It appeared to be still Miss Denholm's turn, and she wound down her window.

'Giddoy,' she called out. One of the farmers returned this standard greeting and waved back pleasantly but they continued chatting, apparently unconcerned that they were blocking the principal Kaukapakapa-Waipapakauri road. Miss Denholm waited a few minutes and then lost her temper. 'Get out of the way, you ruptured old gumboot,' she yelled. This had the desired effect and the tractor started up and drove off. My companions seemed well-versed in the

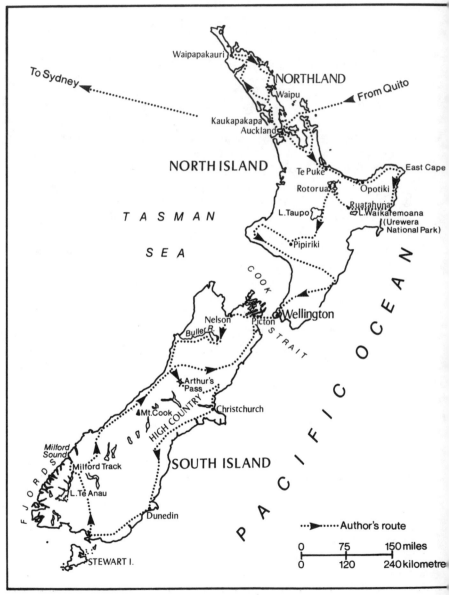

New Zealand

ways of the countryside, but then with only four cities in the country, most people were. I asked where they came from.

'Pukepoto' – this was Mrs Woodruff. 'It's a small place where the neighbours know more about you than you do yourself.' They both tittered. New Zealand's exotic names often made it hard to tell whether the people were swearing or not.

I had arrived in Auckland three days earlier. After flying over both islands my immediate impression was that the land could have been the verdant region of central Chile and this impression persisted, though I later had to add the rolling downs of the English southern counties, the bleak moorland of the Scottish Highlands, and ample pockets of anyone's tropicana. The intensity of green as the plane came in to land was overwhelming and the cows looked very orderly and domesticated in their neatly partitioned fields, but startling in their black and white patterns. (South America had not possessed many Friesians.) The exterior of the plane was sprayed with disinfectant before we were allowed to leave and the same happened to my tent at customs. This measure was aimed at preventing imported diseases from infecting the country's crops, Friesians and eighty million sheep rather than through any direct concern for its three million people.

I had scarcely walked any distance from the airport when a car stopped. The driver, Peter, a well-fed prop-forward type, middle-aged and digging his grave with a dentist's nightmare of a grin, offered me a lift into the centre of the city ('Yeah, hop in, mite. Oil tike ye there'). We arrived in noy toyme at all. The country's chief port, habitation and former capital (1841–65) took up considerably more room than a sheepless population of 700,000 would suggest. The sea would have surrounded it were it not for six slender land links anchoring it solidly between Northland and the main body of North Island. Yet the sea still claimed most of the inhabitants; more than one hundred beaches were to be found within an hour's drive of the city, and Peter was one of 60,000 Aucklanders who owned a boat. Auckland seeped determinedly across the land, diffusing over and around the bulges of extinct volcanic cones which caused many of its streets to tilt. Its one-storey houses and shops doubled in size towards the centre and were dressed in quarried stone, some newly reconditioned, others dark and in need but acceptable on account of being old and arguably quaint. Some of the pavements were only wide enough for two pedestrians side by side, but most were more accommodating and were covered along their entire length by a verandah roof which jutted out from the building and was supported by a row of poles. Its underside was festooned with slim name plates identifying the wares of bakers, newsagents, ironmongers, haberdasheries and small supermarkets. Delivered milk stood in pint bottles on doorsteps, newspapers were sold on the street in coin-operated honesty boxes, red telephone booths ('Press button A to speak, button B to return your coin') copied those once found in Britain, only the better climate allowed the removal of the lower half of their walls on two sides and, perhaps because this was the opposite end of the world, the sequence of numbers on the dial was reversed. Auckland gave the impression of reluctant busyness, of having nothing against the new but finding the old still functioned and managing quite well on it, and an almost tangible atmosphere of trust.

Peter let me out in a street of modern office blocks and electric buses sparking below the ugly web of street wires – Queen Street. At five p.m. the city closed. I stepped off a Queen Street pavement and nearly got run over by rush-minute traffic because I was looking the wrong way and expecting vehicles to approach from the Latin American direction. Aucklanders (whites, Maoris and Islanders – the world's largest concentration of Polynesians lived here) disappeared and there was little life except outside the odd café or bar, and two policemen helping a male in drag into their car. Whether in this little pantomime Cinderella was being rescued from atrocities or helped home after enjoying them, it was impossible to tell. Nightlife was discreet and modest (or else well hidden), and yet Auckland made anything after five p.m. appear wickedly outrageous.

Within an hour of my arrival and buying a poke of fish 'n chips (homesickness), I had been offered three invitations to stay by families with Scottish connections. I stayed with the New Zealand-born McCorquodales whose loo had a wooden seat and, high up the wall, a cast-iron cistern with a knotted string to activate its Niagaran flush, and whose children said 'Goody gumdrops' in glee and 'Golly' in surprise. That this was the opposite end of the world to my homeland was not obvious. My bathwater drained away in a clockwise eddy whereas it would have turned anti-clockwise had I been in a British bath, but apart from this, the accents and the sight of the odd businessman going about the city in shorts, there was little to indicate that this was a foreign land. I looked into the faces of the people and saw the faces of family and friends. New Zealand's easy-going nature and home-from-homeliness won an instant admirer.

From Auckland the road rose and fell through the warped greenery. Our 1968 Ford Anglia straddled the centreline of the trunk road but traffic was thin and respectful towards Miss Denholm's disregard for convention; we passed over single-track bridges and through the occasional copse of wild bush where ferns sat atop black trunks, and cabbage trees looked as if their branches had been decorated with grass pompoms. Miss Denholm and Mrs Woodruff were discussing, in full-blooded language, the result of a rugby match which had been announced on the radio news; Te Hasuku Warriors 9, Pukehou Pukekos 12. I felt completely out of the conversation, could no longer tell when Miss Denholm was swearing (she never said 'Golly!'), and commented once on the large number of sheep.

'We must show our friend Waipu,' Mrs Woodruff suddenly exclaimed, and they kindly made a lengthy detour.

Waipu was a nearby town with a fine old set of bagpipes and a portrait of the austere Rev. Norman McLeod whose piercing eyes sent a shiver down my kilt. His and many other portraits were the meagre collection of possessions the early Scottish pioneers of this area had left behind and they were kept in a building called the House of Memories. McLeod (1780–1866), his legend related, was one of many Scots who left their homeland in the early nineteenth century, a staunch Calvinist and a gifted speaker who led his followers to righteousness with a sway of fear. He once insisted that a boy's ear be cut off as a punishment for some small misdemeanour. He was already seventy years old when he brought his community to New Zealand after fruitless attempts at settlement in Nova Scotia and Australia. On Christmas Day 1862 he preached a sermon out at sea and so entranced his listeners that the oarsmen forgot about the waves, the boat capsized and half the congregation drowned. When McLeod eventually died his pulpit was taken to pieces and distributed among his followers, for it was considered that no replacement minister would be found who was worthy of using it.

It took me one week to complete a circle in Northland and return to Auckland. Hitch-hiking proved to be as effective as owning my own car and it was necessary politely to refuse many generous offers of hospitality simply in order to cover any distance. The miles were embellished by the commentaries of drivers who were knowledgeable to an uncommon degree on local matters. They supplied histories and the names of birds, trees and flowers, and most were able to glance at a mob of sheep from astonishing distances and point out which were rams, wethers, fat lambs or two-tooth hoggets, and which were Merinos, Romneys, Perendales, Corriedales, Coopworths, Border Leicesters, Cheviots, or mixed. These performances overawed me.

It was midsummer and the climate was ideal for camping. The days were hot and soporific and smelt of pollen and sheep-processed grass. My plan was to spend three months on a figure-of-eight route around the two islands, centring on the ferry which connected them at Wellington, and touching Dunedin, the 'Edinburgh of the South', and undertaking the country's most celebrated walk along the Milford Track at its lowest point. Even after only a week I had become quite conceited about my command of New Zealand names and so it was a particular joy to travel east from Auckland and find stretches of coastal road studded with the pohutukawa tree. It only blooms for the few weeks around Christmas, hence its other name (rather dull, I thought), the 'Christmas tree', when it erupts into clusters of fiery red petals.

At Te Puke (easy) a policeman stopped and proudly took me on an extensive tour of the area. There didn't appear to be any criminals here, just thirty-seven millionaires within two miles of the town's post office and land valued at NZ\$ 60,000 (£25,000) per acre. Te Puke was largely responsible for a greengrocer phenomenon, the kiwi fruit's meteoric rise in popularity. These millionaires had once been dairy farmers and soft fruit orchardists who then took a gamble with a fruit that resembles an unshaven potato on the outside and is dazzling lime-green on the inside. It was a bold step because they had to screen their fields from wind, build trestles for the vines to climb, overcome the problem of cross-polination as male flowers often appeared at a different time from the females, and wait five years for new vines to bear fruit.

'Used to be called the Chinese gooseberry, and no one wanted it. Sounded like a cross between the 'Yellow Peril' and a sour hairy fruit. Then they changed the name to Kiwi fruit, did some clever marketing, and . . . thirty-seven millionaires . . .'

When the Chinese gooseberry followed the rush of oriental gold prospectors and reached New Zealand in 1906 it was seen as another threatening inroad being made by the Yellow Peril. The antipodean colonies were painfully aware of their isolation from Britain at this time but now it was proving little loss, and their proximity to Asia was the net gain. No one liked Chinese gooseberries but everyone, including the Chinese and Japanese, liked Kiwi fruit. The Yellow Peril had become Yellow Profit.

This was *my* country! Roads wiggling around hill and along coastline, past sand, crag, bush, daintily painted little village and hayfeverish field. Mine, and Romney's, Perendale's and Coopworth's – already old acquaintances but still just sheep in sheep's clothing to me. I was nearing the East Cape region where the majority of the Maori population now lives, and a teacher, Merle Tupper, with fair skin and luxurious Polynesian black hair, was giving me a lift through Opotiki. She pointed out St Stephen the Martyr's Church which still holds services in the town, and told me its grizzly history as an illustration of the early pakeha (white man) and Maori conflicts.

The church was built in 1859 by a German Lutheran minister, the Rev. Volkner, at a time when activist movements were springing up as a result of the missionaries' teachings. One of these, Hauhauism, was based on the Old Testament and paralleled the Maoris' plight under the pakeha with that of the Israelites under the Egyptians. Volkner had fled from an approaching Hauhau force but returned to his church too soon and was immediately seized by a fanatical Hauhau prophet called Kereopa. The next day Kereopa preached to his followers in the church, inciting them to hysteria and finally demanding Volkner's death. The missionary was brought before them and allowed to pray. He shook hands with his executioners and was then hanged from a tree. Maoris believed that knowledge and certain magical powers could be procured by drinking an enemy's blood and eating parts of his body. Kereopa gouged out Volkner's eyes and ate them. He then cut off Volkner's head and took it to the pulpit, resting it on the edge while he convinced the frenzied mob that by sipping the missionary's congealing blood which was passed around in the Communion chalice, they would be able to speak English and perform miracles.

Such gruesome accounts were not one-sided and the Maoris also suffered severely at the hands of the pakeha. It was in this atmosphere of distrust, resentment and discrimination that New Zealand's two populations passed through their infancy of coexistence. (Kereopa was eventually brought to trial and hanged.)

'I was born in a Maori community in East Cape,' Merle continued. 'During my schooldays forty years ago pakeha children were called "white maggots" by the Maoris. Now it is rare to find a rift between coloured and white children.' And yet the minority Maori population still feel victims of prejudice, she said, despite officially receiving full rights and citizen status. Merle could speak the Maori language, which is slowly disappearing, and understood something of their character. Maoris love games but are not motivated towards solo sport – there are great Maori rugby teams but no great Maori athletes. Her Maori pupils were much more disciplined than whites because of their stronger family bonds and were intelligent but not academically industrious. School certificates provided scant incentive for those who were convinced they would not help them get jobs later, partly because of the high level of unemployment in the whole country but mainly on account of their colour.

To a large extent Merle felt this attitude was justified, as widespread currents of ill-feeling against the Maoris are periodically displayed by the modern pakeha. The issue of land rights causes passionate debate, but whatever the assertions concerning the Maoris' deprivation of land, the boundaries and details of the land in question are usually too vague to satisfy legal definition. There is no doubt that the Waitangi Treaty, guaranteeing Maoris 'the full, exclusive, and undisturbed possession of their Lands and Estates, Forests, Fisheries and other properties which they may collectively or individually possess', was an expedient promise to encourage the 512 chiefs to recognise British sovereignty that day in 1840, and then it was conveniently ignored.

Some pakehas consider the 'equality laws' have overcompensated and it is now the whites who suffer discrimination – anyone proving one-eighth Maori blood is entitled to cheap loans, housing assistance and other perks not freely given to pakehas. 'And yet no other indigenous people have integrated and now coexist with western colonists as successfully as the Maoris,' Merle concluded.

'Yeah, my grandfather used to eat pakehas,' said Kim, tearing at a sandwich, beef, I hoped. He was a muscular Maori sheepshearer chatting to me over a fence during a pause in work. 'But he gave it up when the pakeha started washing. Lifebuoy ruins the flavour.'

The shearing shed stood beside an old community meeting house, a single-roomed wooden building with eaves and pillars covered in a frenzy of carved figures, bloated, foetus-like, seemingly garrotted and staring through silver-green abalone eyes. Kim was one of a gang of contract shearers who worked their way around the country. He said it took five years to become a competent shearer and the whole secret was in learning how to handle the sheep quickly and to grip it in the most efficient manner. They were paid $57 (£26) per hundred sheep (more for bigger rams) and a good man could get through between 250 and 300 in one day.

'These Cheviots here, are they in good condition?' I asked.

'They're Corriedales,' he replied. He studied them for a moment before returning to work. 'Yes, these are good ones. Thick fleece, big, fat, well-grown and long legs.'

It looked a back-breaking task. Big fat long-legged sheep are reluctant to give up their thick fleeces. Each shearer grabs a sheep from the pen, slides it on its back to his stand and holds it in a reclined begging position with his knees, leaving both hands free. The hand holding the power-driven shears sweeps down the inside of a rear leg while the free hand runs over the wool an inch in front of the murderous blades to gauge the undulations in the animal's body. After that the sheep appears to be undressing, and the shearer merely helping it to slip out of its coat. His hands move automatically, swinging suddenly from body to head and barely allowing the vibrating scalpels to lose contact with the wool as they plunge over the forehead, flicking an ear out of the way, nimbly nudging the sheep over onto its other flank, its head pressed between his legs, ending with short sweeps to leave the fleece lying on the floor and the sheep, bald to the eyelashes, bolting down a ramp to the pens. The ideal finish is an even cut as close to the skin as possible, and yet the proportion of sheep suffering wounds is insignificant.

Kim had worked in Australia for several years but he disliked their way of life. He told me that New Zealanders shear with a wide comb because it is faster and more efficient, but the wide comb is controversial in Australia. The owners of sheep stations want it to become standard but trade unions insist on a narrow comb being used as it is slower and effectively lengthens the working season for its members. 'Things are different out there. The merinos in the outback are the worst, so thin it's like trying to shear moving pieces of roofing iron. And the station owners are crazy – like all their sheep to be left bleeding. If the sheep's not covered in blood, they think you've left half the wool on.'

I turned inland towards Lake Waikaremoana and the Urewera National Park, comprising the largest remaining area of native bush in the country. Hill farms gave way to a valley of weeping willows and then to dense interwoven branches of rainforest padded with moss and veiled with cobwebs. The Tuhoe people who once lived in this dank forest led the most spartan and primitive existence as a result of the area's isolation, poor fishing and scarcity of flax for clothing. They were known as the 'children of the mist', and it was easy to imagine them still creeping through the forest's permanent shadows. Other things were also creeping through the shadows.

A trail led me uphill at a comfortable angle, occasionally forcing me to duck under branches and climb over tree roots. I stopped to rest by a stream and was thinking once more how practical a kilt was for walking, allowing freedom of movement and avoiding the chafing misery of trousers in wet vegetation, when I noticed a black thing like a staple on a fence post attached to my leg. It had a trumpet-shaped sucker at each end and was advancing along my skin by releasing one end, looping it over the other which was still gripping and extending its wormy body for two horrible inches. At this point it swung the trumpet from side to side as if looking for something, and then turned it down to fasten onto a new bit of skin. The other end immediately repeated the manoeuvre, and I felt a surge of revulsion on experiencing my first leech. I flicked the loathesome thing away – luckily it hadn't found a bit of me it liked. It spun through the air, landed a couple of yards away and instantly came cartwheeling back towards me. What an incredibly sensitive system they must have for locating a host! This one would have to find another, and I left at once.

After several hours I came to a smaller lake and found a stone shelter to pass the night, hoping my cartwheeling pursuer would not be able to make up the distance before dawn. In front of me lay an expanse of dark water whose banks were a tangled mesh of tree roots and limbs, growing more tangled and grasping in the fading light. They began to look uncannily like leeches. Bell birds called and were mimicked by tuis, also called 'parson birds' on account of white tufts worn at the neck of their otherwise black plumage. I took out a candle and a guidebook, and read about the extraordinary life of Rua Kenana.

He was born in 1867 and lived in the Urewera forest at Maungapohatu, later moving a short distance to the old Tuhoe village of Ruatahuna. Having proclaimed himself to be a modern-day saviour and the younger brother of Jesus Christ, in 1905 he founded his Te Wairau Tapu religion to regenerate the Maori cause. He promised seven wives and everlasting life to his followers and attracted considerable support which reached a peak around 1910. In this year he announced he would demonstrate his miraculous powers by emulating Christ's feat of walking on water. On the appointed day a huge crowd assembled to watch as Rua stood by the water's edge on a rocky peninsula at Whakatane Heads. A profound silence fell over the onlookers as he prepared to take his first step. At the last moment he withdrew his foot. He turned and addressed his audience, asking if their faith in him was so strong that they truly believed he could do it. The crowd shouted enthusiastically, whereupon Rua announced that their obvious conviction made a demonstration pointless and they were all to return to their homes.

The pakeha authorities were anxious to discredit Rua, fearful of his influence over the people. In 1916 the police were sent to Ruatahuna to arrest him for contravening the local liquor laws. Some of his followers resisted the police and Rua's son was killed in the resulting shooting. After spending a year in prison he returned to the settlement where he led a quiet life and continued his teaching. His name is revered by devout followers to this day.

When I visited the hamlet of Ruatahuna the next morning I was invited into the house of an eighty-year-old Maori called Rongo. He had been present that day when the police came to arrest Rua. Maoris were forbidden by law to drink alcohol in those days but Rua and his followers did so secretly. Rongo defended him as being a good man who watched passively when the police arrived. Rua had said beforehand that if they killed him then this would show he had been no more than the son of man, but if he survived then this would prove he was the Son of God. Rongo heard a shot and saw Rua had been hit in the forehead with such force that he was thrown over backwards against a grassy bank. The next moment he stood up and there was only a scratch of blood above one eye – that was when Rongo became convinced Rua was a prophet. No leader ever replaced him after 1937 and his famous roundhouse had collapsed

Rongo still taught a small group of followers each Saturday on the Sabbath. ('Sunday is not the Sabbath. The Bible and – look – even our calendars always give Sunday as the first day of the week.') He lived in a simple house with television, washing machine and framed hand-coloured photographs of his family around the walls.

My route went down the centre of the island and passed the sulphur-smelling mudpots around Lake Taupo, a stance of black and red volcanoes and the green folds of farmland which continued to the lower end at Wellington. On the way I learnt to recognise Lincolns (intensely scruffy, all noodles and ringlets, obscured eyes), but this breed was so uncommon that the knowledge neither stopped nor started conversations. I reached the capital with a young couple whose old Morris had been decorated with spraycan flowers and graffiti. Jim's door read, 'Stop French nuclear tests in our backyard', while Gill's glowed with 'Inactive today, radioactive tomorrow'.

Jim was a bearded self-employed carpenter and Gill was a student of ecology, Lincoln in appearance but in an attractive way. They were proud New Zealanders; they resented the planting of quick-yield *radiata* pine instead of slow-growing native species, had pro-tested against the recent South African Springbok tour which had divided the nation (Miss Denholm would have argued vehemently; sport was SPORT to her and politics had no place between rugby goalposts, unless it helped to keep the ball moving), and they ate well, thought broadly, drank unwisely, and were the sort of people I knew I'd look back on from the other side of the globe with a feeling of reassurance.

We drove through Wellington, one-fifth the size of Auckland and proportionately slower, and went to the top of Mount Victoria. The view showed Wellington falling steeply down to a circular bay, curling round one side and jutting out into it on an indented peninsula. The more level, central areas were modern and gave rise to Wellington's title as the 'Glass City', but this observation seemed blinkered from our standpoint as the overriding impression was of coloured house roofs and brightly painted wooden walls forming a great expanse of confetti suburbs. The whole was hemmed in uncomfortably by beaches and many baylets, and interrupted by the grey scars of the airport and the untainted greens of its hills, parks and sports grounds. Wellington fears earth tremors and so its high rises have been built low; the main dangers now appear that the Glass City may shatter and the Confetti City may have a few of its fringe components shuffled off the inclined streets and into the bay. It is a view worthy of a capital.

Behind us lay Cook Strait, the gap in the country's mountain ridge responsible for the characteristic weather report that Radio Windy announces for Wellington each day. The Strait is notorious as an ill-tempered stretch of water, capable of whipping up a heavy sea without warning. It is at its most treacherous when an outgoing tide is in conflict with Wellington's predominant wind, the southerly, whose gales arrive without interruption from Antarctica. It is scarcely less dangerous under northerlies which are prone to rush down the mountains and lash the sea with fierce squalls known as *williwaws* – and it was in such a storm from the north that tragedy struck the ferry *Wahine* in 1968. Weather forecasters had underestimated the speed of a storm moving south from Auckland as the *Wahine* was travelling north from Christchurch to Wellington. The two met in Cook Strait. The ferry was almost safe when it hit rocks at the entrance to the harbour and, in full view of horrified onlookers watching from their homes and the television audiences across the nation, it sank with the loss of fifty-one lives.

Fifteen miles away across the Strait was the outline of South Island.

'What's it like over there?' I asked.

'It's wilder. It has the Southern Alps, lakes galore, some glaciers and more grassland. Ideal for walking, making electricity and keeping lots of sheep,' Gill summarised. Jim nodded. 'It's certainly different. Mostly Corriedales and Merinos.'

This was the pivot-point of my tour. The ferry from Wellington took a little over three hours to reach Picton and it was during the crossing that I met Beryl Gollner.

She was a small thin woman whose sprightly manner was still irrepressible despite close to eight decades of exercise. Her silver-grey hair was energetically frizzy and her face conveyed kindness when she relaxed the intensity of interest that sharpened her features and allowed coffee and food to go untouched while she conversed. She had been married to a Scots Guardsman and had lived in Britain for many years, which was why she was attracted by my kilt. I was intrigued by her dynamic personality and her immediate confidence ('Will you have some lunch with me? . . . You haven't eaten? . . .

Good! Then you will, won't you?'). Her features sharpened and her coffee went cold while Beryl recalled bygone days. Then she showed me an account she had written of her childhood in New Zealand before the First World War – and she has kindly allowed me to retell the story and quote her own words.

I am a New Zealander, but only just. I was born in a nursing home in Remuera in 1903, three months after my parents arrived from England. Their eldest child had died of peritonitis and my father had vented his anguish on my mother; staying out with other women, coming home drunk at night and being quite inconsolable. His parents thought he and mother would be happier in New Zealand where there would be fewer temptations, so they leased a farm and hired a farm manager and a housekeeper, and my parents sailed out with their remaining child, my sister Doris.

The idea that there would be less temptation in New Zealand was wrong. My mother felt she couldn't endure father's unfaithfulness any longer. She divorced him and remarried – a tall handsome Englishman. My new father worked in a timbermill and we moved to many towns. At Te Whetu my sister and I mixed with rough children and learnt bad songs and rude words from them. We never repeated them in front of our parents but for some strange reason we longed to say and sing them, so we climbed into the hills where no one could possibly hear us and shouted these rude things. We came down feeling really daring and wicked, but not the sort of wickedness we thought God would mind or for which we had to be punished, or forgiven. I think to us, God must have been a very broad-minded and tolerant being. After such sessions we felt we were more like other children but daren't let our parents know we were. We had to be more than good, we were prigs in fact. It has taken me half a lifetime to get over the indoctrination I had.

Then we moved to Pipiriki. We travelled through the bush on two huge timber wagons, each pulled by six big horses. My sister and I rode on one sitting on top of the logs, holding on to our dog. Mother and father followed on the other with mother's little piano which she took everywhere. She was a good pianist and it gave everybody such joy to hear her play. We eventually arrived on the shores of the Wanganui River. It really looked like nowhere but it seemed that this was our destination, for the time being anyway.

We seemed to do that sort of thing all the time. We'd arrive at a place that looked like a real place to live, but we didn't stay there, and when we came to a place that didn't look like a place to live, we lived there. At Pipiriki we got to know a rich family named Hunter. Mother always said that these were the sort of people we should know, that New Zealand was only temporary and not a real place. One day we would all go to England and live properly, so she said. What was *properly*, I wondered? I was quite happy.

The Maoris living in a pa near Beryl's family at this time kept cows but just let them run wild. They never bothered to milk them, preferring to buy condensed milk from the store instead. Beryl and her sister often went fishing or picking cherries with Maori boys, sometimes for the whole day. The Maoris were totally trustworthy and never caused any problems. Beryl's parents made many friends among them and one was Chief Te Tuhi, the last of the Master Carvers of the Tuhoe tribe.

What a wonderful life it was then. Things were for our using. Food was not poisoned with sprays. Fish was safe to eat and we took what we wanted. Our crayfish were not swept away and exported, they were a plentiful source of food, and very cheap. Raspberries, blackberries and peaches grew in abundance in the wild places. The Missionaries had planted them years ago. It was a lovely place and so silent, with a silence that seemed to come from all directions. And there was bush, yes, real bush; everywhere. At seven years of age I cried when they cut the trees down, and I'm still crying now at seventy-seven.

Then Beryl recalled living in a room at North Shore, Auckland.

I loved to hear the postman clop-clopping by on his horse in the morning, and we loved going over on the paddlesteamer to Auckland. We used to sit on the platform and watch the great paddles going round and round, and they allowed us to look down into the engine-room to watch the big pistons going up and down. On the docks there were goats eating up all the rubbish.

Beryl's father had tried to enlist at the outbreak of war but he had been refused because he was forty years old. In 1916 he was accepted.

Father insisted that we take one last trip to Rotorua. He loved it so and felt that he would never see it again. We travelled in Mr Grant's little solid-tyre car as far as Waitapu. We stayed the night at an accommodation house there and in the evening we met a very interesting couple, a Maori man and his Pakeha wife, both teachers. We spent the evening chatting to them. In the morning, when they came into the dining room and sat down to breakfast, the proprietor said, 'Maoris don't sit with Pakehas. You can have your breakfast on the verandah.' My sister and I were furious and picked up our plates and followed them. Mother and father did likewise. Such an incident was not uncommon in those days.

Then came a move to Wellington for six months while Beryl's father trained with the 15th NZ Expeditionary Force, and the whole family made plans to leave for England.

As we were going on such a hazardous journey, mother arranged for us to be confirmed. I had never been christened so I was baptised at the same time. The ceremonies were conducted by Bishop Sprott, whom I really admired because one day during a sermon he banged his fist on the pulpit and said that if the government didn't allow religion in the schools 'we would be bringing up a generation of Educated Devils.' I thought it was great for a man of God to get so worked-up and use such language.

When it was getting near the time for the 15th Reinforcement to march through the streets of Wellington and embark for England, I made small lucky black cats out of thick felt with a safety pin on the back, and gave one to every member of father's platoon. People lined the streets and I handed out my mascots as the platoon passed. We crowded the wharf as the men boarded the ship and gathered on deck. They seemed to cover the whole ship. They threw out streamers to us and we held onto one end and the men held onto the other, then after what seemed ages the boat moved slowly out into the harbour with all the men singing – I can't remember what. Many of us were crying, it was such an emotional moment. As the ship sailed away the men rolled out the streamers until they reached the end and then they broke and dropped into the sea. We each rolled up a wet salty streamer and many of the men kept the piece that had been left in their hands.

A week later we all sailed for England on the *SS Tinui*. We arrived on my thirteenth birthday. It was the end of an era of peace and happiness as a family that we were never to know again. So ended my childhood in New Zealand.

Beryl's family survived the war and soon adapted to the change of lifestyle, although they missed New Zealand's warmth and money was short during the depression years. Her parents were back where they felt they belonged and Beryl settled into studying on an art scholarship, later marrying and living in London. Although she had grown deeply fond of Britain she and her, by then, second husband were persuaded to emigrate back to New Zealand in 1956. Now they worked with handicapped children and lived a simple life in a house surrounded by flowers and a menagerie of pets. New Zealand was as Beryl remembered it. 'I had so few material things, but I had all the riches of nature, the sun, the wind – all things that lived and grew were my playthings, the great trees, the rivers, all gave strength to my body and thinking to my mind . . .'

It seemed we had no sooner begun the journey across the Cook Strait than it was over. My last glimpse of Beryl was of her pausing to refasten the large Greenpeace badge that had shaken loose from her jersey, energetically waving goodbye and then turning to carry her love of New Zealand and all that it contained deeper into the crowd awaiting access to the car-deck.

'. . . strength to my body and thinking to my mind . . .' This last, I felt, was the distinctive feather in the kiwi's plumage.

The Cook Strait was placid that day, without southerlies or williwaws, and when the ferry docked at Picton on the South Island, Beryl set off east and I followed the road west through orchards and shrubs laden with berries. The soft fruit season was well under way and tractors on stilts straddled rows of boysenberries (a three-way cross between a raspberry, blackberry and loganberry), their revolving brushes jiggling and tickling the dark juicy fruits until they dropped into catching trays. Also in season were marion-, aurora- and ollalieberries (all bramble hybrids), a host of stonefruit, early pipfruits, a few citrus families such as tangelos (from the marriage of a grapefruit and tangerine) which had found warmer pockets in the land – and still to come were kiwi fruits, feijoas and thornless blackberries. The fruit situation was as complicated as that of sheep.

The orchards formed a fringe along the coastline and refused to follow the road inland to the gorge of the Buller River, yielding to the greater force of pine trees in vast plantations. It had taken time for this area to recover from the *Wahine* storm, as it has become known, when timber worth millions of dollars had been flattened. (Man-made forests are more susceptible to blow-downs than natural ones, and New Zealand has the largest man-made forests in the world.) The road squirmed around landslides and squeezed beneath the bulges of overhanging rock and accompanied the dancing course of the water on a hornpipe to the Tasman Sea. Had I been dropped unawares into this country it would have taken some time to work out which one it was. South Greenland? – only the colours of the houses were not gaudy enough and insufficient boulders were lying around. Chile? – only here there were more tractors than ox-carts and an absence of Spanish and soldiers. (No soldiers! The contrast to a year of daily encounters with them was suddenly striking.) Honduras? Canada? Tierra del Fuego? – the mountain landscape could have fitted any of them. To me, living only in the present, the name of the country was unimportant. It was enough to be in a place I liked, taking the long way round and finding a continually diminishing need for arrival. Destinations were hard to keep in mind because they concerned the future and threatened to interrupt the slow present with a sense of urgency. However, destinations are expected of travellers, and Dunedin and Ayers Rock were the ones that could be extorted from me by those who considered end-points necessary.

A car driven by Sandy Quintin carried me eastwards up and over the Southern Alps. He was a farmer who owned 28,000 sheep (he understood my predicament and didn't elaborate), and an unusual mongrel which lay on the rear window ledge. It was black and friendly and defied simple metaphor; a canine boysenberry, a three-way cross between a Scottie, Pekinese and a spent lavatory brush. We gained height through lightly forested hillsides, heading towards distant peaks of naked rock made sombre by the early morning shadows. After a section of continuous hairpins set in the remnants of a monstrous rockslide, the road levelled and we came to a sign. Sandy read it out aloud. 'Arthur's Pass Summit; 926 metres.' He stumbled over the last word. 'Damn metrification. What the hell's that in pounds per square inch?'

The lavatory brush barked.

The land became more subdued in colour but wilder in nature, turning to tawny moorland stippled with lighter shades of tussock grass, dark bogs and grey-green rocks of schist. The uniformity of the scene was disfigured here and there by triangular patches of scree whose apex ran up the mountains to touch the ragged skyline. This was the northern end of the High Country, MacKenzie Country, named after a wily Highland shepherd who chanced upon this great mountain basin and who, together with one collie, had it well stocked with rustled sheep by the time it was officially discovered in 1855. Some of the largest sheep stations are to be found here and one of these is Erewhon, taking its name from the title of Samuel Butler's novel set in this region, which he loved even though the simple anagram might suggest otherwise.

The Quintin family invited me to stay with them for a few days to watch a mob of sheep being mustered for shearing. The average shepherd owned several working dogs, typically at least one black and white collie, the 'eye dog', and three or four of the larger, more heavily built 'huntaways'. Eye dogs control the direction of a flock, working up front or at the side to turn the leaders. They never bark, but slink stealthily through the grass and divert the sheep solely by means of their ruthless stare. The huntaways will bark on command and usually work from the rear to act as the driving force.

A shepherd on his way to work leaves an endearing and unforgettable impression. Wearing a squashed brim hat, an old shirt flapping in the wind, shorts and stout leather boots bound tightly above the ankles, he sits hunched over the handlebars of a mistreated trail bike. He has been displaced into this huddled position by a wooden fruitbox which is fixed above the back wheel by ample coils of knotted string. Here he carries his ingredients for smoke-ho, a pair of pliers and his eye dog, or as many as three of them. He doesn't drive fast but he bumps along and makes a lot of noise. The eye dogs stand with their front paws on the edge of the box and take an active interest in everything around them, especially the wake of spiralling dust and the pack of huntaways which bound eagerly alongside. Even from this precarious position, they can be seen eyeing distant sheep. They are unperturbed by sudden stops, unswayed by corners and unbounced by potholes. They just like eyeing sheep and feel at one with their shepherd. And like this they weave across the landscape, along rutted footpaths, over humps, down dips, through bushes and up open hillsides.

There are few more imposing sights than to witness the accord and mutual respect displayed by a shepherd and his dog, especially when they are at work.

'COME HERE, FLO, YOU FLAMING BITCH,' Sandy screamed as the far-off Flo went berserk and split the flock. 'BY HELL, I'LL GIVE YOU A HURE OF A HIDING . . .' (I felt Miss Denholm would have been proud of such an outburst.) He cracked a large whip and the report reached Flo who suddenly became tame and repaired the damage. After this the display was faultless. For every mile that we walked the dogs covered two dozen in the course of combing the hillsides. Sandy worked five dogs at the same time, calling out individual instructions and converting them to whistle blasts when they moved out of voice range. Being fit and trilingual were the essential qualifications of a sheepdog.

'I never hit any of my dogs,' he explained in a quiet moment. 'That doesn't do any good. Instead, I know which dogs dislike each other and I can send in any combination to fight a misbehaving dog, and call them off when it has learnt its lesson. You have to treat them like school-kids really. If a teacher hits a boy, it may hurt but he feels a bit of a hero. If his mates gang up and lay into him, the message is learnt more quickly.'

The hill opposite us suddenly turned into a quivering white mass as an avalanche of 4,200 Corriedale ewes came pouring down from the ridge. Two huntaways were barking at the rear and another patrolled either side, channelling the flow towards the eye dog which zigzagged out in front, turning back strays and countering any resistance when the leaders deviated. The valley floor filled with a shallow zone of dust, thousands of individual shapes became vague and blended into a single obedient body being driven to the holding pens by five dogs. Now that Flo was behaving, it made a remarkably imposing sight.

I didn't stay long in the garden city of Christchurch but took a lift south with a red deer farmer. He soon put the sheep economy in perspective.

'I saw the downward trend a few years ago and got out. Now things are real bad. The market for mutton has gone to hell. Sometimes you can't get a dollar for a carcase. Sometimes the value of the animal doesn't even cover the cost of slaughtering it. Instead of getting a pay cheque from the slaughterhouse, now you can get sent a bill. That's why I moved into deer.' He had built ramps up the perimeter fence of his farm to allow wild deer attracted to the captives during the rutting season to enter, and become trapped. Selling the progeny to other farms was the most lucrative source of income but antler velvet also brought a high return, mainly from Korea where it was sold as a food spice and an aphrodisiac. Almost every part of a deer's carcase had a commercial use, including the eyeteeth which were sold as matching pairs to jewellers, the yellowest ones being the most popular. Once the high cost of fencing the land had been overcome, he believed deer farming yielded a profit per acre three to four times greater than that achieved by sheep or cattle in their prime. While I was still contemplating the relative worthlessness of those 4,200 Corriedales, the deer farmer let me out beside a fort made of whitewashed breeze blocks and ringed with flags. He said the God Squad lived there, and he drove off with a mysterious smile. I went to see who made up the God Squad and what they had done to deserve their name.

A car left the fort as I approached and a man who seemed to be ninety per cent beard and ten per cent beret spoke into a walkie-talkie as he drove by. The main door opened as I reached it, and a man with the other end of the walkie-talkie (and just thirty per cent beard) invited me inside. 'The Lord has sent you,' he extolled. I replied that this was possible. Either Him or Idle Curiosity. He led me through a courtyard where the walls were lined with coats of arms and heraldic figures, and through the Needle Door (Matt.19; 24) which seemingly improved the odds on getting into the Kingdom of God. Then past a wall of honour – Wesley, Luther, Joan of Arc (no sign of the Rev. Norman McLeod) – a swimming pool hewn out of rock, a throne, a mock Bedouin camp and a small arsenal of weapons.

'We are a group of non-denominational Christians,' my guide explained, 'and have built this retreat to survive the impending Apocalypse.' Their intentions were peaceful. (The arsenal was for hunting game after the Apocalypse – they were conveniently close to the deer farm.) 'We follow the code of conduct stipulated by the Bible. We cut our hair but not our beards. We do not ordain women or allow them to preach and we baptise by full immersion.' Most members of the group wore a ring with the insignia of a menorah, and dressed normally. They evidently had everyday jobs and came to the fort, Camp David, at weekends or whenever they felt the Apocalypse was nigh. They had been given the name God Squad by the press after police had raided the fort on the suspicion of finding narcotics, and had uncovered the arsenal of weapons instead.

I didn't doubt my guide's faith or his benevolence but I found his 'because the Lord has moved us' replies shallow and evasive. Furthermore, his persistent attempts to enlist me were becoming oppressive. Somehow we broached the subject of what Jesus looked like and he intimated that he knew. I challenged him to tell me.

'Well, actually, Lord Jesus Christ looks exactly like you.'

This revelation startled me because it was not the first time I had been likened to the Saviour. The other occasion had been in Peru. I was climbing out of a bus in Arequipa as a woman approached to board. She looked up at me and suddenly stopped, let out a gasp and stumbled several paces backwards. 'Are you all right?' I asked. 'Aaaah,' she uttered weakly, and was too choked to speak for a moment. She recovered quickly, and then whispered, 'If only your hair were longer . . . you'd have the face of Christ.' This puzzled me and for the rest of the day I went about my affairs hesitantly, trying not to look at anything for too long in case it turned out to be a sign. Some days later I was visiting a church noted for its paintings when it struck me that Latin American religious art invariably depicted Jesus as a fairly typical gringo: white skin, ruddy cheeks, ungroomed beard and long curly hair. This explanation had brought some peace of mind.

This second likening to Christ was more disturbing. I decided to flee Camp David. I refused the rest of the tour, a meal and the chance of Camp David's salvation. He told me not to delay, the Apocalypse was coming. I bolted through the Needle Door, and felt relieved to rejoin the deer and the fallible

On a rainy day 200 miles to the south, a steep hill led me down to the sea, passing through a hollow which was filled with Dunedin. The name is a simplification of the Gaelic word for Edinburgh, Duneidion, and the city was designed to recall as much of the Scottish capital as possible: Princes, George and Queen Streets, suburbs of Corstorphine and Musselburgh, a monument styled as a Gothic rocket, a statue of Burns (also suffering from pigeons), and a flow of water called the Leith. The New Edinburgh Settlement began in 1847 following a schism in the Scottish Presbyterian Church which resulted in the breakaway Free Kirk. The 'Wee Frees' wanted to start their own colony and the burgeoning opportunities in New Zealand proved attractive at a time when twenty-five per cent of fit Scotsmen were out of work. Within two years of the town's founding the Scots were outnumbered by English immigrants, but they remained the dominant force by virtue of their incomprehensible accents, expertise in engineering, and control of the township's sporran strings. Slow to develop at first, Dunedin was consolidated by the 1860s inland gold strikes which caused its population to leap from 12,000 to 60,000 in two years, and was built grandiose from the glint in gold pans. It was the first city outside North America to build a cable tramway, and it contains New Zealand's only castle, distillery and kilt shop.

At first I thought it had even preserved Edinburgh's weather chart, but in this respect it sides with London, both having 167 rainy days in the year against Edinburgh's 189. Seen from two of the better viewpoints (both occupied by a cemetery) its centre is a dark pincushion of towers, spires and chimneys, blunted by slate and tin roofs. Its prospect of the ocean is obstructed by a peninsula of fields and farmland which juts across from right to left and creates a sea loch which was once favoured by sealers and whalers. At the end of this peninsula is the castle and the world's only mainland breeding ground of what I took to be Maori kites, even bigger than the Inca ones, but they were in fact Royal Albatrosses.

A farmer let me sleep in a barn near the castle, a self-conscious building of grey and brown stone. It gave the impression that its architect had been uncertain what castles normally looked like and had gone for a bit of everything to be on the safe side. A little turret at the top was an offshoot of a three-storey tower straddling, a two-storey block which was partially surrounded by a glass-encased wrought-iron verandah. Underneath was a dungeon where poachers and drunk employees were detained at the pleasure of the owner, the Hon. William Larnach. Between the years 1871 and 1886 the castle's construction cost Larnach the modern equivalent of £1,000,000, for both materials and craftsmen were imported from Europe. He was a successful banker and a popular politician but less fortunate in his private life. This baronial mansion was built as a loving gesture to his first wife and to house their six children in style. He was subsequently widowed twice and in 1898 he shot himself in a room of Parliament Buildings, supposedly as a result of learning that one of his sons was having an affair with his third wife, a French aristocrat unfitly named Constance.

Larnach Castle was only a short walk away and yet a whole world distant from McFarr's Barn. Ian McFarr had got out of sheep and into pigs, hundreds of them. Anyone who still believes pigs are delightful creatures after travelling second-class with them and attending dinner with them, should share a dormitory with them. When pigs are not sleeping they snort and when they are not snorting, they snore. My night was devoured by noise. I left early the next morning, bleary-eyed, well-washed and yet still with an agricultural rawness where Lifebuoy should have been, and hitched into the city – a model of 'Auld Reekie', only the nickname could have been mine – with a shepherd taking his collie to a vet for precautionary treatment against hydatid. He wore a tartan bonnet, and chatted about Auckland. He had been there once but hadn't liked it. The rivalry between the two cities was traditional. Much of Dunedin's gold wealth had been sent to Auckland.

'They don't even have toyme t'soy giddoy t'ye there,' he complained.

'But they said it to me,' I argued in Auckland's defence.

'Yeah? Guess they can turn it on for swivelheads, cribbers and loopies.'

I had to concede this point and ask for a translation. Swivelheads were evidently normal tourists, loopies were those who came year after year and cribbers were semi-resident, owning a 'crib' in northern terminology, a 'bach' in the southern, and a 'weekend cabin' anywhere else. I was hoping he would roll his *r*s but he didn't and just squashed his *i*s and *a*s like everyone else.

The people hereabouts are said to resent Dunedin being labelled the 'Victorian City' because it has plenty of Edwardian buildings. The Edinburgh parallel is also out of favour as Dunedin is regarded as unique in its own right and not a poor copy of any other city. It is compact, meticulously planned and solid. The university and the Otago Boys School elevate themselves above the surrounds of already fastidious architecture, combining ecclesiastical austerity with masonried clowning, and so does the railway station with its pillars, arches, balustrades and white crusting. Getting educated and getting out must have been civic priorities. Dunedin appears sober and parades excessive rectitude. Dunedin on one of its 167 rainy days looks saturnine, tired and somewhat worn – and yet I had a familiar feeling that behind all its bluestone there was a festival of active minds and the tailings of a three-day ceilidh.

My kilt also had a worn and tired look. Exhausted, in fact. The sporran had chafed a hole in the front flap, pleats had been ripped and repaired with stitches of panic rather than precision, and numerous leather patches that had been sewn over those parts where the kilt was continuously rubbed by the base of my backpack and my camera case were peeling away. It wasn't hard to make friends anywhere in New Zealand and impossible for a Scotsman not to do so in Dunedin. The city's inhabitants are neither prim, severe nor damp. I was soon befriended by the owner of a sewing machine, Mrs Duncan, and received a quick lesson on how to operate it. I bought a square metre of neutral grey material (three weeks waiting on orders for Scott tartan), cut off the inside flap of tartan from my kilt and stitched it over the front flap as one large patch, and then filled the gap inside with a flap of grey.

Time was moving on and I set off west for Fjordland a few days later. My departure from Dunedin made it seem as if once again I was leaving home, leaving Edinburgh in a kilt which, from a distance at least, looked brand-new. Dunedin was certainly unique in its own right and as an imitation of my birthplace it was admirable – lacking only the place where I was born and a brooding castle on a muckle rock.

Fjordland has some of the country's most renowned muckle rocks. This area has been designated a National Park and its boundary can be reached by driving west from Dunedin for half a day. A special permit and a fifteen-mile boat trip are then the obstacles confronting anyone wanting to walk the Milford Track, a thirty-two mile trail in a natural trench through the heart of this spectacular park. The walk is popular and there were no permits left by the time I arrived. This only left the possibility of sneaking in and doing the walk secretly, trying to avoid wardens and legal hikers by walking early in the morning and late evening and resting during the day. I got around the initial boat trip to the start by a lengthy detour via the Dore Pass on a route which had been abandoned to overgrowth and stabbed with the notice 'Alpine experience required for this trail'. Ingenious! It was easier to upgrade its status than to repair it.

Fjordland measures its rainfall in feet and receives twenty-five of them each year. One of them fell on my first day. Matted ferns blocked the way, soaking me and cutting my fingers when I slipped and inadvertently grabbed their cheese-wire stems. By the time I passed above the treeline and moved onto the exposed hillsides my kilt was saturated and heavy – my new kilt looked ancient. I camped in the pass and the next morning was rewarded with a view of what lay ahead. The flanks of 6,000-foot mountains fell away with increasing steepness into a glacial valley until they formed a canyon a quarter of a mile wide and several hundred feet high. The Milford Track ran through the middle as far as an unfortunate hill that had apparently fallen into the canyon at a point on the limit of my vision. My map showed the path climbing around the obstruction and then returning to the valley floor (taking a less direct route than the world's fifth highest waterfall) where it remained until its conclusion at a deep fjord.

The descent to the track took little time but then my pace had to become more cautious. From inside the canyon the rock walls seemed to rise to daunting heights, here and there dripping bridal-veil falls from their crest and allowing only a long banner of sky to be visible. The path ran alongside the Clinton River which bubbled and churned impetuously before calming into sluggish pools stained by the depth of peaty sediment. On the second evening I arrived at the fifteen-mile mark without having encountered any other humans. Here the path began to climb the ridge that blocked its progress like a dam, reaching its highest point (3,785 feet) at the Mackinnon Pass. A cairn marked the spot and was dedicated to Quintin Mackinnon who was the first to squelch his way through this area and marvel at the view of encircling snow-clad peaks and the steep drops back down into the trench. The cairn was erected by the curious alliance of the government, the NZ Gaelic Society and Otago Rugby Football Club, and provided a handy perch for several keas. These are large plump parrots with olive feathers, and are noted for being mischievous thieves and aggressive towards sheep. They don't understand man's obsession with views. They believe he makes this 3,785 foot ascent to feed them cheese and raisins.

I found an emergency hut nearby and went inside as darkness fell. It was deserted except for a backpack, and the sight of it made me feel uneasy. A slender cubicle stood close by the hut, perched on the edge of the panorama. It must have had the best view of any privy in existence. I liked the sign beside it, rotating to expose FREE or IN USE for those occasions when a queue builds up in no man's land. In New Zealand privies are called 'long drops' – an understatement in this case.

I began to prepare a meal by candlelight, expecting the owner of

Feeling at home beside Lake Wanaka, South Island, New Zealand

4,200 Corriedales are driven to the shearing shed by one shepherd and five dogs

The Cairns-Kuranda line: taken from the top of a pylon by a kilted cameraman self-consciously holding wild flowers

(*opposite*) A citizen of Broome, West Australia

Wave Rock, south of Perth, is a wall of granite fifty feet high, eroded and stained by rain run-off

Ayers Rock, the birthplace of the world

the pack to arrive at any moment and listening for the sound of footsteps. The air of expectancy became uncomfortably tense as I waited for a stranger to emerge from the darkness and enter this remote hut. Then there was a noise outside. I sat motionless and strained to catch another sound in case it had been my imagination. It came again, right from the doorstep. I turned to watch the door latch but it didn't move. My gaze idly dropped lower down the door until it came to a knothole about one foot above the ground. My muscles suddenly contracted and froze. *An eye was staring at me through the hole.* My shock turned to terror and held me rigid. The room was quite large and I was sitting at an oblique angle to the door. The eye could have been looking at any part of the room but there was no doubting the piercing intensity with which it had narrowed its vision until it was focused on me. It stared hard out of the darkness with the same desperate menace as the Rio mugger, and I was impaled on its hostility. We continued this unblinking stare for what seemed an eternity while my mind sought out the owner of the backpack and found him as a demented maniac from some house of horrors. Then the eye disappeared, and there was the sound of wings. A damn kea! I went to bed alone on my mountain, blushing like a fool.

Two mornings later I reached the end of the track and had to wait for the National Park boat in order to cross the final stretch of water. It was raining heavily; four drops would have filled a thimble. Streams had become raging torrents and every rock face in the area was streaked with veins of white water or lost under a broad cascade. Other walkers appeared at midday – an assortment of noses prodding through holes in phosphorescent waterproofs. I dressed up like them and the boat took us all to Milford Village. No one asked for my permit. I felt slightly cheated.

I had a plane to catch in three weeks' time; Auckland to Sydney. I began to work my way up the west coast, glimpsing the country's highest peak, Mt Cook (12,349 feet) beyond acres of wild lupins and being surprised to find two large glaciers creeping close to the main road. Then I crossed to North Island again.

I shared one lift with an English hitch-hiker who had newly arrived in New Zealand.

'Look at all them bloomin' sheep!' he commented.

'Yes, Corriedales,' I replied. 'Good ones. Long legs.' It was a spontaneous reaction. I was sincerely trying to belong.

New Zealanders call their homeland the 'half-gallon, half-acre, pavlova paradise'. On average they consume half a gallon of beer each day, own half an acre of land and consider pavlova to be the national dish. I disliked the leeches and grew tired of being bamboozled by sheep, but what irritated me the most about New Zealand was the difficulty of finding anything to criticise.

13 · Gooloogong, Bedgerebong, Mulberrygong, Billabong

The young man looked uncomfortably hot, Ayers Rock red, and disappointed. He was about to land at Botany Bay and was dreaming in the way prospective arrivals have little alternative but to dream, in quotes, statistics and the neatly packaged generalisations gleaned from books or hearsay from others. He turned back the centuries and dreamed of the adventure, not the scurvy and fetid stench, of being one of 160,000 involuntary pioneers, transported half-way round the globe for shoplifting a silk handkerchief and reaching the land the Chinese came to know as Hsing Chin Shan ('New Gold Mountain'). Gold never made the news there now, he thought, just everything else that is semi-precious or that Japan can burn, blend, smelt or electrify into profit. Thirty per cent of Australian exports went to this distant neighbour; iron ore, coal and menu-topping steaks of raw kangaroo all fed the Japanese hunger.

He visualised himself bouncing across hot earth with a heavy weight in an elastic pocket between his legs, but this was too agonising to endure. He tried to think of cinder-black natives knocking cockatoos out of the sky with curved sticks but the sad image of a discarded shadow lying crumpled around a beer can came with greater ease. He thought of semi-Americanised New Zealanders without the gumboots, of rugged femininity and muscled gelding-lambs-with-your-teeth manhood, bronzed and bleached by the sun. 'Eighty per cent of the population living on five per cent of the land.' The prospect would thrill any lover of space and wilderness, and he was one. But first would come Sydney, handsomely portrayed by postcards but said by some to be 'the great Australian ugliness on the edge of the great Australian loneliness'. He could only reserve judgement until more of the city came into view and he continued to absorb more facts, underlining some of them as they appeared, void of exclamation marks, in an official brochure: 'The Town Hall in Sydney has an organ with six keyboards, 127 stops and 8,672 pipes. Most of the time it is out of tune.' He felt like someone

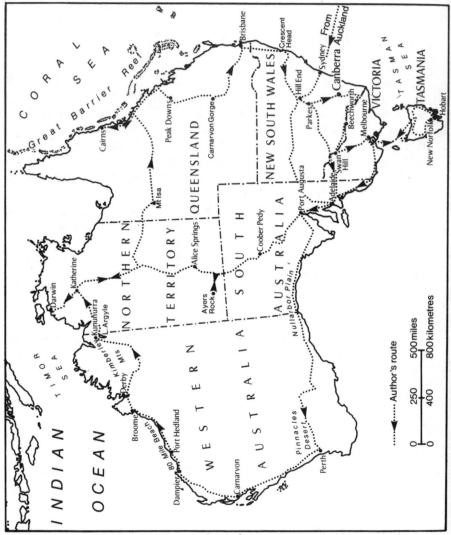

Australia

about to meet a stranger whose childhood had been legendary, and he thanked God (though this was said to be done only in Adelaide) that he was not of the ilk that had introduced rabbits, foxes, rats, sparrows, carp, blackberries, thistles, prickly pears, the Tolpuddle Martyrs (1834) and tetchy shop-stewards to this country.

Arriving is always a delicate, lonely act, full of uncertain anticipation.

He was disappointed because the view below showed Botany Bay to be a container port, ringed with chimneys leaking smoke into a yellow-black ceiling through which the plane had descended in order to land on a peninsula of tarmac. Only Captain Cook had looked on Botany Bay without a sense of irony when he thought up the name. Charles Darwin hadn't mentioned the flowers during his visit in 1836 – only that he disliked Sydney society, but then he hadn't arrived during the Mardi Gras festival.

Phil, dressed in tails, high collar and dark glasses with red pinprick lights in the centre of each lens which he activated through a wire disappearing into his pocket, thrust a can of beer towards the guy underdressed as a Scotsman. No one could walk far that evening without becoming a magnet for beer cans. Only a policeman refused but he was persuaded to borrow Phil's glasses and go through an eye-twinkling tapdance which caused Phil to drop his can in laughter. He had two dozen more in a pack on his back. The evening streets were crowded with a general drift towards a wide avenue where a band jerked on a stage supported on their own deafening acoustics. A vampire ambled past, followed by a huge effigy of the Queen on a float, her arm waving like a windscreen-wiper, and every now and then she let out a rollicking peal of schizophrenic laughter. Everyone wore necklaces of luminous green chemicals, and everyone went under the common name of Moyte.

'Ye'll foind, Moyte,' Phil explained, 'that yer average bloody Aussie is a fairly easygoing sort of a lazy bugger.' Phil said he was a gardener in the city parks. His moyte, looking remarkably natural as a pot-bellied frog, said he was a lawyer. The difference between their two jobs, Phil was quick to point out, was the quality of the surf. Phil got more time off to surf locally during the week, the frog could afford to go further afield and find wilder surf in his holidays.

The sea seemed a part of most people's lives. When a girl called Marge bumped into me (it was possibly the other way around) and discovered I had only just arrived, she immediately said she had a cat and offered to take me out the following day to see some of Sydney's sights. A cat? I queried. A cat, she confirmed. She took a biro and wrote an address and time on the palm of my hand. Then she vanished. It was a bewildering evening. I met half of Sydney, learnt about ockers, and carefully nursed the ink on my hand through hours of wearing revelry.

Phil and the frog were both ockers. It was a term that had recently gained popularity and referred to a new brand of strident nationalism. Had they been eighty years older they would probably have been supporters of the White Australia Policy and been shouting anti-Asian slogans such as 'Two Wongs don't make a White'. Fifteen years older and it would have been 'Bung back a Brit'. A national identity had remained diffuse through decades of Italian, Greek, Lebanese and Slav immigration, a mineral boom and its demoralising slump, and a traditional loyalty to increasingly unreliable business friends such as Europe. Now all immigration had tightened up and Australia was taking a look at her own interests, an introspective soul-searching in the light of new isolation, and was developing the feeling that it was all right for Australians to be themselves, they didn't owe allegiance to anyone, and that Aussie culture had a place alongside everyone else's. Ockerism was as good a word as any for it, unmistakably Australian.

Somewhere in the background the Queen let out another hysterical shriek of laughter.

My aunt, Jean Donald, had visited Australia to play golf for Britain in the days before she became a professional with Slazenger, and I had the address of several of her friends. What few rounds of golf I had played would have been completed more quickly with just a putter, a number nine iron and a scythe. In spite of my handicap, these friends made me welcome. I stayed in a flat, a 'home unit', on Darling Point which was close to the city centre. The view from my room made me feel afloat as water stretched from the garden swimming pool to the Harbour Bridge.

To my relief Marge had not forgotten our meeting and already had the mainsail hoisted by the time I arrived at the boat club. She was in her late twenties, freckled, tanned and cheerful. Her short crinkly black hair didn't react much to a breeze but her strong frame looked well able to cope with one, suitably weighted for leaning from a catamaran's trapeze. She was a physiotherapist and a keen sailor. Her family had always kept cats.

'Have you done much sailing before?' she asked.

'Only a little. You'll have to tell me what to do.' My expertise with small boats (and golf clubs) roughly matched my way with horses. Cats looked flimsy but infinitely preferable; a flagpole with two outriggers at the bottom and a net so that you could look between your legs and see how fast you were going. As we floated away from the shore Marge ran through the functions of the various ropes.

The breeze caught the sail and the boat went skating out into Sydney's vivacious harbour on one hull. The harbour cleaved deep into the city and almost cut it into two equal portions. We were just one of an inexhaustible flotilla of marine craft and the water surface was seldom without the suspense of at least one hundred imminent collisions between wobbly windsurfers grappling with striped sails, dinghies dawdling in wide zigzags, two-legged cats showing off on one, a race of Flying 18s – each keeled over, spinnaker bloated – sedately motoring ocean yachts, waterskiers holding out tripropes in front of Very Large Crude Carriers and nippy hydrofoil ferries which seemed unconcerned and sliced straight through the masses.

The harbour not only dominates the splendid panoramas of the city and subtly inspirits or bloody well inconveniences the lives of the three million people who live round about, but it also exists as a light-hearted unit of measurement: the sydharb. Lake Argyle in north-east Australia, for example, has a surface area of 285 square miles and a volume of nine sydharbs. This is far from being ridiculous because the harbour is a very important and meaningful image to most citizens. The sydharb also exemplifies the 'stralian's remarkable talent for reducing everything to its simplest form or else renaming it with a sobriquet that is bait for their mousetrap sense of humour.

The Harbour Control Tower ('the Pill' – facilitates berth control) stood to starboard as we passed under the famous Harbour Bridge ('the Coathanger') and under some of the 140,000 cars which squeeze into bottlenecks each weekday in order to cross it. Then we came to the arresting sight of the Opera House. I let go of the sheet at this point so we could admire it at a slower pace. It has no universally accepted nickname as it is a fantasy building and tickles everyone's imagination in different ways. You can see it as the popularly cited hotch-potch of clam shells, as sails caught in sequence against the skyline, or less conventionally as Robert Morley's 'something that has crawled out of the sea and is up to no good'.

After sailing for three hours and capsizing once in the surprisingly warm water, we returned to land, changed into dry clothes and then drove around the city in Marge's Toyota. Her standard of living, she believed, was about average. Sydney certainly has its slums like anywhere else but the general atmosphere is of advanced comfort. One-fifth of the country's population live here and the expanding fringe of unsightly ribbon development – ugliness eating into loneliness – is symptomatic of the city's lax attitude, its tradition of laissez-faire and continued delight in its own importance.

'I suppose we still do see ourselves as the capital,' Marge admitted, 'but every Australian city sees itself as something special. It makes for healthy rivalry.' She parked the car near the city centre and we walked about amongst a haphazard assortment of architectural styles, each smugly different and impossible to reconcile with its neighbour – a great feeling of spontaneity and of no winners in the clash between old and new; a mock-Greek temple of ponderous columns with decorated cinctures, an early highrise attempting elegance by incorporating tattoos of red bricks, and a modern no-frills concrete, glass and steel skyscraper beside a little wooden house whose upper balcony was faced with an elaborate matrix in wrought iron. Sydney's considerable charm comes from her gardens, thirty-two beaches and her sydharb, and to a lesser extent from the sheer inconsistency of her assembly.

The air was humid and only the serious tourists were out looking at the clam shells and the Coathanger through thoughts of a drink and the breeze we had just left. The sun that gives Australians the highest incidence of skin cancer in the world was melting a group of stalwart office workers playing lunch-time cricket in a park and delighting the outfield ring of businessmen whose shirts were open and toes bared as they surrendered themselves prostrate before it.

The image of dust-chewing frontiersfolk is misplaced and only adds to the paradox that the world's least densely populated country is its most urbanised. It is as if the vastness of their land intimidated the inhabitants and made them huddle together in cities. While farmers do chew dust and fight against pest, bushfires, droughts and floods, urban Australians look beyond their city limits in terms of a change of swimming pool, beer-coolers, barbecues and four-wheel drive outings. They are essentially a nation of fun-lovers, comfort-seekers and adventurous picnickers, and this is only natural in a land so suited to over-indulgence.

Sydney has everything to appeal to them; international cuisine and entertainment, nightly silhouettes sitting on a balcony in the King's Cross district against the red neon glow of the words 'Australia's Largest Bed', bars, beaches and adequate means of escape. 'The only thing wrong with Sydney is its hellish traffic,' Marge complained as we got stuck in another jam. 'And now they're putting up crazy new signs no one can understand. The papers are full of it.' The furor concerned the attempts by the authorities to reduce the delays caused by those stopping momentarily by the kerb during rush-hours to drop off spouse or friend, the 'kiss 'n ride' drivers, by replacing the old signs with a stronger message to show this practice was illegal. They had hoped to clarify the situation by replacing 'No Stopping' with the new 'No Standing'. Leaflets on road regulations had been amended to explain that '*No Standing* means *No Stopping*.'

A few days later I decided to leave Sydney in order to see a bit more of the country. The stamp in my passport permitted me to stay for six months as a non-working visitor. I hoped to extend this for several months and also to obtain a working permit as it was now fifteen months since I had last earned money. My existing funds were low but not yet critical. Some of my savings from previous jobs had been sent out to me in New Zealand but I needed to find a well-paid job for three to four months if I was to be able to afford a meandering route back to Britain in the final year. Judging from the reports of unemployment in the papers, it was not going to be easy. Hitch-hiking would, I hoped, prove effective, my tent would be adequate for accommodation and my only necessary expenses would be fuel for my stove, supermarket food and entry fees to the places of interest. My daily expenditure seldom needed to exceed an average of between £1 and £1.50 (A$2–3 at this time) except on the days when I had company or when an occasional extravagance seemed essential.

'Where are you heading for?' Marge asked.

I told her of my vague plan to hitch clockwise round the country, first to Tasmania, then to Perth. Australia, like Brazil, looked deceptively manageable on a small-scale map.

'I suppose you realise how far that is? This country's two and a half thousand miles wide and two thousand from bottom to top.' I nodded. 'You'll need the kilt for hitching. You need a gimmick nowadays. I know someone who always hitched with a surfboard. He took it to Ayers Rock – carrying an eight-foot surfboard a thousand miles from the sea!' Then her freckles wrinkled and she looked wistful. 'If I didn't have my job, I'd have liked to come with you . . .'

'Why not come? You can get another job later.'

'Maybe not. Anyhow, I don't have a kilt or a surfboard.'

'You could take your cat . . .'

But she was not to be persuaded. I set out alone on a walkabout which was to take me 12,000 miles, through the outback and to all the major cities, past fragments of history and into the lives of new Australians and the remains of those 30,000 years old, and eventually to the legend of a blushing sandstone monolith.

The main road west rose leisurely into the Blue Mountains, the major obstacle to delay the advance of the early settlers until a way was found through in 1813. It skirted four small hillocks called Rick, Rack, Roar and Rumble and at times was all but absorbed by a forest of eucalyptus gums in a selection of their four hundred wonderful varieties, some with bark flaking away as if to reveal previous layers of paint in glaring hues, and there were ghost gums whose trunks dazzled by day and glowed eerily in the half-light of dawn, dusk and moon, and blue gums which exuded a haze of scented fumes. Gum trees and the bold tinctures of naked rock are the distinctive features of an Australian landscape. An artist requires few colours to capture the character of bushland. The lightest and darkest shades go to tree trunks, the bright reds and oranges are claimed by rocks, while earth, grass and leaves settle respectively for weak washes of browns, yellows and lavender-grey. The rolling mountains in the picture before me periodically parted and sheer walls opened up vistas of canyons and valleys crammed with bush, fading with distance into deeper shades of the vaporous blue that gave this range its name.

An old miner named Rudy took me two hundred miles to Hill End. He shrugged off the miles as he did forty years of hunting for gold. Bent and gnarled beyond his sixty years, and scorched brown, Rudy and his brown dog were exactly whom one would expect to see emerging from the parched scrub that made Hill End ideal bonfire country. They were baked almost to the same dead, dying or struggling to live dryness that must have inspired Australians to stay in their coastal cities and build breweries.

'It's not where you live that matters, it's what you do there,' was Rudy's argument. He had seen his former way of life eroded into museum exhibits and tourism. Gold had never been that profitable to him. His largest find had been a half ounce nugget. Now he earned more making and selling models of washing cradles and the stamper batteries that once pounded rocks continuously throughout Hill End's days and nights, though that had been before his time. He still thrived on the sickness of gold fever, on the hope of a lucky strike, on the feverish heat of the times he came close to beating this place.

In the 1860s representatives of the British government tried to suppress the first reports of a gold strike at Hill End through fear of creating a rush that would draw labour away from more important colonial work. And besides, they had other concerns – they were introducing sparrows in an attempt to reduce the prevalence of caterpillars. A permit was required by law to mine for gold in the mid-nineteenth century but when the first official surveyor went to investigate the reports, he found an industrious community illegally trading in gold and five hundred miners showing the Australian's enterprising and characteristic dislike of authority. (The hero of *Waltzing Matilda*, the alternative national song, is a swagman who has stolen a sheep and prefers to commit suicide rather than be caught by the police.) With the exception of the quarter-ton lump of rich ore dragged out of the Star of Hope mine one evening in 1872, Hill End was not a spectacular or long-lasting goldfield. 'When gold became scarce,' Rudy explained, 'the town experienced a second boom by phoney speculators who planted valuable samples in worthless mines or shot streaks of gold into the walls with a shotgun. A gold mine became known as "a hole in the ground owned by a liar" in those days.'

Hill End today is a frugal collection of occupied houses and as many derelict ones interspersed among rusty steam engines and stamper batteries. The town now has a population of eighty mortals and uncounted ghost gums and ghosts. History is hard to preserve when it is built of perishable mud, timber and sheets of crinkly iron. In Australia it is predominantly the towns founded on (dare I mention it?) the presence of convicts – gaols and court-houses – that were afforded the luxury of preserving their past in solid and neatly hewn stone. The historical towns of Bathurst, Richmond, Beech-worth, Port Arthur, Hartley and many others all have noble old buildings, and all would have appeared on a nineteenth-century criminal's list of places best avoided.

Hill End was a damnable place to wait for a lift because of the heat and flies – as much a part of the Australian scene as rocks and gums, and merciless in their attention. Swarms instantly converged on any human who came into sight. They flew into my eyes, lingered on my lips while running their stethoscope tongues over my skin and nipped onto the back of my hand when I raised it to swat them. They were too quick and numerous for my murderous swipes to have any effect and eventually I could do no more than try to ignore them, occasionally directing a snort of air at the more impertinent indi-viduals assaulting my nose. That evening I came across a newspaper cutting from *The Age* which told me more about these flies.

An article entitled 'No bull, we need beetles' related that the average cow (and bull) drops ten cowpads of twelve-inch diameter each day. Australia has 30 million cattle and accordingly 300 million daily cowpads. Dung-beetles are not found in Australia as they are in other countries with indigenous creatures that create sizeable pads, so these pads are not turned into the ground and disposed of as organic manure. Instead they lie on the surface, making the sur-rounding grass rank and providing the perfect breeding medium for flies. In experimental areas where dung-beetles have been intro-duced, the report maintained, there has been a significant reduction in the fly population and an improvement in pasture.

I wished the dung-beetle health and success as the flies drove me westwards to Parkes, a town dominated by the two huge skeletal saucers of its radio telescope. Here I studied the map to find the most direct route to Canberra. This appeared to be via Gooloogong, Boorowa, Yass and Murrumbateman. It was slightly longer via Bedgerebong, Bribbaree, Thuddungra, Wallendbeen, Stockinbin-gal and Wee Jasper. But to have included Diddah Diddah, Daddah Daddah, Howlong, Toolong, Yackandandah, Yarrangobilly, Burumbuttock, Wantabadgery, Mulberrygong, Mair-jimmy, Yal-lakool, Womboota, Jincumbilly and Suggan Buggan would have been quite possible but absurdly roundabout. The car-drivers who took me to the capital were almost as varied as the town names. They included an outback farmer whose telephone lines had been brought down twice in the last month by high-bouncing roos, a baritone singer with the Australian Opera Company – he considered the acoustics of the Sydney clam shells to be 'pathetic' – and finally with a psychologist working for the WHO, who said very little.

Canberra is clean, spacious and looks dully efficient. This purpose-built capital is sited midway between Sydney and Melbourne, and its foundation in 1923 marked a compromise solution to the dispute between those two rivals over which should hold the title of leading city. Some Canberrites see their home as having a sterile atmosphere. It was built to plans prepared by the American architect Walter Burley Griffin whose first job had been to design an incinerator in Sydney. Canberra employs eighty per cent of its population in national administration. Where you would expect to find a central area of busy shops and the most important offices, Canberra has a man-made lake which blows a tall fountain into the air. Where you would expect to find the central fringe of lesser offices and an up-market residential area, Canberra has a large park. The park does in fact contain several principal government offices and the palatial white parliament building set at the end of a broad avenue of lamp-posts, but the city proper has been banished to the outskirts and camouflaged as another park. It has all been done very tastefully. The city's fifteen-mile spread and poor public transport make it exasperating for the pedestrian, but it is a delight for the motorist because the wide roads, lined with two million trees, were planned for a fierce rush hour which has never happened.

On top of Capitol Hill, which lies closer to the centre than the city, stands the War Museum, an enormous mausoleum displaying a fascinating and intensely depressing collection of ANZAC memorabilia from both world wars: intact planes, tanks, guns, bayonets, bombs and the other things that make death child's play; medals, personal possessions from the trenches, flags, models of battles, photographs of corpses tangled in barbed wire and the names of 100,000 war dead individually listed, gold letters in granite, 62,000 of them from the First World War, the event that, tragically, first gave Australians a sense of national identity.

I found the presentation beautiful, the effect charitably ugly. I spent several days in and around Canberra but found that the War Museum dominated the view, and my thoughts. More than anything I felt troubled by the words 'Their name liveth for evermore' and 'Lest we forget'. The same inscriptions had appeared on the Roll of Honour in my school cloisters and on lonely Celtic crosses near

Highland villages, and always jarred. The words rang empty, condescending and almost treacherous, penny payments for hundred-pound sacrifices. The names might live for evermore, or for as long as there was granite, but they no longer lived in the minds of the living, in whom man's two inherent flaws remained: his ability to see his own discontent as a crusade towards peace, and his inability to see that there can never be peace as long as he is prepared to fight for it.

I found consolation, in Canberra, at Forest School which was attended by the sons and daughters of Australians and the city's foreign diplomats. When the schoolbell rang, the children from fifty-five different nations came out together to play.

The Snowy Mountains stand lumpishly and show little eagerness to gain height. Organised ski races took place here as early as the 1860s, but the ski tows stretched and dangled idly above slopes of alpine flora when I made the ascent of Mt Kosciusko, an unprepossessing mass and yet Australia's highest at 7,316 feet. It was early autumn and one night in a tent on the near-freezing summit was enough to tempt me down to the near-roasting lowlands – it seemed to be a land of fires, frying pans and one fridge – where I found a campsite among snow gums and beside a small billabong, a river bend which the main current had bypassed.

I was awakened at dawn by the loud raucous squawking of cockatoos as they flashed white overhead in a chaos of heavy wingbeats. This seemed to activate the charming kookaburras, like large smug kingfishers in drab feathers, and they began to inspect their territory with outbursts of infectious laughter. It wound up in a crescendo until the birds were quite hysterical . . . *Hoo-hoo-hoo-woo-Woe-ho-ho-ho-Ha-ha-Hahahahahaha.* A rock wallaby hopped unawares towards my tent and then sensed danger, bouncing gracefully away on tiptoes, its solid tail held out as a counterbalance as it nimbly ducked under fallen trees and fled over branches strewn on the rough terrain. Then a harmless four-foot-long goanna lizard waddled by and climbed a tree to search for insects.

Australia's wildlife was a constant marvel. A tablespoon of newborn red kangaroos contains four creatures which can each grow into seven feet of muscular bounce capable of inflicting fatal wounds by slashing an adversary with the long claw on its hind feet. In times of food shortage a female kangaroo can suppress conception for several years until conditions become more favourable, and her eggs will then develop without further mating. There is the adored koala bear which is generally bad-tempered and can be vicious when it is not sitting dozing against the bole of a tree. Its ground cousin, the wombat, has a similar temperament and a particularly solid body which even truck-drivers dread encountering on a road. Koalas, roos, wombats and wild camels – the offspring of those which escaped from Afghan camel trains once used in the desert regions – are common enough in some areas to appear on warning roadsigns ('Wombats for the next 15 km'). Australia possesses a frog which carries its eggs in hip-pockets, the Port Jackson shark, the only egg-laying member of its species, and the world's only two egg-laying mammals, the spiny anteater – a sharp-nosed porcupine – and the retiring platypus. When the first preserved specimen was sent to Britain, zoologists looked at this otter with a large duck's bill and a poisonous claw on one of its rear legs, and dismissed it as a hoax.

Some of the world's most venomous creatures also find a home inside Australian territory: stone fish, sting rays and jelly fish frequent the seas while the lethal funnel web spider and at least six types of venomous snakes live on land. A fresh black snake releases enough venom in a single bite to kill two sheep; the copperhead, nine; the tiger snake, 118; and the most deadly land snake in the world, the taipan, can theoretically dispose of 1,062 with one bite. These statistics were disturbing to one sleeping on a creased ground-sheet.

From the Snowy Mountains I rode with a truck for a long lift westwards, descending into a bumpy landscape of scorched grass and cattle which lay in the shadow of trees looking glum and uninterested in the production of pads. We passed a livestock auction where farmers sat in shorts on fences and surveyed a horizon of holding pens crushed with enough sheep for fifty or sixty good taipan bites. Irrigated fields of sunflowers and tobacco surrounded the town of Beechworth and here we stopped for a glass of Tooth's beer. The main street contained wood and brick houses cheerfully renovated from last century and antiquated hotels with warped verandahs and intricate wrought-iron railings. It is a mining town but remains better known for its solid stone gaol and as the haunt of the outlaw described by the historian M.H. Ellis as 'one of the most cold-blooded, egotistical and utterly self-centred criminals who ever decorated the end of a rope in Australia'. Edward (Ned) Kelly is nevertheless still revered as a folk-hero. Apart from his colourful contribution to Australian folklore, Ned Kelly's painful achievement was to expose and ultimately change an inefficient and corrupt police force.

He was born in 1855 of Irish parents; Red, his father, having been transported from Tipperary at the age of twenty-one for stealing two pigs, Ellen, his mother, having emigrated during the potato famine. Ned was the eldest of their seven surviving children and early on he developed a hatred for the police who constantly harassed his father because of his criminal past and suspected illegal dealings. Both Ned and his brother Dan had frequently fallen foul of the law by the time their mother was arrested for attempted murder, having struck a policeman with a shovel when he called at the Kelly home. The facts of the incident are unsubstantiated but it was alleged that the policeman had come to arrest Dan (without a warrant) for horse-theft and found the brothers gone. He had attempted to rape Ned's sister, Katie, and her mother had rescued her. Ellen Kelly was sentenced to three years in Beechworth gaol and here she bore and raised the baby she had been expecting at the time of the offence. The local populace tried to free her by setting fire to the wooden grid at the entrance to the gaol but the attempt failed and the grid was replaced by metal bars. This proved to be one humiliation too many for Ned and Dan. They recruited two others and the notorious Kelly Gang set off on its short but successful career.

In one of his many addresses, Ned was later to vent his feelings on those representatives of law and justice who had abused his family:

> '. . . and is my brothers and sisters and my mother not to be pitied also who has no alternative only to put up with the brutal and cowardly conduct of a parcel of big ugly fat-necked wombat headed big bellied magpie legged narrow-hipped splay-footed sons of Irish bailiffs or English landlords . . . ?'
>
> *The Jerilderie Letter*, 1879

The Kelly Gang robbed banks, held up entire towns and locked the police in their own cells whenever possible. It was during this period that Ned's reputation as a 'Robin Hood' figure originated. Although easily capable of violence, the Kelly Gang usually committed robbery with compassion and on one occasion at Euroa, Ned drank whisky with the bank manager whose vaults he had just emptied and then took him, his wife, two servants and seven children for a picnic at Faithful Creek. The outlaws were hunted for over two years before the police finally surrounded them in the Glenrowan Inn. After a long shoot-out Ned made two desperate dashes for freedom wearing a coat and helmet of home-made armour weighing ninety-seven pounds. The first time he was driven back but the second time he ran a considerable distance unharmed, deflecting volleys of bullets until his unprotected legs were hit. Remarkably, he fell unnoticed and possibly could have escaped but he returned to continue fighting and was captured. He was hanged in Melbourne in 1879, aged twenty-four. His skull rested on a shelf as a tourist attraction until it was stolen in 1978.

It took me a four-hundred-mile detour to discover that Ned Kelly's way with words is a trait that has not been lost. Swan Hill was far off the direct route to Melbourne but I was timing my arrival in Victoria's chief city with its annual Moomba festival which was still a week away, and it was pleasant to drift westwards through the vineyards and wine-tasting parlours which follow the course of the Murray River towards Swan Hill, a port for paddlesteamers in the days of river traffic, and noted for its reconstructed Pioneer Village, a well oiled and inhabited museum. Craftsmen were at work demonstrating traditional skills; a shop sold stone-ground flour, tallow candles and posters (printed on an old press) showing the Mona Lisa picking her nose; a horse operated a treadmill and powered antique machinery for short stints, and old methods of transport gave rides around the complex.

The driver of one horse and cart was a young man wearing a cowboy hat, sporting the early stages of a beard and a cigarette which he contorted from side to side across his mouth in the manner of Clint Eastwood with a cigar. His cart was empty and he sat sprawled on the seat watching an elderly couple approach. They were both smartly dressed and walked arm in arm even though the man was slightly lame and used a stick. They looked charming and faintly aristocratic.

'Gidday,' said Clint, and rolled the cigarette over his lips.

'Be a good man and take us up the hill there,' said the gentleman.

'Can't be doin' that, sur,' replied Clint, and he explained that he had a set route and he was not permitted to deviate from it.

The gentleman dismissed this with 'Oh come, come. It won't hurt . . .' but Clint stood firm and repeated that it was not possible.

The hill was not on his route. The gentleman tried to persuade him once more but Clint interrupted him and responded with a polished performance on the theme of duty and punishment in the 1870s. The couple tolerated this, thinking he would agree to their errand after this playful repartee. When they realised he was serious, they were clearly affronted.

'You're just a typical Australian,' shouted the lady vehemently, 'not wanting to do any work.'

'I'll report you to the management,' threatened the gentleman.

'Take it to parliament if you like, sur, for all the good it'll do,' Clint replied amiably.

'Young man, I hope your wheels fall to bits under you . . .' snarled the gentleman, '. . . and your horses die of colic,' interjected the sweet old lady.

'And young man,' this was the gentleman again, his face red, angrily tapping his stick against the wheel, 'I hope your horses fart in your face.' With that they stormed off.

Australians are indisputable masters in the art of insult.

The journey from Swan Hill to the southern coast passed through the splendid Grampian Mountains, wheatfields and the poor waste-land around Ballarat that yielded the gold that made Melbourne prosperous. Ingram Collins gave me a lift for most of the way in his mobile pulpit. He was a cantankerous amateur preacher who happened to be old and Scottish. (I think about five per cent of my lifts came from religious pedagogues.) He spoke largely in biblical verse or unacknowledged quotes and sounded ineffectual when he had to connect them with words of his own. Collins explained how he had been a struggling insurance broker until he discovered the power of prayer. At the time he felt he could better pursue his spiritual calling if he owned a private business, so he prayed to this end. He began in a small way hiring out cement-mixers and soon extended this to heavier construction machinery, and 'with the Lord's help' he had bought out all his rivals within five years. The moral of this account was evidently the power of prayer, not the relative speed with which divine assistance could crush business competition.

'All Scotsmen love to die dramatically,' Collins expounded, 'and if they can't die dramatically then they won't die at all.'

His wild driving almost ended the lives of two Scotsmen with suitable ostentation but we managed to reach Melbourne safely that evening. I had another golfing contact in this city and, feeling something of an impostor, found a telephone directory to look up the number. I succeeded in making contact after a lengthy search hampered by pages of Papadimitropouloses and Papaconstaninouses, a reminder that only Athens contained more Greeks than Melbourne. The MacLachlans welcomed me and explained how to reach their house by tram.

Trams are a hallmark of the city. They were designed by the same Scottish engineer who built Dunedin's cable-cars, and recently the exteriors of old trams had been decorated by some of the city's leading artists. I travelled inside Black Birds painted by Clifton Pugh and ultimately inside Les Kossatz's Sheep. I had heard all the jokes about Melbourne's conservative image, bad weather and obsession with school ties but, trundling along in a motorised work of art, looking out on well-behaved traffic, wide avenues of stately buildings and fashion-shop windows filled by gilded mannikins, on a pleasant evening and in the company of theatregoers, children in fancy dress burrowing into cocoons of candy floss, and two wobbly drunks, I felt unable to take sides in the Sydney versus Melbourne rivalry.

The MacLachlans, Betty and her husband McCloog, lived in a fashionable district; their children had grown up and now lived in other parts of the city. McCloog was tall and thin and spent long hours running a store which had been in the family for four generations. Betty was an artist; large, delightfully extrovert and with an irresistible power to raise laughter. 'McCloog always says the best part of my paintings is my signature.' She said one day she would like to paint a Melbourne tram. If that ever happened, McCloog maintained, he would walk to work.

I went with Betty to watch the highlight of the Moomba festival, the Birdman Rally. We climbed inside Psychedelic Waves (by Don Laycock) and were transported to the Yarra River which flows through the middle of the city. Melbourne lacks the immediate impact of Sydney's magnificent setting but it has retained a sense of dignity. It was obviously founded, whereas Sydney seems to have just happened. The streets are meticulously laid out in a grid and their architecture represents the era of grandeur and solidity before the advent of poured buildings. Inevitably gaps have developed and been filled with interloping highrises, but these are made to look embarrassed and humbled by the sheer volume of hewn stone surrounding their bases.

'I adore Sydney,' Betty said, when we were discussing the two cities, 'but I'd find it too hectic to live there . . . Of course you know that *Melbourne* was built by free labourers, not convicts . . .?'

This city is the commercial centre of the nation and those free labourers constructed it to look the part. If Sydney conveys the impression that Australians dislike work, Melbourne made me believe some love it. Another difference, I felt sure, concerns their organs. It is difficult to imagine Melbourne ever allowing one of its organs to go out of tune, but unthinkable that it would announce the fact to overseas visitors in its prospectus. The two cities are wonderful counterpoints. Like Poms and Aussies, they deserve each other. I felt no need to take sides.

Melbourne normally goes to bed at a wholesome hour but during Moomba (this Aboriginal word is usually given some hellfire translation such as 'Let's get together and have fun') it sacrifices sleep and sheds whatever stolid reputation it may have. This week of exhibitions, processions and communal activities gets less people together for less fun than Sydney's Mardi Gras, but the Birdman Rally cocks a worthy snook at the festivities of the north. A platform is erected forty feet above the surface of the Yarra River and a prize of A$10,000 awaits the first birdperson to glide for fifty yards before touching the water.

As we made our way from the tram stop to the crowds lining both banks of the river Betty told me more about the contest. 'It's a real hoot! Some people take it very seriously but most just go in for fun. No one has ever won the prize but I think the record stands at thirty-eight yards. They say it's almost impossible as the rules are very strict.' Wing-spans are not to exceed twenty-six feet, and engines, gear cogwheels, assisted launches and any form of stored energy (including gas balloons, momentum propellers, gigantic rubber bands) are not supposed to be permitted. Many contestants blatantly ignored these regulations but they were all allowed their turn.

A Mexican *bandido* jumped with a sombrero covered in air-filled balloons which plummeted almost as quickly as its owner. A body was launched in a coffin as a naval funeral and a witch riding a broomstick took a flying leap which was officially recorded at seven yards on impact, one of the more respectable final results. The hero of the afternoon, however, had constructed a huge biplane. It was a ponderous contraption made of the tubular frames from old gala day seats, plywood flaps, sheets of doped paper and about half a mile of wire. It was designed around a bicycle which powered a weighted propeller. This made it ineligible for the prize but nevertheless it looked extremely effective. Days and possibly weeks had gone into the biplane's construction and yet when people saw it, they laughed. It was just a folly. It was obvious the thing would never fly. Eight men had to be recruited from the spectators just to drag it up the ramp onto the take-off platform. The pilot was a puny youth and his slightness caused another snigger to swell and echo along the ranks of expectant onlookers. He climbed in and began pedalling furiously. The propeller turned, picked up speed, faster and faster until it was a blur. The crowd fell silent. The pilot reached out, released the handbrake, and to everyone's surprise, the plane surged forward. It had covered perhaps three feet when there was a sharp report like a pistol shot, the fuselage broke in two, a wing fell off and the pilot was ejected, tumbling onto the platform. The biplane stood there inert, only a matter of inches short of becoming airborne, and the birdman lay sprawled alongside, inches short of the starting line.

At the end of the week I boarded the *Empress of Australia* for the overnight voyage to Tasmania. I had heard there was a chance of finding seasonal work in apple orchards or shellfish factories. Betty came to see me off but she seemed absent-minded at my departure. I waved from one of the decks as she stood on the dock below but it took some time to catch her attention as she was staring at the vast expanse of white ship as if it were an empty canvas.

The *Empress* docked early in the morning and by the end of my first day I had acquired an instant liking for the island and its people. The Tassies are just as warm-hearted as other Australians but more reticent. They shrug off the blessing of owning one of the most beautiful regions in the country, but their apparent indifference does not conceal the zealous way they cling to their identity and their island. Their way of life is slower than the mainland's, and their outlook disarmingly simple.

In Devonport I fell into conversation with an old man standing in a garden swallowed up by flowers.

'Have you lived here all your life?' I asked.

His vision had been wide, encompassing hills and sea, but at that moment it narrowed and came to focus on me with what I felt was resentment.

Then he laughed. 'No. Not yet.'

14 · Looking Smart in Wes'tralia

Tasmania is a state of mountains, small hill farms and generous concentrations of untouched wilderness. A fifty-mile track runs from Cradle Mountain in the north of the island (not far from the ferry terminal) to Lake St Clair located close to its centre, and this walk was my introduction to Tasmania's wild splendour. The track passed typically through great mires of button grass and gum forests abounding with wallabies, below tall crags of red granite which frequently dominated the horizon, and alongside ample lakes and tarns to ensure a timely reflection of sunset skies. The Scott Kiliert Hut was one of several trailside refuges; it was named after two walkers who had died near the spot in a blizzard – a sobering thought to anyone with a general view of Australia as a marginal desert, and particularly to anyone with a surname in common.

Tasmania's hilly, crotchety terrain is not intended for easy living (it was once host to two of the severest penal colonies) but, as with many places of outstanding beauty, it is ideally suited to adventurers and damp vegetation. From Lake St Clair radiating outwards towards the coast of basalt cliffs and beaches, the rest of the island appears as a felicitous blend of dense forest, fields, pasture, mining communities, fishing villages, and the fine city of Hobart with its graceful bridge and half of the country's four casinos. The Tassies are perhaps best known for their apples although the government has been paying orchardists to uproot their trees and find alternative crops as the industry has been in decline since Britain joined the EEC, and for its hydroelectricity projects which have caused environmentalists hard fights. Their island has the country's highest rate of unemployment.

Tassies share the national apathy towards litter and the country lanes were strewn with beer cans and bottles every few yards. I passed a town whose sign plate bore a large blank space before the word 'Penguin'. It had in fact been called Upper Penguin until recently when the inhabitants had petitioned for it to be changed, having finally tired of the predictable titters whenever they answered the question 'Where do you come from?'. The zinc, lead, silver and gold mines of Rosebery had no work, the manager at the office of a hydroelectricity scheme near Tullah showed me a deep pile of job application forms awaiting the first vacancy, and the same happened at Queenstown, a shocking area of stark yellow rock denuded by the acid rain resulting from the sulpur discharge of its smelter.

Launceston had a church with a noticeboard on which someone had scrawled 'We are the soul agents for this area', but it had no vacancies for labourers. I met a group of about sixty motor-bike enthusiasts who had gathered for a rally. I asked for suggestions as to where to find work. The consensus of opinion was to try the scallop factories on the east coast where casual splitters were employed to open the shells. A dab hand at splitting could earn $125 in a day but they said it took years to perfect the knack to that degree. I took a road which went up Bust Me Gall Hill and then down Break Me Neck Hill, and visited the scallop factory at St Helens. Poor catches, no work, 'maybe next week'. This was offered as encouragement but the words had the empty ring of a Latin American mañana.

The apple season had not started in the orchards south of Hobart, and the capital's leading newspaper had devoted extra columns to Situations Wanted. Hunting for work over those few days was miserable and I was feeling in low spirits when I reached New Norfolk. I arrived at one of the district's largest farms late in the afternoon. My mind was so geared to the expectation of a refusal that the offer of a job picking hops took a moment to penetrate. Then I had accepted before the farmer could finish explaining the details, and was shown to a bunkhouse where there were other workers whom I could ask what the farmer had been talking about.

Hops were new to me. The vines were trained to grow up string held taut between the ground and a fifteen-foot-high trellis. During harvesting they were first cut at the base and then two tractors worked in tandem along each row; the first pulled a trailer on which two people stood, collecting and stacking the vines. Above them worked two cutters, slashing at the tops with machetes as they stood in a crow's-nest held aloft in the arms of the second tractor. It made a strange sight, but it was effective.

My job alternated between stacking and cutting, the latter being much less tedious but requiring a trustworthy companion. We worked within an arm's length of each other and the machetes were kept brutally sharp. My workmates were local men and their wives working their holidays, most of the men being dockers who seemed to spend more time dealing in and creating the things that fell off the backs of trucks and ships. The exchange of wit and constant banter made light of the work but first I had to learn Strine, so that I could translate such terms as 'Emmachizzit', rhyming slang and antipodean jargon. Beer didn't come in cans or bottles but in tinnies or stubbies. You were ill if you were crook but kept chickens if you had chooks. Cowboys or novice station hands were jackaroos or female jillaroos, rubbery-dubs were pubs, sharks were Noah's arks and an impending calamity was called 'she'll be right, mate'.

The bunkhouse had individual rooms and a communal kitchen where we prepared our daily packed lunch and other meals. Work began at seven-thirty a.m. and finished at six-thirty p.m., including two smoke-hos, an hour off for lunch and an hour of overtime. The standard rate of pay was A$6.31 (£3.50) an hour. The vital spark of the workforce's entertainment was Ivan. He was a tall wiry character full of the boldest talk compatible with a fear of having to prove his words with action. During working hours his head was permanently crushed into a small bucket-shaped hat which concealed his rattish features from the nose upwards. He chainsmoked cigarettes to the last puff and I always expected his ginger moustache to catch fire at any moment. Ivan was a jovial champion of abuse and regurgitated humour, mostly obscene but losing none of its flavour in the retelling. ' 'e's that crude,' admitted his wife, 'at times I'm ashamed of 'im.' This was a very lenient opinion.

'C'mon, *hop* to it everyone,' Ivan said at the start of each day and then began hours of work among the bitter-smelling vines.

During a lull in the crow's-nest with Ivan, I was alarmed to notice a spider with the diameter of a teacup walking up my leg. ' 'e won't 'arm yer,' Ivan said, picking it up. ' 'e wouldn't 'arm a fly . . . well 'e would 'cos that's all 'e eats.' He threw it down towards Dick the tractor driver, who was leaning back yawning. The spider just missed the open mouth. Dick was the foreman and Ivan's chief scapegoat. He was fat, dreamy and fortunate in being partially deaf and brontosaurusly insensible. Work resumed for several rows until Dick hit a post and almost jolted us off our high perches. Ivan was slumped over the crow's-nest railings. 'You bloody idiot,' he shouted, 'you daggy half-wit.' He turned to me. 'I'll tell you this, cobber – if they ever hang Dick as a tractor driver, they'll hang an innocent man.'

The job lasted only two weeks and then the last field had been stripped. My wages came to A$600 after tax had been deducted, and by then I almost felt crook at the sight of hops. With the prospects of finding more work in Tasmania so bleak I decided to head directly for Western Australia where the country's largest iron ore deposits were to be found. Mining in the outback was said to be well-paid but a dull life and this meant a high turnover in the workforce.

A small Morris 1100 took me north from New Norfolk to the ferry terminal. The trees were glorious in their autumn colours and the early morning light seemed to lend the farmland the alluring serenity of a Constable painting; the light of departure is often tinted by nostalgia. And yet it was not at all obvious that this was a departure. The Morris puttered along at a crawl – slow transport or preachers always picked on me when the longest distances lay ahead: 3,000 miles to Perth! I tried not to be impatient and looked out for butterflies, recalling the slow lift in Ecuador when one had over-taken the petrol-tanker I was travelling in.

'She's not going too well,' said Mr Knowles, content in his retirement.

'No, she's not,' I agreed.

We negotiated bends that felt no different from the straights and descended the occasional favourable gradient that never altered our slow speed.

'Just wait till the second corner from here,' he said suddenly, 'she'll go like hell.'

I watched trees go past and marvelled at the detail it was possible to see at eight mph. Then the engine revved up, the trees began to flash by and I glanced at the speedometer to see the needle touching 40 mph. Perth began to feel closer.

'Second corner,' said Mr Knowles triumphantly. 'She always does that.'

The journey went smoothly to clean sedate Adelaide (known as the 'City of Churches', it was founded by Presbyterians – the congregation-drowning Rev. Norman McLeod settled here before moving on to Waipu in New Zealand), stuttered as far as ugly Port Augusta and came to a halt on the red ground beside Iron Knob, a town whose distinctive geographical feature had been mined away. Before me lay an expanse of wheatfields ploughed for the winter, stretching to the horizon, and beyond them lay an area where cartographers seized on any object over three feet tall and marked it on their map. It was the stretch of road I dreaded more than any other in Australia; the thread of tarmac crossing 900 miles of the Nullarbor Plain. To hitch-hikers around the world it was rated as severe a test as the Alaskan Highway and being caught among triple-level flyovers in Los Angeles. Only the trans-Sahara hitch produced a more phobic response. It was late afternoon, and a dense hop-scotch of flies played on me relentlessly. I prepared for a long wait beside a roadsign whose scratched messages reinforced my apprehensions. They recorded waits in hours, sometimes in days, and snippets of the things that went through lonely minds under a hot sun: 'Men are so necessarily mad that not being mad is just another form of madness . . . Starry was here . . . Life is not a destination but a journey . . . Starry is still bloody here.'

After two hours a car took me to the next township which absorbed all traffic into its incestuous circulation. Several more hours of fruitless waiting followed and then I went to camp by the side of the road. I awoke with the cold around midnight and heard a regular flow of heavy trucks going past. I couldn't sleep with the thought of missing all those potential lifts, so quickly packed and took up my stance by the road to hitch through the night. At three a.m. a truck finally stopped and I climbed the ladder into the cab.

'Bloody hell, I thought it was a bleedin' sheila standin' there,' said the driver, a vague shape in the reflected glare of his headlights. 'God strike me down dead. I don't normally go around pickin' up guys in bloody skirts, my bloody oath I don't. You must be off your bleedin' head.'

'My bloody oath as well,' I replied, 'I don't normally go around accepting lifts from people who can't tell the difference between a sheila and a guy with a beard.'

After this introduction he became more affable and, despite his disappointment, he agreed to take me on condition that I kept talking to prevent him from dropping off to sleep. The darkness seemed interminable as we drove through the small hours and conversation became desperately hard to maintain when Kevin responded to every attempt with one-word answers. Only on the subject of trucks did he show any interest, and so we talked Macks,

Whites, Scanias, Louisvilles, Kenworths and double-overhead cams until dawn. We stopped for coffee at Penong which was notable for windpumps raising water from artesian wells, a few houses and a pack of curs. The wheatfields and grazing had ended and the flat land was given over to scrub dominated by the stunted stems of spindly mulgas. Then they disappeared abruptly and there was nothing as far as the eye could see to break the expanse of blue bush and saltbush which dotted the ground as glaucous clumps on russet-grey sand. The Nullarbor Plain blended into the arid desolation of the heartland: the Great Victoria, Simpson, Sturt's Stony, Gibson and Great Sandy deserts. The explorer Sturt was unaware of this when he set out north from Adelaide in 1844 to look for a great inland sea. He and his party dragged a whaleboat into one million square miles of desert. And somewhere to our right stretched the Trans-Australian railway line with one section of 297 miles of dead straight track.

After several hours of this monotonous view it came as a shock, and then a relief, to see a roadsign. A shock as it was so long since we had last seen one, and a relief to be able to focus our attention on a point of interest. It was a warning. 'Camels next 10 km'. Then it flashed past and the view reverted to how it had been. We stopped at the Nullarbor Roadhouse where the tapwater was salty and undrinkable. We drank a stubbie and ate fried eggs on toast. (They don't seem so bad together in a desert.) Kevin told one of the sheilas that his egg was 'ratchet' and her cooking was the same. Next, with admirable brassiness, he turned his attention to chatting up this lousy cook.

The road ran close to the coastline as we neared the state border of Western Australia. From the elevation of the cab I could make out the striking combination of red cliffs, pure white sand and the prussian-blue sea. It looked inviting.

'Don't let it fool you,' said Kevin, still smarting over his unrequited hungers. 'Sea's soddin' cold there, and crawlin' with Noah's arks.' He yawned and merged it into a groan. 'God, I feel Donald Ducked.'

He had been driving for over twenty-four hours without sleep but by then we were in a state where truck-drivers were not bound to log their hours at the wheel and he wanted to make a few more miles, secure in the knowledge that the law had no hold over him. He was determined to pay off his A$127,000 truck within four years and this meant taking all the work he could get. Some months he averaged over 20,000 miles. We maintained a steady 65 mph even though Western Australia's section of the road was ragged and bumpy. After dark my eyelids felt like hinges rusted shut. The road was still so straight that the lights of oncoming cars shone in our eyes for twenty minutes before they passed us. We stopped around midnight, too tired to continue and having exhausted our discussion on trucks. I slept on the open trailer under the cargo of farm machinery.

The night was still, with the stillness of a shunned land. A whisper would float a thousand miles. There was no sound of insects or birds. My thoughts drifted back to northern Chile. 'Singing birds don't like deserts.' No canaries here. No sparrows either, and none in the whole of Western Australia. Sparrows couldn't fly the Nullarbor. A million square miles of desert, and my goal in the middle. Ayers Rock was still a distant whisper, floating across this infinite expanse. Everything was reduced to geometrical simplicity. I slept as a point on a line which had no end. The Nullarbor extended forever, silently withholding its third dimension.

We reached Perth the following night.

In 1925 the commuter train from the suburbs of Bassendean took nineteen minutes to reach the centre of Perth. Today, more than fifty years later, it still takes nineteen minutes. Despite Perth's extremely modern and polished appearance, and its evident pride in being the only city of any importance in the west of the continent, it has retained the happy-go-lucky attitude of those days before the 1890s Coolgardie gold rush when its existence was founded on the uncertain need of filling a blank on the map, a need given urgency by the fear that a French colony was about to be established on this coastline. It has expanded into a handsome city, balancing its streets of mirror-faced office blocks with parks and ornamental flowerbeds, and allowing the Swan River to snake decoratively through its limits as a playground for windcraft rather than as a convenient drain. Perth occupies more ground than Greater London and yet has only one-twentieth of the population. The pride (and shame) of its old buildings are collectively found in the port of Freemantle where 120,000 live sheep periodically embark onto one large ship for the journey to a controversial slaughter in Muslim countries. Perth has a few less salubrious areas, but most of its suburbs measure poverty by the scanty size or the lack of swimming pools.

West Australians see themselves as a separate entity. Their state is eleven times larger than Britain, four times the size of Texas, and so far from Sydney that it is cheaper to fly to Indonesia for a holiday. Perth stands content as one of the world's most isolated cities, and its lack of competition affords it a more relaxed atmosphere than could be found in the east. Bustle finds privacy in its open spaces. Some bustle, however, was obvious on the day of my arrival; rising tension in the Footy league (the Australian version of rugby, played on a cricket pitch), a notably busty exodus to the beaches, the regular swing of restaurant doors – and this city has more restaurants per head of population than any other – and, eschewing distance, the Grimethorpe Colliery Band were on a tour from Yorkshire. In short, Wes'tralians do not regard isolation as loneliness, their business is seldom pressing, and they still consider it a pleasure to be transported across the city of Perth. There is no need for the Bassendean train to go any faster.

I had long since given up trying to compare one nation's degree of friendliness and hospitality with another – Australia's was equal to the best. My last antipodean contacts lived in Perth and they invited me to use their house as a base for an indefinite period. Peter and Hester were not golfers but attended dog-shows when they weren't working eighteen hours a day at running their own furniture business. They owned three Lhaso Apsos with long pedigrees and a cat called Cleopatra with long claws. Their house was situated away from the centre in a suburb of medium-sized swimming pools near Innaloo, which I thought would have had its name changed for the same reason as Upper Penguin. I began the hunt for work my first day.

Nothing feels as heavy as the feet of the unemployed. The streets of Perth became long as I trudged around the mining companies, their inevitable lifts seemed additional obstacles to an atmosphere of trespass and even the most candidly smiling secretaries were merely harbingers of rejections. There were forms to fill in, several interviews and the embarrassment over what name to use. I had found it impossible to obtain an official work permit owing to a small clause which prevented visitors from changing status once they had entered the country. Anyone who came as a tourist could not become a worker without leaving the country and reapplying. This only left me the possibility of lending an unofficial hand to help Australia's productivity. The kilt was packed away and it seemed prudent to adopt pseudonyms for my services, only I made the mistake of using the first name that came to mind on each occasion and then forgetting which one had been used. One interviewer came into the room where I was sitting as a Mr Forbes with other applicants, and called for a Mr Clarke. No one stirred. 'Is there a Mr Clarke here?' he asked again to give the candidate a fair chance. It only occurred to me after a further expectant pause that Mr Forbes had applied to Amax and here at Hammersly Iron I was Mr Clarke. Mr Clarke was then faced with the dilemma of acknowledging his identity and appearing dim-witted or letting this opportunity slip away by remaining silent and casually taking his leave after a few minutes. I chose to appear absent-minded but, understandably, this was not considered an asset for the post of Explosive Technician's Assistant. 'I'm sorry, we want someone with experience' and 'You need to have a state driving licence' were commonly cited with a sympathetic frown.

After only three days, but very intense ones, I had the choice of two similar jobs and picked the one in an office of a mineral exploration company. (I was Mr Burke. In a penitential sort of way it was easier to remember.) The position was menial, operating a printing machine and hand-colouring seismic survey charts with crayons but I was simply happy to have found work and a change from constant travelling. Apart from Tasmanian Dick the tractor-man, I don't think I ever met a dull Australian, and the staff in this office must have been handpicked for their particularly lively personalities. I don't know if they ever found any minerals but they paid me a wage of $250 (£140) each week so presumably they must have found something. During the three months that I worked there my most interesting discovery was that the pot plants, and the office had dozens of them, were rented from an outside company who charged $25 each week for each plant. Any plant that wilted was replaced and a girl was sent over every few days to water them and polish their leaves. This never ceased to amaze me and made me feel less guilty when accepting my high wage for a slack week.

Now that I was established with a five-day working week, I found weekends frustrating. They were too short to cover any proper distance for sightseeing once the immediate area had been explored, so it became an obsession to use this period of confinement to earn as much money as possible. At first I bought a bucket and window-cleaning paraphernalia and went around Innaloo (district) to test the demand. Perth was built and still thrives on a spirit of enterprise.

Aware that East Australians continue to regard it as a city of only parochial importance and a convenient border peg, Perth welcomes success in order to enhance its national prestige. It is known as the 'achiever's city'. Some Wes'tralians would have turned a bucket and chamois into a multimillion dollar business in no time, but I undersold myself. Window-cleaning earned me a handful of notes, enough cups of tea to fill my bucket, a rebuke for crushing a geranium, and a dogbite. I turned to the paper which often carried 'Bar Staff Wanted' adverts but found most of them added '. . . must be able to fit 30–40 in. skirt'. I resisted the temptation to apply in my kilt. There was no alternative but to hunt on foot and each evening after work I trailed around restaurants. On my thirty-fourth attempt (and with an officially estimated 776 to go) I met with success.

Mescas, an expensive seafood restaurant, agreed to hire me (Mr Lewis) as a wine waiter on Friday evenings. It was owned by two Spanish brothers and the job became mine when I said '*Buenos tardes*' to them, and fortunately they didn't search deeper into my credentials besides asking if I had served wine before. They smiled, slapped me on the back and told me to start the following evening. Black trousers and a white shirt were the only requirements. Trying to select suitable clothes from a wardrobe that was a motley backpack seemed a problem at first, but my black hop-picking corduroys seemed presentable after a wash and iron, and I had a cream-coloured nylon shirt which would probably suffice in subdued lighting.

After work at the office the next day I changed into my renovated outfit and walked into Mescas, pausing on the way to comb my hair in front of a café window and below a broken sign which read 'FIS & IPS'. It was necessary to bob up and down for a while in order to locate the best reflection of myself in the glass but when it appeared, the image was unrecognisably smart. I winked at it several times just to make sure it really was mine and then realised that the proprietor inside the café was staring rigidly in my direction. I nodded politely and hurried on to Mescas with a plastic bag of casual clothes under my arm. The dining-room was empty except for Tony, a silver-service waiter who was as spruce as a penguin.

'Good to see you, Alastair.' (I always kept my first name.) He glanced down at my trousers and continued setting the table. 'There's a room at the back where you can change.'

This caused a moment of consternation. I clung to a weak smile. 'I feel fine thanks, but it would be nice to leave this bag somewhere.'

José, the chef and one of the brothers, had appeared at the door to the kitchen and watched me disappear towards the backroom. He was waiting outside when I emerged.

'What? You theenk you can work here like zat? Theese eze high class restaurant.' He had already entered into the spirit of a bullfight. 'Zee trousers have no crease, zee shirt eze not white . . . I do not beelieve eet! You say you are expee-rienced barman?' (That was true. I had worked in a hotel bar before.) He turned and walked out of the room cursing, his arms bandaged around his head. Tony came to my rescue with a spare pair of trousers. We were roughly the same size. José then reappeared in time to catch the end of my apology for not realising a tie was required. I had been too long on the road.

'Qué? No tie?' he shouted. I do not bee . . . oh, *qué mierda!* . . . ' There is no finer language for swearing than Spanish. Its rasping gutturals allow you to hiss and spit, its long rounded syllables crush with their weight when screamed, and its hard stiletto consonants come sharp and stabbing. José was a virtuoso. He turned pepper-red while he liquidised me. Then his voice suddenly slipped from anger to sufferance. It was obvious that had it not been so close to opening time, I should have found myself in the street. Tony again produced a spare and told me to do up my shirt buttons. All went well until the collar and then to my horror I found the top one was missing. I almost gave up at that and offered to go but Tony's resourcefulness was astonishing. He was securing my collar with a stapler when José once more made an entry. This time he said nothing but squeezed his face into wrinkles and quickly returned to the kitchen. The next moment came the sound of violent chopping. But my metamorphosis was complete – from the trappings of a walkabout to the livery of a wine waiter, and within ten minutes I was welcoming the first customers.

The ritual of serving wine soon came back to me and I must have removed over twenty corks from a variety of bottles without mishap, when one table ordered a bottle of 'Bin 77'. It was at the lower end of the expensive range, although none of the Australian labels meant anything to me. The bottle was approved and in the dingy light I began to run the blade of my pocket knife around the bottleneck to remove the foil. It refused to peel off and my two attempts to pierce the top and engage the corkscrew also failed.

'Here, let me show you how we normally do it,' one of the diners offered, and he gently unscrewed the cap.

The busy evening went on until two a.m. and then it was time to leave. I stopped in the doorway. 'Bye! See you next Friday,' I called to José and turned to face the street, pausing before allowing the door to close. To my surprise there was no angry response and no contradiction. During the following days I scoured second-hand shops and bought a good pair of trousers, a white shirt and a bow tie, and continued my search for part-time work. The response to my enquiries when visiting restaurants dressed in my finery and ready to work was amazing. At the end of my third week in Perth I had one full-time job and four part-time ones.

Wednesday and Saturday evenings were spent (as a resurrected Mr Clarke – I now had a method of remembering the names) behind the bar of a Mexican restaurant called Aztec Annie's. My boss was a grouchy man, always ready to pounce on the slightest mistake, and he worked alongside me. It was hard enough trying to remember what went into such cocktails as Island Paradises, Golden Dreams, Harvey Wallbangers and Freddy Fudpuckers without him fussing over the extravagance of supplying an extra maraschino cherry as decoration. One evening was memorable when he accidentally dropped a glass of beer into a customer's lap. This caused me to wear a supercilious grin for about an hour. Then he gave me a tray of three Pina Coladas to deliver. 'For Pete's sake don't spill these. They're hell to clean up.' 'She'll be right, mate,' I had replied, determined that nothing was going to ruin the evening of my boss's first mistake, and I wouldn't normally have tripped, but a woman had left her handbag in a narrow passage between two tables. Three sticky yellow Pina Coladas fell down the back of a girl wearing a low-cut red dress. And yet Aztec Annie's didn't fire me either.

The International Function Suite employed me (Mr Wills) as a black and white barman on an irregular basis. These evenings were always the longest as the staff had to clean up afterwards. An Aboriginal Reunion dinner-dance left a fearsome turmoil after three vicious fights which involved both men and women. It looked incongruous to see them running riot in their respective suits and dresses with gold and silver brocade, but their carnage was modest compared to a Greek dinner-dance. Give the Perth Greeks a simple combination of salt, pepper, paper napkins and a jug of water, and they will concoct a mess of staggering proportions. Add to this some drinks and three courses with a choice of vegetables, and they will create the culinary holocaust that is their idea of a good night out.

My fourth job was under a forgotten name (the method was unreliable) as a casual waiter in Agile Ernie's. This was a trendy fast-food joint which never closed. They employed me for a full day shift on both Saturday and Sunday. By this time I had very few evenings off and my workload had escalated into a demanding schedule. The bus system broke down after midnight and became erratic at weekends and this meant I usually had to try to hitch the eight miles home in the small hours. On Friday and Saturday I would take my sleeping bag to work and sleep on a park bench for the few hours remaining between the end of one job and the start of the next. I returned home weary on Sunday afternoons but after a good night's sleep, things didn't seem so bad by Monday morning. It was just necessary to look at the effort in terms of the goal.

Agile Ernie's demanded of its workers speed, efficiency and a cast-iron disposition to cope with up to two hundred weekenders who crushed into its multi-level salon and around its forty huddled tables. We squeezed through the pandemonium with armfuls of plates and large-print menus over a yard long, wearing jeans and Agile Ernie sweatshirts. It was pressure work and one afternoon it almost caused me to crack.

It was a Sunday after a hectic week and two consecutive all-night sessions which had permitted only a few hours rest on a park bench. Sundays were normally quiet but towards the end of my shift the room suddenly filled and people were clamouring for attention from all sides. There were tables to be cleared, the cutlery tray was empty, the coffee pot almost dry and then some pernickety bitch turned back a plate of bacon and eggs for the second time; on the first occasion the bacon had been too crispy and then she said it was underdone. And she didn't give a damn about the bacon. She sat there filing her nails over a cup of coffee, using her saucer as an ashtray, smoking and filing and chatting to a friend. That was it. She was out to impress her friend by having the audacity to return a plate of humble bacon and eggs, twice. I wanted to say to her, 'You ruptured old gumboot. Why do you come and bother us? Why don't you go and pester FIS & IPS down the road?' But the customer was always supposed to be right.

I was returning to the counter with her plate when a hand grabbed my Agile Ernie's sweatshirt and stretched the material so that it bulged and then hung distended like a piece of spent bubblegum.

'Gidday. Are you a Born Again Christian?' asked the owner of the hand, a youth.

No, I told him, I was just a waiter. This didn't satisfy him and he rambled on about BACs. I could have revealed to him the popular opinion that I had the face of Christ but instead I excused myself and explained that there was this urgent bacon and eggs to deliver. He was persistent and still wouldn't let me pass.

'Probably half of your customers here are Born Again Christians – don't you realise how many of us there are?' He seemed incredulous.

'Look, mate,' I said in best Aussie, 'I just work here taking orders for Banana Smoothies, Bacon Big Boys, Dole Bludgers and everything else on this three-foot menu. Much as I'd like to sit down over a Chocolate Bomb with each of my customers and discuss their religious convictions, I don't have time. So how the hell am I supposed to know who is a Born Again Christian when they eat Agile Ernieburgers, ravage my clothing and spill their Mint Dewlips as often as the flaming pagans?'

I hadn't intended such an outburst but it was the bacon and egg issue that had sparked it off. The next moment I was accosted by a table of eight. Large groups were always exasperating because at least half would find the menu a mental obstacle course. True to form they hummed and hawed and giggled, and finally asked 'What's nice?' An honest answer would have conceded that precious little was nice. Most of the offerings had been resuscitated with a microwave and glamorised with enough kitchen cosmetics to confound an autopsy . . . But I am dishonest and smile and suggest the things that are raw or have had the least interference from ourselves. Eventually they manage to select something. Then one makes a new discovery and they all change. I crumple up my list and start again but now they are on their third thoughts and racked by indecision. I say I'll come back in a short while.

The coffee pot is empty once more, the Born Again Christians have spilt a Mint Dewlip, Mrs Connoisseur Bacon and Eggs looks as though – heaven forbid – she enjoyed her meal and might order the same again, and behind me, eight imbeciles are contemplating a choice of ten ice cream flavours and settling for one that isn't on the menu. I lean against a wall for a moment, close my eyes and think, 'Dear God, why don't we just drag everything out in a large trough and charge them an average for the amount the level drops?'

* * *

Mid-way through my stay in Perth, during a period when my five jobs had kept me away from news reports for some time, I was walking to work along a different street for a change and passed a newspaper vendor. The words on the billboards brought me to an abrupt halt and I stared at them in disbelief. 'BRITAIN ON THE WARPATH.' 'BRITAIN SAYS "WE'LL FIGHT TO THE END".' 'BRITISH TROOPS CAPTURE 180 – RETAKE SOUTH GEORGIA.' Nine months had passed since the Argentine consul had thrown a party for an international bunch of waifs, and we had drunk a toast to 'Libertad'. I could still recall the taste of that wine.

Every day my walk from the bus station to the office was flanked with news of the war. For one week there were no casualties and then the *Belgrano* was sunk and 350 Argentinians were killed. My thoughts returned to the night spent with young army conscripts in the bothy at San Martín de los Andes. They had thought my country must be 'nice' because it had no compulsory military service. I wondered if any of those who had shared their food and quarter with me had been on the *Belgrano* and had perished in the icy seas. 'Britain 1, Argentina 0', sprang up as graffiti on a wall, but the next day the *Sheffield* was sunk. Already the stonemasons would be chipping away 'Their name liveth for evermore', 'Lest we forget . . .'

It seemed to be a time of intolerance and discontent both within myself and my small world, and within man and his larger one.

My visa was extended for two months, and then one week I shook a lot of hands and said a lot of goodbyes with a lump in my throat that was not caused by anything on a three-foot menu. Messrs Burke, Wills, Lewis and Clarke (and an Agile Ernie's waiter) had worked a seventy-six-hour week for three months, and earned A\$5,250 (£2,940). Now they were wanting to explore again. They combined into one who set out on the road to the north, hoping to fill his diary with accounts of happier things.

15 · Dreamtime

One hundred and fifty miles north of Perth the blood-red blooms of Sturt's pea (the state flower) come to an end and here, within sight of the Indian Ocean, lies the Pinnacles Desert. The pinnacles are an average of ten feet high and made of a tinted limestone. The land around them is a former seabed covered with shells, and the pinnacles were created through the action of rainwater running down the trunks and roots of trees which once grew in this calcified layer. The pinnacles formed over thousands of millennia, growing downwards as underground stalactites, and in time they were exposed by surface erosion and sculptured into their present shapes. They protrude from acres of sand-dunes as a crowd of yellow, bluish and reddish megaliths. It is very much as one might picture an open-air cash 'n' carry of Druids' standing stones, and a remarkable sight in the early morning or late afternoon when the time can be read by the long shadows of a thousand sundials.

It was here that I planned my next route, or rather came to a decision about my direction. The route was fixed as there was only one road, but half-way along it there was a branch which gave the possibility of travelling a loop around the eastern half of the country in a clockwise or anticlockwise direction. The eddy in my draining bathwater (now about to become infrequent), and Southern Hemisphere vines growing up poles, all favoured clockwise and this trend suited me too. Basing my mammoth decisions on something trivial brought me simple pleasure and encouraged the carefree nature travel should be allowed to instil. If Australia were depicted as an oval at rest, I was in the bottom left corner. My route would take me up the left side, across the top, down the right almost to Sydney, half-way along the bottom to Adelaide and then straight up the middle to Ayers Rock and eventually to Darwin, 8,500 miles away.

The land to the north of the Pinnacles Desert resembled arid tundra, interspersed with swaths of wheat fields around each isolated settlement. A banana belt encircled Carnarvon, salt evaporation tanks gave Dampier an Arctic landscape but everywhere else depended on iron ore stripped from open-cast mines which formed deep scars in the red ground. For hundreds of miles the only signposts pointed to mining towns – Tom Price, Mt Newman, Marble Bar, Goldsworthy – or warned 'Beware kangaroos'. Cars and trucks carried a solid roo bar in front of their radiator and this accounted for the sporadic carcases of roos and cattle lying on the wayside in the constant trail of littered tinnies and stubbies. New carcases trembled with crawling flies as they rapidly dehydrated under the fierce sun, and each represented one mouth less to have to nibble sustenance from the green shoots of spinifex bushes which covered the flat terrain with vicious spikes and grew into tangles of natural barbed wire.

Traffic dwindled to a few vehicles per hour and at Port Hedland I was let out beside a long line of hitch-hikers waiting at the north exit. One group of five headed the queue and thereafter individuals were spaced out at two-hundred-yard intervals. One person had been waiting for three days. Following the ethical code of hitching, I walked to the far end and took my place. Flies, heat, few cars and fourteenth in line all made a depressing prospect. I made a sign 'THE LAST!' and hoped that between it and the kilt, someone might be induced to stop. After two hours numbers three and fourteen (it's a gamble) were taken aboard a truck for the 400-mile ride to Broome, passing close to Eighty Mile Beach for most of its length. There were two people sunbathing on it.

Broome is a small village, once inhabited by the Japanese who chanced upon its rich oyster beds in 1883, and then bombed by them in 1944; now it cultivates pearls and waits patiently for the tourist industry to discover its miles of sand. There is little to distinguish the towns of the north-west. They all look the same whether it is the dry season or the mad wet season when humidity rises sufficiently to crack the tolerance of a Buddha and forces a slight increase in their suicide rates. Now, in August, it was dry and hot and three months ahead of madness. Derby was typical. It was the next town after Broome, a three-hour drive through scrub and a profusion of anthills which rose high into the air like gingerbread cathedrals. I had thought of horse-racing but Derby seemed to sweat simply standing still. It is the centre of the region's beef industry but a few of its 5,000 inhabitants, mainly the third that are white, drill nearby ground and find oil with the help of seismic charts hand-coloured in Perth. Derby has two wide main streets and a grid plan of lesser ones where bungalows either cringe under trees for shade or stand on concrete

legs looking for a breeze. Private swimming pools are essential,
doormats not. It has shops, milk bars, a video library, a leprosorium,
a bloated boab tree that once served as a prison, and two pubs whose
shadows contain a littering of Aboriginals during closing time.

In the bar of the Spinifex Hotel I again met Dave Simmons, the
bank manager at Derby. This establishment was cramped and drab
enough not to offer any distraction from the serious task of drinking.
For this reason it was popular. Dave said he only came here very
occasionally in the hope that it might have improved, but now it had
put him in mind of the leprosorium.

Dave, his wife Kirsty and three children had rescued me from a
lonely highway earlier in the day and given me a bed in their house.
He was in his mid-thirties, a quiet and considerate man who made
relaxing company. He had an opinion if required but no shoulder-
chips waiting to be offloaded. He seemed to have everything worked
out, where he was and where he was going, and although not
without professional ambitions, he was unusual in having learnt
how to extract the maximum contentment from the present. This
had rubbed off on Kirsty and she conveyed the same impression of
steady fulfilment. Their standard of living was moderate, and
certainly no worse for being in the isolated north. Apart from being
on stilts their house was like any other to be found in the south
(Upper Penguin or Innaloo) and contained gadgets of modern
necessity rather than luxury. Dave said that one of the reasons he and
Kirsty had given me a lift was because they thought it important for
their children to meet people from different countries and back-
grounds. In this respect they showed more tolerance and understanding than others in the Spinifex Hotel that evening.

'Sure I like Abos,' growled a loud voice from the bar. The owner
was a marsupial trucker, a broad white hulk of a man wearing shorts
and a T-shirt ballooning over the contents of many tinnies safely
stored in his pouch. 'I think every family should have one chained to
their garden.' The man's companion looked bored. The Aboriginals
on the other side of the room ignored the remark. I suddenly noticed
that the bar counter was in the shape of a horseshoe and although
there was some movement of colour around it, essentially the blacks
sat and ordered their drinks to the left of the point while the whites
stayed to the right.

I was shocked. 'Do you have apartheid here?'

Dave looked embarrassed. 'It's not that strong. Don't let that loudmouth influence you – not many think like that. But yes, there has always been a tradition of separate sides for black and white here. It's not strictly enforced but most people usually comply. It sort of prevents *incidents.*'

But there was an *incident* brewing. Two Aboriginal girls kept moving into the white section and asking for cigarettes or a light. The truckers ignored them, some told the 'filthy gins' to go away. When the bar closed and everyone had wandered outside, one of the gins had an argument with a white girl. The next moment they were rolling on the ground, kicking, punching and tearing at each other's hair. The truckers and Aboriginals listened to the screams and watched with mild interest until someone shouted that the white girl was pregnant. They were separated even though it took some time to prise open the black's hand and release the white's hair. The black began lashing out at a trucker. She was thrown forcefully to the ground but immediately leapt up and went at him once more. After a short violent struggle she was thrown lengthwise over a fence and hit her head against a stone on landing. Slightly dazed, she shook her head and in no time she had climbed back over the fence and was screaming abuse. A police car suddenly appeared and pulled up beside her. Without asking any questions the officer bundled her into the car and drove away. People wandered off. It was evidently just another night in Derby.

The tragedy for the Aboriginals is that they are not part of Australian society. They came in the same lot as the deserts.

Before the modern changes came about, this primitive people roamed a land whose every feature was a totem from the Dreamtime, that period when the Aboriginal ancestor heroes conducted journeys and quests on a continent still in the process of formation. Through their initiation ceremonies, walkabouts and Dreaming, later generations of Aboriginals sought to strengthen these totemic bonds. They led a moral life in strictly structured tribal societies. Strangers were introduced to a community not by name but by an assigned title. A man might be designated an uncle depending on his station in life so that the community would know the degree of respect and the privileges to accord him. Marriages were arranged by parents, and a woman who did not have children or was unable to bear any, was given a child to adopt so that she would achieve the esteemed status of motherhood. The Aboriginals knew how to extract water from certain trees and the roots of shrubs, and hunted with spears and boomerangs that flew straight towards an object. (The returning boomerang was a toy for their own amusement and was not used for hunting except on occasions to curve up into a flock of birds.) Their language had no written form but they were inventive rock artists and prodigious story-tellers.

The first white men to see these hunters and gatherers who had lived from animals and plants in waterless places for over 30,000 years depicted them as lean and lithesome. Today they wander around as a lost people, largely indifferent to a past that cannot return, indifferent to a future that appears empty, and usually searching for no more than another beer. Some are still lean, as skinny and frail as mulga twigs, but most are as out of condition as their more relaxed fellow whites. They lose their teeth early through an unhealthy diet, and both male and female support the pot bellies of dispirited zoo creatures. Their skin has the sheen of ebony, and the same darkness which is enhanced through contrast by the ghost gum white hair of the elderly.

As Dave drove us home we discussed the English pirate William Dampier, who had visited the area in 1688 and commented, 'Dry, dusty – the most miserable people in the world.' Doubtless he had been put in a bad mood by the area's exceptionally high tide variations, and possibly by the crocodiles.

'The saltwater ones grow up to eighteen feet,' Dave elaborated, 'and they are devilishly cunning and fast. When they seize a victim they dive and disorientate it by spinning round and round until it's drowned.' He described the process so vividly I could have believed it was from personal experience. Crocodiles are found all along the northern coastline. Dave had seen a newspaper article on a man-eater which had been hunted in Queensland. When it was finally shot and cut open, inside was found the body of a man intact from the knees upwards. Dave had seen a photograph . . .

Dave didn't find Derby people at all miserable but he had experienced great difficulties with the first Aboriginals to open cheque accounts at his bank because they had regarded each cheque as the right to make an unlimited payment. Now the bank stored their chequebooks in one large suitcase and advised Aboriginals on each transaction whenever they came to make a payment. 'This also enables us to identify the account-holder as few of them can write and most have to sign with a cross. Some are orphans raised on a mission and have no more than a nickname. We've got accounts held in some weird names: King Billy, Steak 'n' Onions, Buggalugs, Willie Wheaties and Limmerick.'

Back in the Simmons' house our conversation turned to the plight of the Aboriginals in general. It was a passionate subject with Kirsty. 'Their demise began with the expansion of white settlers in the outback and the resulting conflicts over land rights. As late as the 1930s there were instances of poisoned food being left out by station owners to rid themselves of the "black vermin", as they called them.' Their situation continued to deteriorate under a succession of governments who managed policies of open aggression, negligence or benevolent incompetence. One of the biggest mistakes, Kirsty believed, was to have allowed the Aboriginals easy access to alcohol. Their chemistry was different from that of whites, their nervous system was less acutely developed and their genes were recessive. Their rapid addiction to alcohol was not just a result of centuries of abstinence but, she maintained, was also due to a different congenital level of zinc in the Aboriginal's liver. Her gloomy picture was only brightened by enterprising new communes being created where drink had been voted out and the Aboriginal culture, and pride, were being revived. These were funded partly by the government but largely by the royalties accruing from mineral rights on certain Aboriginal lands. 'But it's a small step,' she concluded. 'The truth is that the modern Aboriginal, still deeply rooted in his Dreaming, still baffling white doctors with the successful techniques of his *ngangkari* – medicine man – still a master of survival in dry regions, is dying in the ones that are no longer dry. And it's here that most of his people are to be found.'

She pulled a book from a shelf, *From Massacre to Mining* by Janine Roberts. 'I think you should read it,' she said. I did. It documents a history of genocide and ethnocide as gory and cruel as that suffered by the Red Indian, and alarming medical statistics: 30 per cent of the total Aboriginal population are diabetics (against 2 per cent of whites), syphilis and trachoma are rife – over the age of sixty, one in four is blind – and the Aboriginal's lifespan (49 for a male living in Melbourne) is twenty years less than that of a white. Only 2 per cent are educated beyond third form in secondary school and no more than twenty Aboriginals have ever graduated from a university, mostly in the arts and none in medicine.

I decided to move on. Derby was offering me nothing happier to put in my diary. Maybe the mine at Mount Isa would, or the Great Barrier Reef?

It was with a marsupial truck-driver that I set off the next day on the 850 mile journey to Katherine, the first crossroads of any importance. He drove a road train, a truck tractor pulling three trailers ('dogs') to form a race of freight 160 feet long, weighing 110 tons, running on sixty-four wheels and carrying ten spares in case of punctures. The land rose and fell in gentle folds, shrubs and bushes clung thirsting to its rusty surface, and kites rode the thermals in ever-hopeful circles. Each day brought a flawless blue sky, the smell of heat and dust, and the same great expanse of uniform bush. It was always 200 miles further to reach anywhere in particular and when we reached there, I could have sworn it was the place we had left five hours earlier. When we crossed the Fitzroy River, named after the far-blown captain of the *Beagle*, the road dissolved into a dirt track for 200 miles and red powder dust filled the cab and formed a deep layer on every surface. Then we flanked the Kimberley Mountains which pulled the land out of its hapless collapse and raised it into small folds whose edges had frequently been shattered into crags. This extravagance of emptiness appealed to me and the character of the Kimberleys, assuming an expression of quiet wisdom and eternity, won another convert to the totemic power of the Australian outback.

'Diamonds, plenty diamonds in those hills,' whispered the truck-driver from the corner of his mouth. His artful confidence made me wonder if anyone else knew this but later we passed crude hand-painted signs which showed that the area had already been carefully prodded by geologists. Then the landscape changed dramatically at Kununurra where fields paraded in fertile colours and paddled in the spillwater of the mighty man-made Lake Argyle (nine sydharbs). Since the dam's completion in 1973 the area had failed as an attempt to create an important agricultural oasis despite the eagerness of certain crops to grow well. Cotton had been decimated by plagues of insects, rice had been devoured by tens of thousands of magpie geese, peanuts had suffered plummeting market prices and sugar cane had met with political opposition from Queensland which feared the rivalry. The area had now been turned over to agricultural research and some production of sunflowers, sorghum, soya beans and mixed fruit, though at a fraction of its potential.

We were skirting the inner sanctum of the great Australian loneliness; million-acre properties where doctors, teachers and neighbours have hazy faces, talk with crackles and are known only by the sound of their voice. My driver indicated one turn-off to the beyond. 'That station there – two million acres! They sell 15,000 head of cattle every year! Have to muster with a helicopter and use a loud horn to scare them in the right direction. Some of those creatures never see a human till the day they're sold!'

When the road train dropped me off in Katherine, where I washed off my layer of dust by swimming in a gorge of crocodiles (a harmless freshwater variety), there remained the same distance of unremitting scrubland separating me from Mount Isa. I arrived there with my 2,288th hitched lift of the trip (the tally was logged each day in my diary), a short lift lasting fifteen minutes. The driver was a frail woman who, despite an acquaintance of only quarter of an hour, remains one of the most vivid personalities in my mind. Gwen Taylor was almost sixty years old and being eaten by arthritis. Her arms and legs and neck were in special braces which enabled her to drive for short distances. Gwen smiled and joked the whole time despite being in constant pain. She stopped the car by the roadside before reaching the town and asked me to help her get out to see some flowers she had spotted growing in the parched sandy soil. We walked over together, she resting on my arm and limping heavily. She said these flowers were called vincas and they only grew in hot dry places. She bent down and ran her fingers lightly over the petals. 'I love them for their courage,' she said. We drove to the base of a hill in the centre of the town where Gwen let me out and I climbed the hill to camp for the night. Whenever times have subsequently become hard and cause me to feel poorly, I recall this 2,288th lift.

Distances appear to have been compressed in this corner of Queensland, and anyone looking down on Mount Isa would find it hard to believe that it is officially recorded as the world's largest town in terms of area. Its City Council administers a region of almost 16,000 square miles, twenty-five times the area of Greater London. It is a mining town of 35,000 people where at any one time during the day or night one thousand of them are underground extracting simultaneously the ores of copper, lead, silver and zinc.

That evening I went through the daily ritual of writing up my records, and noted my impressions of mine work gained during the day's visit.

The guide leads us into the main lift which can hold 180 miners, and we descend 3,000 feet into the earth; the journey takes one minute. We are trussed in bulky one-piece suits which are almost double thickness with all the pockets. Men wear white, women orange, 'otherwise it's hard to tell the difference', the guide says, though I don't see why anyone needs to 3,000 feet underground. We wear plastic safety helmets which hold a two-brightness lamp; a dim general beam (lasts 28 hours) and a concentrated bright one (14 hours). The lift stops at the twentieth level and Old Jimmy, the guide, tells us to switch on because none of the shafts have lighting beyond the entrance.

The atmosphere is sultry and grimy, and smells of old railway stations. The tunnels are big, arching to fifteen feet in height and being the same in width. They are painted white to reflect any light and are studded with bolts; rock control, not rock support. Old Jimmy gives us some figures and I jot them down on a scrap of paper; 250 miles of road, 125 miles of railway track, 75 trains and 300 diesel machines, all underground. (Helmet lamps are handy for writing but make conversation painful with their dazzle. And you certainly can't unobtrusively leer at an orange uniform.)

It doesn't feel like me under all this gear. It's 45°C at 100 per cent humidity in this shaft, and they say the new level being prepared at 6,200 feet will have a rock temperature of 75°C! Just as well they advised us to wear these overalls over nothing. My senses are dulled as if looking at everything through a telescope – seeing it all as it is and yet the experience appears impersonal, detached from reality. Everyone is puffing and sweating – strange how quickly coiffeured tourists lose their composure. The air is so oppressive you can feel its resistance.

We are nearing the crusher and odd tunnels lead off from the main one, but even the concentrated beam of our guide barely penetrates the murk of dust, and it's thrown back into our faces. We go through rubber flap doors and enter a large cavern where the noise is deafening. A colossal chain with half ton links is slowly moving up an angled shute and encountering a deluge of rocks which it ignores. The rocks bounce and tumble through the links, getting smaller each time, and land in a set of ceaselessly chewing nutcracker jaws which disgorges them into the depths below.

Then we go down another tunnel. Already I feel lost. It is a long walk to the next point of reference and the party becomes spread out. I am at the front and look back into the darkness. The sound of the crusher has faded to a dull rhythmic throb, inseparable from my heartbeat. Close my eyes, and this could be a stroll down one of my own dry arteries. Then the resonant echoing tramp of advancing footfall dominates and I open my eyes to the sight of single points of light bobbing up and down, each disjointed and with its own pattern, a lilting movement, conjuring up the eerie image of the Klu Klux Klan marching torchlit through the night.

We turn into a short side tunnel where a man is operating a drill against a rock face targeted with white crosses. The area is floodlit by two lamps and here the three oppressive elements of heat, dust and noise are at their worst. I can't tell if the man is dark-skinned by birth or just occupation but he is black. I hope he gets well paid. He deserves to. This one wall will take him five hours to prepare and then he'll move on to another. Work goes on round the clock so it doesn't matter what shift you are on as it's always night down here, and day only exists in terms of your headlamp.

We are suddenly ushered into an alcove as a roar rounds a corner and moments later a back-end loader rumbles past, illuminating us in yellow flashes of its strobe light. The machine fills the passage so completely there seems no margin for error and I am again transported into a surreal world, this time of science fiction. The driver is in the middle of the machine, sitting sideways to his direction of travel and looking along his shoulder. His face is dehumanised by helmet, goggles, breathing mask and ear muffs. He stops at the end of the tunnel, discharges his load into a shute and throws the gears into reverse before the bucket is completely empty, spilling fragments of rock. There is something desperate about the furious pace of his work. He pauses to mark his notebook and then returns at full speed, looking along his other shoulder now, charging past, oblivious of our presence. 'Bonus rates' . . .

Then we are back at the lift and, one minute later, being blinded by the brightness of day.

My next destination was another world of muffled sounds and restricted senses, the Great Barrier Reef. On my way from Mount Isa to Cairns where the reef came closest to the mainland, I collected a letter from home at a poste restante address. Amongst the pages of news was one that caused me to recall some words of Robert Burns with a sense of gloom. 'Oh wad some Pow'r the giftie gie us to see oursels as others see us!' he once wrote, but he might have wished for something less severe if he had received a letter similar to the one that had been waiting for me. It contained the giftie. On the relevant page my parents said that some time ago an Australian called Terry Cowlam had written to them to say he had met me and to offer reassurance that I was in good health and spirits. (Terry and his wife had been one of the first kind families to adopt me, and one with whom I had instantly shared a close rapport.) My parents had appreciated his letter and quoted an extract which had amused them even though it had brought them no reassurance.

> Dear Mr and Mrs Scott,
> It was a lovely day, a lovely spring day in Australia last Sunday when I was travelling home northwards from Sydney to Crescent Head, one of the chosen places on this earth.
> Leaving Newcastle and turning right over the iron bridge that crosses the Hunter River, I came across an incredible sight. By the side of the road there appeared an amazingly old and well travelled kilt, oft repaired and faded from the clan's true tartan, fronted by a patched and hairless sporran which held more written notes than those offered in exchange.
> Curiosity led to a stamping on the brakes and out of this pile of clothing, fit only for a museum or charity, came a rosy-cheeked bearded laddie with clean eyes and . . .

That evening I did a lot of sewing and was thankful for clean eyes.

Burns's words seemed to be the theme of the week and the Great Barrier Reef provided another insight into how 'others see us' a few days later when I exchanged an amazingly old kilt for shorts and joined a party of tourists setting off on a snorkelling trip. My interest in the reef had been aroused ten years earlier by alarming reports that Crown of Thorns starfishes in plague proportions were nibbling into the formation at a devastating rate – but now things were normal again in the coral garden 1,260 miles long . . .

Sunlight filtered through the surface in parallel shafts and lit up bright blue staghorn coral, perfect replicas of the antlers protruding from the walls of many a Highland shooting lodge; bulging globes of brain coral, their cerebral patterns formed by a maze of convoluted segments; mushroom coral whose domes were filigree creations as delicate as skeletons of leaves; other types of coral shaped like fans, doughnuts, concertinas and a bewildering variety of their permutations in greens, reds, yellows, browns, disspirited greys and the whites of those that were dead. Some corals were soft and rubbery while others were hard and scalpel-sharp, and among them squatted giant clams with their characteristic crinkle-edged grin; these were once almost exterminated by the greed of Asian divers, and are usually unfairly portrayed as being the ocean's gin-traps. In fact they close so slowly that a hero or villain has to be very patient in order for his foot to become trapped. Scattered liberally about the corals were jewelled anemonies whose tentacles pulsed and swayed hypnotically in the current and offered shelter to angel fish with dashing stripes – only angel fish are immune to the stinging tentacles, and only to those of their particular host; they lure fish into the poisonous arms and share in the meal.

Sea slugs up to one yard in length, coloured like trails of fruit salad, nosed their way along the seabed. One of the more colour-conscious members of the species, the Spanish Dancer, hovered in post-office red, rippling its frills in a silent flamenco. The rest of the fish came as incomputable varieties of brilliance and soon convinced me that genetics was a spurious theory to explain this astounding menagerie, and that an artistic god was the only answer. Every swimming form was splashed with undiluted colours.

Here were butterfly fish, red demoiselles, little neon blues with false eyes on their tails, the grouchy dragon fish trailing so many red and white striped ribbons it could hardly swim, and the clownfish, possibly the most beautiful of them all. He (or maybe she) was turquoise with a purple edge demarking each individual scale. Orange streaks ran off in a star pattern from his mouth, his chin was cobalt blue while his fins fluttered translucent sky blue. His tail was marked by an orange crescent followed by a mosaic of those colours you see on a church floor when sunlight passes through stained-glass. He swam up to me and then darted off to play hide and seek with his own kind, doubtlessly finding *homo sapiens* tediously white when stripped of his chintz and tartan.

I floated out beyond the edge of the reef and peered down into the dark blue of deep water before catching sight of a solitary barracuda out of the corner of my mask. It stayed twenty feet away from me and swam slowly, a four-foot silver streak with the evil grin of a pike. I quickly returned to the boat because of the horrible suspicion that it found my whiteness attractive.

You can tell this sort of thing if you have the giftie.

'How far is it to Peak Downs?'

'Coppabella is only one stub from here and then Peak Downs is about six stubs further on. We measure distances in bloody stubs in these parts,' said an increasingly groggy Stan. He was driving a Telecom van with a crate of beer bottles beside his seat. A stub was the distance covered in the time it took to drink one stubbie. (My mind played with exciting new possibilities; *Lake Argyle has a capacity of nine sydharbs and a surface area of approximately fifty square stubs*.) Stan had given me a lift from Mackay on the coast and said his route would pass close to my goal of the Carnarvon Gorge National Park, a full day's journey inland, but first he had to check the telephone junction box at a large mine. We had to be almost there as the last few stubs had disappeared in no time, but I had my doubts as to whether we would get much further even though it was only midday.

Peak Downs was an open-cast coal mine which fed an awesome herd of titanic machinery. Dragliners stood on the edge of great holes, their cables casting out a bucket which alone weighed fifty tons and raking it along the surface to clear the overburden from the seam of coal. They were huge cranes weighing up to 3,000 tons and capable of walking on two cam-driven feet at a rate of two yards per minute. Stan said they could clear as much dirt in eight hours as one million Chinese with shovels could manage in twenty-four. ('I say Chinese because they work hard. The comparison would be bloody useless with Aussies.') The coal was shattered with explosives and then scooped up by front-end loaders. The gaping mouth of their bucket could have comfortably held eighteen Footy players posing for their annual team photograph. They loaded the coal into 200-ton Terex trucks which were driven by women. Women were given this task because it was more convenient to give work to the wives of miners rather than have to recruit outsiders who would need extra accommodation. Terex trucks had right of way at all times and a raucous siren sounded automatically whenever they were put into reverse, for it was up to any object behind them to make sure the path was clear. It was disconcerting to stare up at the hubcap of a Terex wheel twelve feet high and weighing almost six tons. Each truck had ten of these wheels and in the event of a puncture, a new tyre cost £9,000 at this particular time.

'You'd think a bunch of butchers ran the place, wouldn't you?' Stan asked when his job had been completed and we were driving away through the mutilated landscape of black mounds and fractures, 'instead of the Church.' He waited for me to give a questioning frown . . . 'Yes, sir. The Utah Mining Corporation. The Mormons are sure leaving their mark here.'

Stan had now reached the point where some inverse law of inebriation came into play; it was only because he had enough stubs to hand that he remained level-headed and kept going. He let me out that evening on the edge of a ribbon oasis, a narrow canyon of white rock cutting twelve miles into the barren land. The canyon was lined with gums and cabbage-tree palms whose slender spiked fronds formed gigantic fans which wavered in the breeze. Against the sun they lit up in radiant pea green or banana yellow, ribbed by the converging dark lines of their stems and the whole acting as a backcloth for the shadow-play of more distant leaves dancing in the upper canopy. A small river moved silently through the canyon, its clear water curling into numerous pools along its leisurely course, its surface rarely ruffled except at the junction of a more active stream jumping down from narrow ravines on either side of the main gorge. After crossing eighteen sets of stepping stones I found a grassy glade by the water and wriggled into my sleeping bag beneath a clear sky. But if this had the makings of a rare halcyon day, then it was ruined at the end by frogs. When darkness fell they set up a fiendish breeping and belching chorus which kept me awake for hours. Had I dreamt, it would have been a nightmare; trapped amongst an agitated flock of sheep burping in an echo chamber.

I awoke the following morning as garrulous cockatoos disputed the dawn, to see sunlight creeping stealthily down one side of the dark canyon walls and creating a band of bright rock against which the branches and leaves above me assumed indentities of bold outlines. I have seldom been able to enjoy watching the progress of early morning sunshine from my bed without a feeling of having slept in, but this occasion was an exception. A kite drifted by on slender wings, tips curled upwards, and a kingfisher, opaline but dulled by shadow, sat on a rock watching the water and bobbed eagerly in moments of anticipation. Some rainbow birds – small bee-eaters – cavorted through the air, flying spirals and tight loops to catch red dragonflies. The frogs had switched themselves off by dawn and had mysteriously seeped into the idyll where they lay invisible, recharging themselves for another night of mayhem.

While retracing my steps out of the canyon I met a warden who directed me up a side-path to some cave drawings which he said were amongst the best preserved in the country. It was a short walk to reach the spot where hand impressions, boomerangs and emus adorned the walls in simple colours and outline forms. I felt uncomfortable in the place, perhaps because I didn't want to be reminded of the Aboriginal's plight, like so many, regarding it as an intrusion into the tranquillity of my beautiful day. But no escape was provided and there they were, matchstick men, lifesized hands, spindly emus and assorted weaponry – posing the question of what the modern Aboriginal would draw if asked to depict the dominant features in his life today. It wasn't hard to imagine. And then, inside a visitor's book kept in a box tacked to the wooden railing which protected the rock face, I found the last word on the Australian Aboriginal; sorrowful, regretful, but appreciative, written two weeks previously: 'What a shame the white man ever came to this place and destroyed the original people. But we are glad their artwork has survived for us to enjoy.'

For the writer, history had overtaken the event. Their name liveth for evermore.

'Welcome to Queensland. Adjust your watch ahead five years,' signs on the state border announce with a brassy wink. This state sees itself as Australia's California. It boasts a strong economy, the ideal climate, the greatest diversity of scenery and vegetation, and is generally regarded by everyone except Tasmanians and West Australians as the in-place to be. In politics it leans well to the right, weighed there by the immovability of its long-serving premier, Jo Bjelke Petersen, and yet maintaining a tradition of innovative thinking. It was Queensland that introduced the dungbeetle to dispose of its share of 300,000 daily cowpads, and it eradicated the former pommy menace of prickly pear cacti by importing a little Argentine moth with the delightful name of *Cactoblastis cactorum*, whose larvae ate only this cactus and died out when there were none left. Many old people are in a similar situation, devouring their retirement days in Queensland because they know that when there are none left, they can quietly disappear without being charged death duties.

I didn't carry a watch to adjust. It had been lying at home since the start of my journey and was now nine years out by Queensland reckoning. Nevertheless I was aware that only one month was left in which to find the place where Bulari gave birth to the world – it was page eighty-six of the picture book, just ahead of Machu Picchu – and to reach Darwin. My visa was hounding me to the end of the continent and to the end of my fourth year on the road.

Brisbane failed to delay me. Cities can entertain me for a while but soon they dull. They obstruct my vision and do not suit my temperament or camouflage. Australian cities made me feel less exposed to predation because of their lack of serious intent – only Melbourne looked as if it meant business – but Brisbane was much like the rest, a vast indifference of red-roofed pop-up suburbia attractively centred on a monumental bridge. I passed quickly through and positively sprinted away from the Gold Coast. This was my image of the great Ugliness and Loneliness compressed into one. Surfer's Paradise was its epitomy; a hotbed of speculators; a euphoria of estate agents; dollar-eyed tenants; a constructor's heaven. I ate at the Gobble 'n' Go restaurant, 'n' fled.

The *real* Australia began at once and as my route notched up another thousand miles, travelling down the right-hand side of the oval and along the bottom to the edge of the Nullarbor once more, I realised how much the outback had ceased to be an object of fear for me and become one of fascination. Perhaps also the awareness that I should soon be leaving this dehydrated land which looked so thirstily on me enhanced the special quality of its barren beauty. The enormity of its space awed me, but often I yearned for the sight of a contented cow up to the tip of its tail in lush grass. And I was secretly pleased that its endless similarity finally absolved me from the need to write my diary. There was nothing new for comment, except that once a cloud appeared; the first in ten days. It looked lost, over-dressed and in a hurry.

My direction changed abruptly at Port Augusta and turned north up the Stuart Highway which slices the country in half. 'Highway' is kind; 500 miles of it are dirt road. A young miner hurrying home to

Coober Pedy gave me my first long lift. His name sounded like Zolf. The roadside was flanked by creeping vines which bore yellow fruit like lemons. We flew along at speed, not worrying about hitting the lemons and trying to maintain the correct momentum which would carry us along the tops of the road's corrugations, and hoping to avoid the potholes which had filled up with bulldust and looked innocuous. The car was old and dilapidated, making me fearful that it would end up as another of the wrecks which lined this notorious road. If a car broke down in this remote area the cost of rescuing it was prohibitive for all but the most expensive models. Most of them were abandoned and soon plundered for spare parts by passing motorists, some being left upside-down and standing on their roof. I counted eighteen wrecks to Coober Pedy and thirty-nine in total to the turn-off for Ayers Rock. Discarded tyres were even more numerous, averaging five to each kilometre and totalling 4,585 for the same stretch.

Zolf had once broken down on this road a few miles from home. He had sent his passenger to bring help while he stayed with the car to protect it from looters. His friend soon returned with a mechanic and they were tinkering around under the bonnet when another car stopped. A man hopped out with a jack and set about removing a rear wheel from Zolf's car. Zolf asked him what he was doing. 'C'mon, fair dinkum,' replied the other, 'you help yourself to the engine. I just want the wheels.'

The town of Coober Pedy is unique in that it is embedded in the world's richest opal mine. Zolf let me see his underground house, typical of many, having been hewn out of the white rock. The town also has an underground church and an underground youth hostel. Zolf explained that these were ideal dwellings because the interior temperature stayed pleasantly mild all the year round and if he ever wanted another room, he only had to burrow outwards. He worked a mine outside the town limits and showed me some large chunks of iridescent opal. I thought it sounded an easy life, picking these stones out of rock walls. Zolf laughed and said he had thought so too when he first took up fossicking for gemstones, but now he realised he would have to dig a mansion to find enough opals to be rich.

I wondered what would become of Coober Pedy when the mine ran out. Would that be the end of the town and its particular species of inhabitants, *Opaloblastis opalorum*?

*   *   *

A certain fanaticism is essential in order to see Ayers Rock. It is not simply something one looks in on while passing for it is situated 150 miles off the country's most unsociable highway. A Land-Rover containing an extended family of Aboriginals took me the final distance in three stages, each stage being determined by when we ran out of petrol. The first time we waited for two hours until another passing Aboriginal driver stopped and sold us a few gallons. This took us by an unnecessarily indirect route to a camel farm which sold petrol and here they purchased enough fuel for roughly half of the remaining journey. On this stage we passed a truck of Aboriginals who travelled by the same method and we stopped to say we had no petrol to spare. When we duly coasted to a halt with a dry tank for the second time, we had to wait three hours before managing to solicit enough fuel to complete the final leg.

A thirty-four-year-old Aboriginal was driving with his wife in the passenger seat, and two young girls were huddled together in the middle, each gripping an end of a cassette player. I was in the back with two old black men and a two-year-old boy who sat naked in the lap of one of them and seemed mesmerised by the can of coke held in the hand of the other. It seemed incongruous to see a gnarled black hand with the veins protruding in stark relief clutching the bright red can with its twisting, billowing white stripe. The old men frequently smiled, exposing crooked yellow teeth and gums as red as the can. Every now and then they would throw out an arm and point to the distance. Only when their arms pointed in different directions did this elicit shakes of the head and some brusque comments until one murmured assent and moved his arm to align it on the same spot. Once I asked if they were pointing at a distant rock. The eyes of the nearest lit up and he nodded. It was one of their sacred places.

We drove on amid silence and unanimous pointing for another hour until we came to the dried-up Finke River.

'This is the oldest river in the world,' said one.

I raised my eyebrows, nodded and turned to the two girls on the front seat. They were listening to the ponderous electric beat of Cold Chisel at high volume which made conversation hard in the back of the Land-Rover and impossible in the front. Their parents didn't seem to mind and the girls looked as if they didn't care anyhow. Was this *their* Dreaming, I wondered? Then I looked back to the little boy. He had been given the can of coke and clasped it to his mouth, his large round white eyes stared down the length of the can as he knocked his head back. Coke poured out, he slurped greedily, coke trickled from both sides of his mouth, ran down his chin in racing rivulets, down his chest and over his bulging belly; the fizzy black liquid left wet scars on his black body, black on black, merging together until they became assimilated in shadow. The old men were still pointing but the volume of the music had now been turned even higher and each could no longer hear what the other said. They pointed in different directions. Three generations had become en-capsulated in Cold Chisel's electric fantasia – the older Aboriginals no longer agreed, the younger ones no longer pointed.

They let me out at a summer camp of their people. I thanked them for the lift and wandered away through a mess identical to the non-biodegradable middens of the Greenlanders; tins, bottles, plas-tic bags, paper wrappings and the rubbish discarded by a people who for centuries had been accustomed to returning the left-overs of their kills to the wilds. Or was that a generous interpretation? Were they really as spiritless and derelict as they appeared through white eyes? Once more I thought how hard it is to blunder into a strange culture with the hope of winning confidence and understanding at a glance. But I wished these Aboriginals had offered me more evidence of my misunderstanding.

Ayers Rock, or Uluru, was a sacred place to the Aboriginals long before the explorer William Gosse first climbed this monolith in 1873 and magnanimously named it after Sir Henry Ayers, the then premier of South Australia, rather than himself. The rock resembles the Sydney Opera House in that it too looks as if it has 'crawled out of the sea and is up to no good.' It stands as a solitary mass 1,100 feet high on a flat plain like a stranded sandstone jellyfish. The sheer magnitude and abruptness of this naked rock make it visible from far away, and the approach seems accordingly all the longer. Gradually its unworldly shape and texture become apparent. Its rounded sides rise steeply, bulge with an impression of inner power, undulate to the top and then sweep down in parabolic curves or occasionally plummet in vertical cliffs pockmarked with cheddar cheese holes. The rock's smooth surface appears to have been carefully polished into this aesthetic shape – if it were smaller and painted white I should have expected to find it inhabited by the Brazilian govern-ment, or, if minuscule, elevated on a plinth in the Tate Gallery – but it results from standing proud to the forces of erosion for over 100 million years.

Rain rarely falls in this region but when it does, water pours off Ayers Rock in hundreds of streams, waterfalls and cascades. Wild flowers burst out into colour and an eccentric species of frog which spends most of the year hibernating three feet down in the sand makes a rare sojourn amid the desert flora. It had been an unusually wet year and flowers seemed especially abundant in the prickly vegetation around a carpark called Sunset Boulevard. I stood there my first evening with three hundred other tourists waiting for Ayers Rock to perform. Sunset Boulevard has been strategically sited so that the Rock in its entirety will comfortably fit into the viewfinder of a standard instamatic camera with a generous allowance on all sides for unintentional cropping. In every other respect the site is ill-chosen and its perspective yields shadowless lighting which fails to accentuate the shape and texture of the stone, and robs Uluru of its unique character.

We were all waiting for the celebrated change of colour, and camera arms were getting weary. 'Now, take it now . . .' came an excited voice.

'Wait till the sun's gone down,' came another.

'Have we missed it?' asked a third.

At breakfast-time that morning, the rock had assumed a maroon tone. During coffee at eleven it had been the colour of cinnamon, fading to fawn at lunch-time. By afternoon tea it had turned pale orange, already imperceptibly rusting so that now (shortly before supper) it was bright red. The changes were dramatic but gradual and subtle in their sensationalism. They came about through the sandstone's faculty for reflection, its response to the intensity and quality of ambient light. After supper and after those who were disappointed had gone to bed, Ayers Rock glowed in the moonlight, deep crimson like a dying ember alone in the night. I sat watching it for a long time feeling deeply content, and grateful. This monolith could have blown all my expectations apart with a single monochrome sulk. Instead, it had behaved magnificently. Bulari rested petrified before me and in those consummate moments the world that was her issue appeared soft and gentle. I climbed into my sleeping-bag and tried to fall asleep quickly before the image could bruise.

After a restful night I left the official campsite early in the morning. The climb to the top of the rock was sharp and exhausting, and hot in a kilt, but it must have been worse for the other obvious foreigner hauling himself up the cable which served as a handrail. Near the top I met a young Japanese cyclist toiling up with his pushbike laden with panniers over his shoulders. From the top we could see tour-camping buses beside ranks of identical three-man tents (sleep two but require three to put up). The scene was wriggling with noise and activity. The rubbernecks and swivelheads of Golden Holidays, Pacific Highways and Ansett-Pioneer were rummaging for wood, lighting fires, converting sausages to smoke, vibrating frothy toothbrushes in their mouths or shouting hearty greetings from camp to camp with the intimacy that comes from sharing early-morning awfulness with strangers in an ablution queue.

The view then swivelled our heads through three compass points and unrolled itself as an expanse of plain with little variegation in hues, but on the fourth it rose up into another dramatic outcrop of rocks called the Olgas. The odd gum tree thrived around their base and so did the hardy desert oak, rearing high above the ground shrubs, each ten inches of height representing the growth of one century. When I visited the Olgas on my way back to the main north–south highway, I found them to be every bit as charismatic as their more famous neighbour, and more astonishing in shape. Their only fault is not to have been created as a single piece of rock. Several walking tracks have been created up and around them and on one of these stands a marvellous sign. It is an official park sign, carved in wood and varnished. 'This portion of the track is BLOODY difficult.' The language of the Australians is refreshingly pure.

The South Australian Postmaster-General Charles Heavitree Todd gave his name to a river on which, for a few days each year, a premium is actually paid to insure against its containing water; his wife donated hers to some nearby springs; and sadly, in what I feel to be a rare lapse of humour, little has been made of Heavitree. The town of Alice Springs is situated in the Northern Territory which comprises almost one-fifth of the continent and was the 'northern territory' of South Australia. (Not that this state was ever enamoured of its possession. In 1877 it tried unsuccessfully to sell the Northern Territory to Japan.) Alice Springs is a friendly town of low houses built in a hollow between cliff walls which turn carrot red in low sunlight. It would be overlooked if it were situated in any other part of the country and even here it would be bypassed if any alternative route existed and were it not necessary for motorists to refuel. Alice Springs depends for its survival on mining, tourism, passing traffic and, I felt, a seductive wink. It is one of those places that catch your attention at the time but later leave you wondering what on earth was so special. Apart from the charming way it exists at all, Alice Springs is unusual for holding an annual boat race without having any water. The Henley-on-Todd regatta takes place during the summer in the town centre on the course of the Todd River which is usually powder dry at this time of year. Teams clamber into bottomless boats rigged with sails and race the vessels on foot. The Australian author Thomas Keneally describes it in his book *Outback* as being 'the best sort of joke, it is spitting in the eye of the gods who made the dry, un-European Centre. It is a case of addressing the Australian God of Weather, Hughie, and telling him to stick his bloody rain.'

The God of Weather has done just that. The final thousand miles to Darwin are waterless, ideally suited to a long cruise aboard the Henley-on-Todd fleet. Sluggish sinewy rivers and crocodiles return nearer the coast amongst red escarpments rearing up from thorn bushes and tinder-dry savannah. The land here seems crudely put together; hunks of rock in brazen hues and daubs of soil equally unabashed in colour are thrown higgledy-piggledy amongst the modest shadings of herbage and scribblings of wiry shrubs. The outback can be harsh with its excess of heat and paucity of moisture, but it is bloody honest in this respect and displays the same frankness as its people. Only Hughie has a fickle temperament and it was in Darwin that he retaliated for all that eye-spitting.

Traces of Charles Darwin had lurked around several corners on my route since I had left Mexico two years earlier: Argentina, Tierra del Fuego, Chile and now Australia. He never reached this part of the coast but the *Beagle* came here in 1839 and discovered the site of what became the town of Palmerston. This link was considered firm enough to change the name to Darwin in 1911. The inhabitants are extremely genial and, like the town, noticeably young. This Darwin sprang out of the rubble and utter desolation left behind when the former town was flattened by Cyclone Tracy. On Christmas morning in 1974 the cyclone was recorded at 167 mph before the airport anemometer broke. It was the third time Darwin had suffered severely from a cyclone but this occasion was the worst, devastating

ninety per cent of the buildings, killing 65 people, injuring 150 and
sinking 25 ships. Now the city is tidy, laden with bougainvillaea
and scrupulously modern.

It has an incompleteness about it which comes from 50,000
strangers having been hastily gathered together in one place. It seems
soulless and temporary, and you feel at once that Hughie has won.
His hot sticky breath hangs over the town and confines silly season
life to indoors or the beaches. One morning the local newspaper
reported that 'Garbage carters in New South Wales received a big
pay rise yesterday – and a promise of more protection against savage
dogs.' It continued at length about the hazards facing garbologists
(as they were termed) and the ethics of garbology. The capital of the
Northern Territory is quiet. You have to go a long way to find your
news.

It was a time for catching up with repairs, collecting letters,
reassessing my luggage and tying up administrative loose ends. At a
savings bank I closed my Perth account and withdrew my earnings.
A letter from Peter and Hester in Perth was waiting for me at the post
office. They said they had received many requests for a return visit
from my window-cleaning clients. It was pleasant to think I was
being missed, and yet it deepened my own regret at leaving.
Australia had wooed me slowly but won me nevertheless.

I felt unsettled in Darwin and I ascribed these feelings to various
factors. The impending step from one land mass to another was
another ending and a new beginning on my long world safari, but it
was different from many of the others. It was the end of the second
stage and the start of the homeward leg, a goodbye to the easy and
placid travel of kindred countries. New Zealand and Australia had
pampered me and thinking about having to face the unknown again,
having to cross, of all names, the Timor Sea to enter the uncertain
hurly-burly of the third world again, aroused in me both excitement
and niggling fears. And there was the question of transport. For
some reason private yachts had been banned from entering Indo-
nesian waters and cargo ships refused to take me, so it was to be
flying again. I resented being catapulted into a new land and deprived of the pleasurable reward of a gradual arrival and of savouring a
slow infusion into the Orient.

My kilt weighed on my mind. It had evolved into an international
hybrid of the original clan colours, an assemblage of materials from
twelve countries which was continually disassembling or wearing

thin; a large expanse of leather was sewn across the back and patches taken from shirts, a towel and a Colombian airline sleeping mask reinforced it from the inside. As to whether it could endure one more year of rough travelling and whether it would even be worth taking to the Orient in case it evoked *torero* hostility, these questions remained unresolved. Preoccupied with thoughts of excitement, trepidation and disintegration, I began to go for long walks. These jaunts took me increasingly further afield until, the day before my departure, I came across Frank Watt.

He lived on a beach among a clump of palm trees in a conglomeration of fish boxes, driftwood, corrugated iron and plastic sheeting which he had fashioned into a sturdy hut. When I approached this fabulous construction he was sitting at the entrance in a folding chair that had seen many repairs and would shortly need to see some more. He looked old and shipwrecked, engrossed in a magazine, wearing a pair of glasses resembling safety goggles with thick rubber frames and heavy wire arms. His face was tanned and gaunt, making his skull pronounced and his nose stand out a long way in front of his deep-sunken eyes. He was balding and yet retained tufts of white hair which stuck out in unattended shocks, startling and wraith-like, his chin bore several days' growth and wrinkles formed expanding rings around his features, but, as I was about to find out, he had a cheery smile which split this image of decrepitude. He wore a fawn collarless shirt and an ill-fitting navy-blue jacket with arms cut off at the elbow, fastened around his waist with a piece of cord and almost long enough to conceal a baggy pair of brown shorts. There were no shoes on his feet, his arms were thin and his frail legs looked scarcely strong enough to support him as they dangled down, not reaching the ground and making him appear marooned and helpless in his chair. I approached him cautiously, having to call three times before he looked up and stared at me and my kilt's equally eloquent appearance. He beckoned me over, we introduced ourselves and slipped easily into conversation.

Frank still spoke with a strong trace of a Yorkshire accent as he related how he had been born in Bradford in 1899 and had lived there until the age of eighteen when he was able to enlist in the army. After the war he worked for a few years in a chemical factory making dyes before being invited to Australia to work on his uncle's farm. When the farm was sold early in the Depression he set off walking north to Queensland to see if the sugar plantations had work, ' 'n' that's what started me off wanderin' as a swaggie 'n' humpin' me bluie' (sleeping blanket). There were thousands of swaggies in those days. One in every three men was out of work.

He found some work in Cairns and liked the area, but after a while he felt he wanted to return to an industrial job. So he walked the thousand miles back to Brisbane, setting off in April and arriving there in December. He found work in a chemical factory which was an offshoot of the company he had worked for in Bradford. This was in 1932 when oatmeal cost 1s 6d for 7 lb and came in calico bags. After this he would work for up to a year, go back to Cairns for a few months and then periodically wander between the two.

'What! A thousand miles each time?'

'Aye, but it's a rare walk.'

Then he retired from this lifestyle and hitched a lift to Darwin 'for a change'. He had found this spot which he liked, built the cabin, survived the cyclone with little damage and had been living here for the last twenty-eight years. He had amassed a library of books, mostly on chemistry and natural history, and local residents occasionally brought him magazines. A radio kept him in touch with world affairs but otherwise his contentment and amusement came from books and nature. Some relatives had died over the years and he had inherited a small amount from them, barely enough, but he refused to collect any welfare benefits. His diet now consisted of oatmeal, coconut and cheese, with one tin of meat every six months. He could still walk into town and back but his rheumatism was getting bad. He smiled his charming smile, and said he always managed to make ends meet.

I asked him if he was ever lonely in this place.

'No. It's people that's lonely, not places. I've never been the lonely sort. An' loneliness is not like solitude. Some folk suffer solitude. I like to think I've achieved it.'

He was a remarkable man for his simple contentment. He showed no particular enthusiasm, and neither hatred, love, hope nor regret. Yet he was positive, not negative. He followed no specific philosophy, religion or creed except that he had found a place he liked and stayed there. This in itself was enough to satisfy him. He seemed to be hermit and hippy, a white and quietly wise Dreamtime figure in an Aboriginal landscape.

We shook hands and I left, pausing a few minutes later to look back and wave. Already he was up and tidying his little niche in the world as he had done for the last twenty-eight years, and I had come and gone and was forgotten. Throughout our conversation one thing had frequently crossed my mind; when his time came, who would bury Frank Watt? Then I carried on down the beach knowing that Frank Watt didn't care in the slightest. His funeral was someone else's. He would always be beside some billabong waltzing through time.

Unlike Frank, I had not found a niche in the world with which I could be wholly content. At times it seemed I had come close to it; Southern Patagonia, New Zealand and Tasmania had tempted me to stay. There had been nothing wrong with any of them but, in truth, I wasn't searching for a place to stay. My goal was still to complete this my journey, not to bring an end to travelling but as a reason to continue travelling. Perhaps I was changing from being merely a dedicated traveller to a diehard vagabond because the experience of looking had become as rewarding as finding. The world was daunting when seen in terms of miles but endlessly absorbing when seen through the eyes of a Mexican who measured his corner of it in the number of Fantas needed to cool an overheating engine, or an Australian who measured it in stubs or the suspense of running out of petrol.

Perhaps one of the most warming compensations of travelling, of having no one home, was the feeling that behind one lay a trail of countless homes. Every departure meant a new arrival, leaving an old home but stepping closer to a new one. When I was leaving one Australian family, my host pointed north.

'Go on,' he said, 'I think your Destiny lies that way. But if it ever takes you full circle then you'll always be welcome here.'

This fortified my spirit and I left Australia feeling invigorated. Ahead of me stood the open door to a temporary home called the Orient. It was a rare walk, humpin' me bluie, kilt and camera through the slow unveiling of life, and myself.